D0053486

THE PRESS

THE PRESS

ELLIS COSE

WILLIAM MORROW AND COMPANY, INC. NEW YORK

Library of Congress Cataloging-in-Publication Data

Cose, Ellis.
The press.

Bibliography: p.
Includes index.
1. American newspapers—History—20th century.
2. American newspapers—Ownership—Political aspects—History—20th century. 3. Press monopolies—United States—History—20th century. 4. Press and politics—United States—History—20th century. 5. Journalism—United States—Objectivity—History—20th century.
I. Title.
PN4867.C63 1989 071'.3 88-32919
ISBN 0-688-07403-0

Ptinted in the United States of America

First Edition

1 2 3 4 5 6 7 8 9 10

BOOK DESIGN BY JAYE ZIMET

For Jetta Cose
and in memory of Raney Cose

AUTHOR'S NOTE

No book of journalism can be written in the cloister. I owe a great debt to the nearly two hundred newspaper people who sat for lengthy taped interviews—in some cases, over the course of months—sharing their feelings, memories, and hopes about their work.

In an age in which reporters and editors are sensitive (and properly so) to the potential conflicts of others, the reader deserves to be informed of my own interests in the institutions about which I write.

Before beginning work on this book and in my capacity as president of the Institute for Journalism Education at the University of California, Berkeley, I received funds from all the major journalism organizations profiled here. As a journalist, I have worked for Gannett and Knight-Ridder. And as a fellow of the Gannett Center for Media Studies, where much of the research for this book was completed, I received support from the Gannett Foundation.

In no way is this an authorized account. A few individuals were asked to verify quotes and specific factual material, but none asked for (or received) the right to approve the manuscript.

I am grateful for the cooperation offered by A. O. Sulzberger, James Batten, Robert Erburu, Al Neuharth, Don and Katharine Graham, John Quinn, Tom Johnson, and Jerry Friedheim. I am also grateful to those colleagues—including Everette

Dennis, Loren Ghiglione, James Hoge, Jerry Sass, Oliver Cromwell, Tom Winship, and Jane Coleman—who read and offered criticisms on portions of the book.

My task was made immeasurably easier by two first-rate research assistants (Michelle Levander and Marchene White), an attentive agent (Michael Congdon), a loving muse (Lee Llambelis), and a network of supportive friends.

John Rothman, of the New York Times Archives, and Terri Dickerson-Jones, of the American Newspaper Publishers Association, were marvelous in tracking down obscure bits of information.

I am especially thankful for the work of my editor, Harvey Ginsberg, whose markings on the manuscript with his stiletto of an editing pencil sometimes drove me to the edge of hysteria. Upon reflection, I always realized he was right.

I, of course, accept responsibility for any errors or omissions.

CONTENTS

PART THREE
THE CATHEDRAL: THE *NEW YORK TIMES*

PART FOUR
THE CHAINS: GANNETT AND KNIGHT-RIDDER

PROLOGUE

That Camelot became a metaphor for John F. Kennedy's presidency was perhaps inevitable. The musical opened on Broadway the month before his inauguration. Richard Burton's young, idealistic king and Julie Andrews's beautifully innocent queen captured perfectly the spirit of Kennedy's New Frontier. And King Arthur's "one brief shining moment" lament eloquently described the loss felt with the president's death.

Kennedy's was a short reign, more memorable for its promise than for its results. And yet his death—*Where were you when Kennedy died?*—stands as a watershed for an entire generation.

Benjamin C. Bradlee, then Washington bureau chief for *Newsweek* and John F. Kennedy's friend, grieved deeply. And in the tormented hours following Kennedy's assassination, he elegized the president in a magazine article—later published as a book—declaring, "John Kennedy is dead, and for that we are lesser people in a lesser land." Even had Kennedy lived, 1963 would stand as a year of thunderous change. His was not the only murder that year foreshadowing trouble ahead. President Ngo Dinh Diem of South Vietnam was felled in a bloody coup. Medgar Evers, a civil rights worker in Mississippi, was ambushed and slain on his way home.

Several world leaders stepped down: Konrad Adenauer of West Germany, David Ben-Gurion of Israel, John Diefenbaker of Canada, Harold Macmillan of Great Britain, Amintore Fan-

fani (temporarily, as it turned out) of Italy. Détente crept into the general vocabulary, Betty Friedan published *The Feminine Mystique,* George Wallace became a symbol for racial segregation, and Martin Luther King, Jr., ignited the hopes of two hundred thousand who marched from the Washington Monument to the Lincoln Memorial and bore witness to his dream.

"Martin Luther King Jr. has made it as a man—but also as the representative of his people, for whom 1963 was perhaps the most important year in their history," wrote *Time* publisher Bernhard Auer, explaining why King was man of the year.

Addressing Columbia University students, James Reston, chief Washington correspondent for the *New York Times,* declared: "Change is the biggest story in the world today, and we are not covering it adequately; change in the size and movement of our people; change in the nature, location and availability of jobs; violent change in the cities and on the land; change in the relations between village and town, town and city, city and state, state and nation, and, of course, change in relations between the empires that are falling and the empires that are rising."

News, in short, was exploding all around; much of it tragic, much of it confusing. And for those thrown by profession into the maelstrom, the sixties in general and 1963 in particular were a roller-coaster ride. For a few, such as Bradlee, private grief and public tragedy came together. Three months before Kennedy was killed, *Newsweek*'s publisher and Bradlee's close friend, Philip Graham, shot himself in the head and died. The next year Bradlee's sister-in-law was murdered walking her dog along Washington's C&O Canal towpath. He recalled that period nearly a quarter of a century later as one of slogging through "a lot of piled up violence and tragedy."

Difficult as that time was for Bradlee, it was infinitely more difficult for his new employer, Katharine Graham, Philip's widow, who felt compelled to take the reins of the Washington Post Company, steel herself against her own deeply felt fears, and keep it on course.

Among newspaper families, Katharine Graham was scarcely alone in having to deal with the shock of unforeseen events. That summer, the *New York Times* and other New York newspapers ended the longest and most bitter strike in their history. Less than two months later, publisher Orvil Dryfoos died. He had held the job for barely two years, having succeeded his father-in-law, Arthur Hays Sulzberger. Dryfoos's death thrust his brother-in-law, thirty-seven-year-old Arthur Ochs Sulzberger, into the most important job on one of the most important newspapers in the world, a seat Sulzberger had not planned to occupy for a number of years and a role for which he was thoroughly underprepared.

"Dad had this great system worked out," said Sulzberger, in which Dryfoos would serve a long, fruitful tenure and then young Sulzberger would take over. "The only trouble was that nobody conveyed all of that to the good Lord and . . . Orvil died of heart disease."

Nineteen sixty-three was a pivotal year for newspapers in the United States. Not only did Graham and Sulzberger begin their stewardships, but others destined to become giants moved into positions of power.

Abraham Michael Rosenthal, a Pulitzer Prize–winning reporter at the *New York Times,* took over the paper's metro staff, planting his feet on a course that would take him to the highest editing position on the *Times* and that would take the *Times* into the modern age of newspapering.

Allen H. Neuharth, a senior editor with the *Detroit Free Press,* moved to Rochester with Gannett, a relatively small regional newspaper company. In due course, he would become chairman of the corporation, launch a flashy national newspaper called *USA Today,* and make Gannett the largest newspaper chain in the United States.

In June 1963, Victor Ridder died. Three years later his brother Joseph would die, leaving only Bernard of the three ambitious brothers who had built their small German-language newspaper into a national chain. In 1969, the (John and James) Knight and Ridder families would take their companies public. Five years later they would merge, creating Knight-Ridder Newspapers—a behemoth of an organization boasting the largest combined circulation of any newspaper chain in the country, although Gannett would soon zoom ahead.

The year of Victor Ridder's death, Times Mirror, little more than a holding company for the *Los Angeles Times,* was preparing to list itself on the New York Stock Exchange. It would be the first general-interest newspaper firm to do so and thereby edge across the line separating family business from public enterprise.

That fall, Wyatt Thomas Johnson, a poor kid from Macon, Georgia, was starting work on his master's degree at Harvard Business School. Years later, he would become publisher of the *Los Angeles Times,* the first *Times* chief executive not to belong to the Otis/Chandler family, a most visible symbol of that newspaper's full acceptance of the rules of the corporate age.

In an address before the American Society of Newspaper Editors in 1947, Arthur Hays Sulzberger, publisher of the *New York Times,* had commented: "Personally, I am not in favor of chain newspapers. I believe that newspapers should be leaders in the community but, at the same time, hold that the thinking that precedes that leadership should be home grown."

John Knight, head of Knight Newspapers, later thundered in response, "Unfortunately . . . 'home grown' leadership is not always of the moral and ethical character typified by Mr. Sulzberger. In too many American cities, the home grown flavor stems from public utilities, railroads, political machines, banks, and industrial directorates.

"In several situations with which I am thoroughly familiar, 'home grown' leadership was in effect no leadership at all.

" 'Home grown' leadership was actually 'home grown' protection: protection for the real estate interest which opposed public housing, protection for the utilities, protection for the manufacturers, protection for the gamblers who were corrupting public officials, protection for the rich and powerful business connections of the publisher."

In more than one sense, Knight had the last word. For by the middle 1980s, the New York Times Company had become—by any reasonable definition—a newspaper chain, and owned more than two dozen dailies scattered around the country.

In fact, by the 1980s, virtually every daily newspaper of national stature (and even most of those totally lacking in stature) in the United States was owned by a chain.

Ironically, the same forces that led newspaper companies to develop into (or join) gigantic chains made the emergence of politically potent media barons less likely than in the age of William Randolph Hearst, when the stock market was not a factor and when readers and advertisers were significantly less sophisticated. For in the market, with its hunger for growth and demands for efficiency, would-be press lords have found a force more powerful than any individual newspaper or group of them could hope to be. And that market considers political propagandizing an irrelevant distraction.

That family ownership should begin declining when it did was virtually inevitable. Many of America's most important newspaper families acquired their properties near the turn of the century. And as the third, fourth, and fifth generations arrived on the scene, the emotional ties to the newspapers typically loosened and ownership became more dispersed—creating an increased likelihood of conflicts among family members. At the same time, estate taxes loomed. Owners, with their wealth tied up in newspapers, were looking for ways to cash in their equity. Stock market offerings provided a perfect solution—a means of holding on to part of a company while also getting cash.

Yet, once the move to the stock market had been made, what followed took on a life of its own. Companies, which could not expand simply by printing and selling more papers in their original markets, were compelled to buy into other markets. Nearly every aspect of newspaper companies' operations was subjected to intense reassessment. The role of labor came under particular scrutiny since control of labor costs held the key to much of the efficiency that the market sought.

For years, most newspapers had a more or less equal partnership with the unions, which held the power to bring their presses to a halt. But as alternatives to newspapers proliferated and newspaper failures became common, owners saw their prosperity increasingly dependent on successfully bringing the unions under control. So the labor battles fought in the 1960s, 1970s, and 1980s were of a fundamentally different nature from those of an earlier time. More than simply skirmishes over benefits and wages, they were wars for survival—often of the union, sometimes of the paper—and were frequently extremely ugly.

The rise of the new corporate culture affected the content of the papers at least as strongly as it did their organization. Certainly newspapers delivered information and hence had an obligation to defend the public's right to know. But to know what? The real color of Madonna's hair? The reason for Michael Jackson's glove? Or to understand, despite a political process that worked against enlightenment, where various policies or presidential candidates would take the nation?

What the marketing experts often had to say was, to tradition-bound journalists, something of a surprise. Personalities, it seemed, were more interesting than ideas. Advertisements were, to the reader, nearly as important as the news. And the nice distinctions journalists loved to make—about what in a newspaper was news and what wasn't—were incomprehensible to subscribers.

In the past, many editors prided themselves on their ignorance of the "business side" of the enterprise. Today's editors routinely find themselves consorting with marketing gurus and management experts.

Previously, news executives and professionals were likely to have deep ties in their communities. Now, like other workers in an increasingly mobile society, they are apt to be corporate carpetbaggers ready to move on when a new job opens up.

Indeed, over the past quarter of a century, even the physical environment in which newspapers are produced has drastically changed—so much so that a journalist visiting from the early 1960s would feel hopelessly out of place.

Reporters have graduated from the typewriter to the computer. Newsrooms have changed from carnival-like arenas of nearly nonstop pandemonium (with reporters screaming for copy clerks, who rushed stories to editors, who placed them on noisy conveyer belts, which would take them to the composing room) to quiet, orderly offices. Cold type has given way to offset. Black and white has given way to color. Printers, pressmen, and stereotypers have been pushed toward obsolescence.

At the same time, the social context in which journalism is practiced has also been transformed. Newspaper executives have had to cope with legal challenges to sexism, racism, and the right to special privilege, to adjust—in short—to the changing nature of work and life in the latter part of the twentieth century.

In the mid-1980s, the *San Francisco Examiner* produced a series of television commercials starring William Hearst III, its handsome, balding, mustachioed publisher and grandson of the legendary William Randolph Hearst.

The spots were playful and clever. In one, Hearst III sits beneath a portrait of his grandfather, pondering what the patriarch would make of his grandson's attempt to modernize the paper—a riddle unresolved as the announcer proclaims the *Examiner* the paper of "the next generation."

The message, Hearst explained later, was that his paper was to be a paper for his generation—not that of the man in whose shadow it had matured: "I am less impressed with the weight of my grandfather's tradition than I am with the here-and-now concern to make this a success."

To Hearst that meant adopting an approach radically different from that of his grandfather—a mass marketer who went after the biggest audience he could get. Hearst III felt compelled to aim at a narrower target: "at people who are desired by advertisers, mainly in terms of purchasing power."

Dave Laventhol, president of Times Mirror, made much the same point: "The daily newspaper . . . is published for people who read and for people who consume. . . . It's largely a middle-class publication."

Some editors are uncomfortable with that viewpoint and would desire the best of both worlds: a mass market but also a focused market. A task force of newspaper industry executives, after lamenting the decline in newspapers' share of advertising dollars, concluded that newspapers could continue to flourish as a mass medium. The television audience, said their report, was becoming so fragmented—with cable, pay TV, and numerous independent and educational stations—that newspapers should be sitting pretty. Yet the argument ignores the fact that newspaper audiences have also become fragmented, despite the increasing number of one-newspaper towns. Competition has arisen not only from specialized and community newspapers, but from city magazines, mass mailers, and a huge array of other sources.

Editors unhappy with the new bottom-line mentality were advised by Michael Fancher, executive editor of the *Seattle Times,* that those who resisted playing by the new rules were doomed: "Sooner or later, their journalistic options will be proscribed by someone else's bottom line." In other words, the demands of business will take precedence over the desires of old-fashioned editors and reporters; the financial stakes are too high and the market too unforgiving for any other outcome.

Times Mirror chairman Robert Erburu echoed that view: "I see editors today much more oriented toward, much more concerned about . . . taking much greater interest in the business side of the product. . . . They'd better have a successful product or they're not going to have the product."

* * *

Though daily newspaper circulation hovers near sixty-three million, the number has not grown substantially since the 1960s. And though the industry remains profitable and has annual revenues of roughly forty billion dollars, newspaper industry meetings are studies in self-doubt. Publishers worry that direct mail will steal their advertisers, that television and computerized networks will steal their readers, that sly investors will steal their companies, and that their own mistakes will rob them of credibility. Their world and their communities have changed so fast that even the marketing consultants have been hard-pressed to keep up.

Larry Jinks, senior vice-president of Knight-Ridder, observed, "I grew up in an era in which mostly white English-speaking males put out newspapers with a little bit of help from white English-speaking females." Yet the cities in which his company publishes newspapers are becoming less white and less English-speaking and his work force is becoming less male—all of which presents difficulties and opportunities unimaginable a few years ago.

At the same time, the newspaper fraternity has become less insulated than in the old days. Though several companies have taken measures to protect themselves, others are all too aware that they are vulnerable to being taken over by anyone with access to substantial capital. That reality compels them to act with more prudence than their forebears.

Not all newspaper executives welcome the new age. "The invasion of investment bankers into the buying and selling of newspapers has led to too much talk about . . . 'building asset values,' " protests Jim Ottaway, Jr., chairman of a chain of small newspapers owned by Dow Jones and Company. "We ought to be publishing newspapers—not running banks," argues the bespectacled heir to Ottaway Newspapers, Inc.

Yet newspaper companies seem fated to remain major players in the financial markets. The compulsion to grow remains strong. And the deals continue to get bigger.

In 1976, S. I. Newhouse purchased Booth newspapers and *Parade* magazine for three hundred million dollars. "It was likely to remain the biggest American newspaper deal of the twentieth century," wrote author Richard Meeker. Yet even before Meeker's book was published, Gannett acquired Combined

Communications for four hundred million dollars and later acquired the Evening News Association for more than seven hundred million dollars, even as Times Mirror bought the *Baltimore Sun* and affiliated properties for six hundred million dollars.

William Thomas, editor of the *Los Angeles Times* since 1971, was less than sanguine about the marriage of journalism and high commerce as he looked forward to his 1989 retirement. His successor, Thomas believes, will have to worry a great deal more about Wall Street than Thomas did. For the pressures from the Street, in his opinion, can only increase.

"As long as the family publisher is in the corner next to you, there's a different relationship . . . between the newspaper and the [corporation] . . . than there is after he leaves and goes to the corporate floor or wherever," said Thomas. Two of the nation's other great papers, the *Washington Post* and the *New York Times,* he pointed out, are still very much dominated by the families who have owned them for years—families that he believes have been able to stave off some of Wall Street's demands. "So I know more about [corporate pressure] than Ben [Bradlee] does or Abe [Rosenthal] does, by far. But everybody's going to learn. . . .

"It used to be that if a publisher had enough money, he'd say, 'Okay, I want the best damn newspaper we can produce. Just don't spend me broke.' Those days are gone."

Also gone are the days when well-matched daily metropolitan newspapers slugged it out in America's great cities. Instead, the United States has become a nation of one-newspaper towns—as both Knight-Ridder chairman Alvah Chapman and Gannett chairman Al Neuharth pointed out in seeking permission from the U.S. Justice Department to combine their newspaper business operations in Detroit.

"In the early to middle 1980s, it became apparent to me that the situation in Detroit was comparable to the situation in other major American cities, such as Philadelphia and Cleveland and Washington and Buffalo and Baltimore and others, where two competitive newspapers, two independently owned profitable newspapers, could not exist in the marketplace," said Chapman.

In December 1986, A. M. Rosenthal, nearly sixty-five years old, retired as executive editor of the *New York Times.* He had been totally devoted to the job and to the paper. Many colleagues thought he felt he should hold the position forever.

His mandatory retirement was preceded by much speculation—about when he would leave, who would succeed him, and what would be the effect on the *Times.* Prominent among those speculating was the *Washington Post,* whose "Style" section ran a three-part series by Eleanor Randolph examining Rosenthal's record, the people around him, and the paper he had built—and whose own executive editor, Benjamin Bradlee, turned sixty-five in August 1986.

GRASPING FOR THE KEYS TO THE KINGDOM, read the headline to the final article in the series, which began: "With the impending retirement of Executive Editor A. M. Rosenthal, The *New York Times* moves into a period of waiting, a pretransitional limbo when the newspaper focuses much of its formidable talent and energy on its own internal upheaval."

Shortly after the series ran, Bradlee heard that Rosenthal had taken to telling his friends, "When I'm about to retire, the *Post* runs a three-part series. When Ben Bradlee retires, the *Times* will run a paragraph." Incensed, Bradlee dashed off the following note.

> Abe:
>
> Here's the paragraph.
>
> Benjamin C. Bradlee retired as executive editor of the Washington Post today, after 30 years in the job. He is 70.
>
> OK
>
> Ben

The message was obvious: that Bradlee would have the last laugh, that Bradlee was allowed to break the retirement rule Rosenthal had been unable to bend. But underlying the barbed dig was an inescapable reality, that soon Bradlee too would retire, as would his colleague Bill Thomas, as would Rosenthal's boss, A. O. Sulzberger, and Bradlee's patron, Katharine Graham, as would the chairmen of Gannett and Knight-Ridder, as had the chairman of Times Mirror.

Times Mirror's Otis Chandler, seeing no Chandler capable of taking over from him, had bet the company's future on outsiders. Gannett's Al Neuharth and Knight-Ridder's Alvah Chapman, outsiders themselves, had no such family concerns (there being no Gannetts involved in running the company, no Knight ready to demand a top management job, and the only Ridder in the line of succession clearly understanding that he would get no free pass). Graham and Sulzberger, seeing great gifts in their progeny, had positioned their eldest sons in important jobs. All, in their way, were preparing for the next generation, at a time when the passage into tomorrow promised to be quite different from the way it had been for them.

The environment the younger generation is entering will be less tolerant of oddballs and erratic visionaries—brilliant though they may be. The emphasis will be on collaboration, on building compatible teams, on taking fewer risks.

An increasing number of newsroom executives will come from finance or general management and have responsibility for controlling costs and managing process. Though they will not be editors, they will inevitably force editors to question some of the practices followed in the past.

Newspapers will try harder than ever to identify their markets and to tailor their products to meet them. They will be under growing pressure to concede that they cannot serve all the readers in a community and that it may not be in their long-term economic interest to try. Some of the most prestigious papers will become more regional, trying to extend their reach and strengthen their upscale demographics as their municipal bases erode.

Newspapers will further tailor their products for special classes of advertisers, increasingly trying to ensure that the ads and news stories are related to each other.

Even papers owned by different companies will resemble one another more strongly than ever, as they standardize formats for advertisers and follow identical advice from marketing analysts.

The price of papers will rise more rapidly than in the past as publishers become less and less concerned about poorer readers (or those outside their advertising target area) who would be hardest hit by higher prices but whom advertisers generally don't value as much as they do more affluent consumers.

Recently, a former *New York Times* manager who resigned to go to another large newspaper was asked whether he missed his old publication. He admitted that he did and added, "It's nice to have something bigger than yourself to believe in." Now, he said, he would have to create that something. At the *Times,* it had been created for him. Other journalists have felt similarly about their own papers; for, as journalists, they saw themselves as keepers of a sacred trust.

That feeling comes harder these days, not only because papers stand for less, but because, like other institutions in society, they are absorbing a generation of young people who see loyalty to any institution—even a newspaper—as secondary to individual fulfillment. Even the *Times,* one current editor confided, could no longer depend on its name and reputation to attract or hold the young journalists it coveted.

In the pages that follow unfold the stories of some of the largest and most successful communications companies in the nation: great newspaper concerns that have survived the transformation from family businesses into corporate giants. Taken together, the Washington Post, Times Mirror, New York Times, Gannett, and Knight-Ridder control roughly one fourth of daily newspaper circulation in the United States—and the percentage is growing. They also control a farrago of magazines, broadcast outlets, and other communications vehicles. Their influence, however, extends well beyond their circulation and broadcast areas. Harrison Salisbury, writing in *Without Fear or Favor,* described the *New York Times* as an institution that had such power in setting a national agenda that it represented no less than a "fourth coequal branch of government." The description is too extreme to be accurate, but without doubt papers as prominent as the *Times,* the *Washington Post,* and the *Los Angeles Times* command serious attention in America's legislatures and boardrooms. Moreover, other communications companies—less successful, less prestigious, or less secure—watch them for hints about how to behave.

As representatives of the public, as its eyes, ears, and wielders of its pen, newspapers have a responsibility to the public at large arguably just as great as their responsibility to their public shareholders: a responsibility to weigh all commercial decisions in the light of those who bear a public trust.

Such accountability was alluded to by one of the brightest of the new breed of managers as the reason his company had lost the auction for some highly valued media properties. To successfully bid on them, he said, the company would have to pay such a high price that it would have no choice but to gut them—by cutting into the news organizations' ability to successfully cover the news and by terminating circulation that costs more than it brings in, making the publications of significantly lower caliber than they had been. And that was something his company refused to do.

His view is not shared by many of his contemporaries, particularly those who outbid him at auction; but it sums up the dilemma of applying the standards of commerce to news organizations.

For the most part, the executives profiled in these pages don't dwell on abstract issues. Like leaders in any industry, they are too busy dealing with the business at hand, groping along, day by day, making decisions, good and bad, trying to steer their organizations safely through the difficulties created by all too human failings. Yet when they do stop to reflect, one is struck by how demanding they can be on themselves, and how uncomfortably they endeavor to serve two masters—commercialism and conscience—that do not always agree.

In many respects, the stories of these organizations represent not so much a tale of newspapers as of corporate behavior in the United States since the early 1960s—a period that has already gone down in many books as the last age of painless prosperity. Every company that sells a product and tries to make a profit has dealt with questions these newspaper executives face—questions of market, positioning, and corporate responsibility. And they all, newspapers included, are bearing witness to the death of an exquisitely American dream—that there is a mass market, that there is one America, that any medium can speak to (or for) all the members of one nation under God.

PART ONE

THE UNDERDOG: THE *WASHINGTON POST*

CHAPTER 1

AN EDITOR AND HIS *POST*

Occasionally, an individual and an institution mesh in such a manner that they become infinitely more consequential together than either could have been apart. The *Washington Post* and Benjamin C. Bradlee interacted in that way.

All the President's Men put Bradlee in the movies, but the gravelly voiced tough guy that Jason Robards brought to the screen had been on stage nearly all his life. The film did no more than complete the circle, allowing the editor who already had conquered Washington to conquer Hollywood as well.

And Bradlee was meant for Hollywood in the same sense that a complicated, explosive story is meant for the front page: The message simply fits the medium. The reality rivals any image the celluloid fantasy factories could crank out. With his dark hair slicked back and head held high, he seems taller than his six feet. Part of it has to do with his confident stride, part of it with the way he solidly fills his suit, and part of it with a wide, charming smile that makes it clear that Bradlee has his role down cold.

He has managed something few public men ever do: to blend so completely into his persona that even those who know him best have difficulty telling where the actor ends and the myth begins.

Years after a break-in at Democratic headquarters launched Bob Woodward into journalistic stardom, Woodward argued that Watergate, the biggest story the *Washington Post* has ever chased, paled in institutional impact beside the man who presided over the newsroom. Watergate "had an impact, obviously, but I really think it's just kind of one more thing in Bradlee's career." The *Post* got the story, in Woodward's view, because Bradlee created an institution that encouraged hard, investigative reporting. And although the Watergate period was "probably Bradlee's finest moment," Woodward believes Bradlee has enjoyed a lifetime of fine moments.

Given Bradlee's pedigree, a good life was virtually his birthright. For Bradlee, born in Boston on August 26, 1921, entered a world of unlimited possibility. "I was born with a silver spoon," as he puts it, "which stayed in there for eleven years until my old man went broke in the Depression."

That silver spoon was handed down from his father, Frederick J. Bradlee, a financier, athlete, and—like his own father and Ben—a product of St. Mark's preparatory school. His father was, rhapsodized Bradlee, a fast-tracker from minute one, "an All-American football player who was, in a way you can't imagine, kind of a golden boy in Boston, at Harvard"—one whose ascent up Bancamerica-Blair Corporation's leadership ladder was fore-ordained in an almost biblical sense.

But with the Depression, the Bradlee household lost its maids, cooks, and cachet. And Benjamin's father went from one odd job to another, selling commercial deodorant, working as an administrator at Boston's Museum of Fine Arts, even mopping out a smoking car on the regional railroad.

At St. Mark's, young Bradlee went on scholarship. He fondly remembers the school for its determination to do something more than coddle the children of the rich. It provided him with a solid grounding in the classics, encouraged a certain patrician social responsibility, and even motivated Bradlee to spend two summers working in a Big Brother camp. St. Mark's, however, was far from heterogeneous. The only person of Jewish origin he recalls attending the overwhelmingly WASP school was a practicing Catholic.

When Bradlee was fourteen, personal tragedy touched him in a way the Depression had not. Along with some 18 others of the 180 at St. Mark's, he got polio. One student died. For three months, Benjamin was paralyzed from the waist down, able to do little more than lie in bed in a brace. His father would place him in a hot tub in the morning before going down for breakfast and put him back in bed once he had finished his meal, repeating the process at night. His parents built a set of pulleys over his bed so Bradlee could hoist himself up, an exercise Bradlee credits for his still ample chest. An older friend would often stop by and encourage Ben to try to walk. Eventually he could, though he needed crutches for several months, wore a corset for nearly a year, and never regained his former speed.

Bradlee's bout with polio was the most difficult test of his childhood. But even before he contracted and defeated the disease, Bradlee had learned from his father to be a fighter. And despite the polio, the Depression, and his mother having to go to work in a dress store, he recalls his as a great childhood: "The Depression . . . brought our family together in a way that was very constructive." And though cash was short, the prospect of better times was always just around the corner: "Mind you, there was always a little dough in the offing . . . if the right people died."

Also, the Bradlee family sat out the Depression in relative luxury, on a twenty-acre estate in Beverly, Massachusetts, provided by family friends on the condition that the Bradlees maintain it. Moreover, Bradlee's father and St. Mark's had instilled the attitude that for people like him, adversity was an unnatural condition, a temporary state that inevitably would change. So when the time came for Benjamin to get his ticket punched at Harvard, "It was just assumed I would go there. I never knew there was another choice."

Though slowed down by polio, he went out for football his freshman year "because I thought my father, even though he never said anything to me about it, would like it." Bradlee couldn't make the team, and played baseball and squash instead—and prepared himself for a war, which to him, as to most young Americans of his generation, seemed inevitable. Hitler marched into Poland the same month Bradlee entered Harvard.

From the minute he signed up for naval ROTC, he knew that he would go to war; he knew also that he would go in style. The ROTC commanding officer, with a buddy in the navy's personnel bureau, worked out a deal for the young Harvard warriors. All were to get good front-line assignments—cruisers, destroyers, and submarines. Thus motivated, Bradlee dropped his work on the Harvard *Crimson,* stopped cutting classes, stepped up his pace, and graduated in less than three years: "There were twelve of us, the first twelve of my class to graduate, three of them from that little WASP boarding school. . . . I graduated, was commissioned an ensign, and got married, in that order, on one day, August 8, 1942"—two and a half weeks before his twenty-first birthday.

After training in Key West, he went to Kearny, New Jersey, and was shipped off for destroyer duty in the Pacific Ocean, where he stayed for three years. "I remember being amazed at how much responsibility I had. . . . This brand new fucking destroyer that cost five million dollars and, for four hours or eight hours a day, I ran it." He also wondered how he would respond to gunfire and discovered, to his immense relief, "I didn't wet my pants. I didn't jump overboard. I was scared shitless, but I did what I had to do."

He was good at his job as a combat information center officer and at helping his men understand what the struggle was about. Possessing what he termed "an oddly primitive social conscience," Bradlee led discussions that attempted to unravel the big questions of the war and of life. "What are you fighting to do?" he would ask. "What kind of world are we going to build?"

He saw much battle action, made many friends, and decided a naval career was not for him. Among other things, naval officers spent so much time at sea that they sacrificed a normal home or social life: "You couldn't get laid. Hard to get laid."

Having left the cocoon of upper-class expectations and entered the military and manhood simultaneously, Bradlee was ripe for shaping by the war. In *Conversations with Kennedy,* Bradlee's 1975 book of his off-hour chats with the nation's thirty-fifth president, he wrote: "This record is sprinkled with what some will consider vulgarity. They may be shocked. Others, like Kennedy and like myself, whose vocabularies were formed in the crucible of life in the World War II Navy in the Pacific Ocean, will understand instinctively. There is nothing inherently vulgar in the soldier's description of a broken-down Jeep. 'The fucking fucker's fucked.' Surely, there is no more succinct or even graceful, four-word description of that particular state of affairs."

The war toughened him in a way that St. Mark's, his father, polio, and Harvard could not. He spent much of his last year, for instance, as the forward area representative for the new commander of the Pacific fleet of destroyers, going from vessel to vessel via "britches buoy"—a canvas bag with holes for cable lines that would carry the bag and Bradlee to the next ship.

The war also gave him experience in management. And he found he liked molding lives and even flirted with the idea of teaching high school.

But probably most important, World War II put Bradlee on a big stage where exciting ideas and heroic leaders struggled for dominance. No high school classroom could be so enthralling; perhaps journalism could.

So in January 1946 Bradlee visited New York's major newspapers, determined to hold out for a job befitting one who had commanded a destroyer. Both the *Times* and *Herald Tribune* offered to hire him as a copyboy: "And I decided I just wouldn't take that after all the responsibility I had had. . . . I wasn't about to schlepp coffee for anybody."

At loose ends, Bradlee signed up for a writing course at the New School for Social Research. His aim was to dredge up the great American novel that lay in his gut; he found that it didn't exist. He heard, however, that some acquaintances—one from St. Mark's—were starting a paper in Manchester, New Hampshire. With five thousand dollars of his great-uncle's money, chutzpah, and his preparatory school connection, Bradlee elbowed his way in.

Theirs was a sixty-four-page paper with four sections and comics called the *New Hampshire Sunday News*—designed to answer the need for a Sunday newspaper in the region. Bradlee did a little bit of everything except run the place. He was copy clerk, janitor, and black market newsprint purchaser. He also helped to produce and deliver the paper and, in his spare time, practiced investigative reporting.

"We won the AP award for all papers, dailies and others. We beat Boston, beat Providence, beat Hartford, beat them all; put five or six guys in jail; had a hell of a time." After that "you couldn't have blasted me out" of journalism.

Nonetheless, by late 1948 his wife, Jean, was pregnant and the paper was nearly broke. Bradlee was making fifty dollars a week, which his wife supplemented by working as an interior decorator. With responsibility closing in, he and his partners sold the newspaper to publisher William Loeb.

Bradlee hustled letters of introduction to the *Washington Post* and *Baltimore Sun* from a well-connected friend of his father and took a night train from Boston. As the train rolled into Baltimore, the pounding rain convinced Bradlee to stay put. The *Sun* could wait, he told himself, until the weather improved, and he continued on to Washington and the *Post.*

A reporter had quit the previous day and Bradlee was hired at $80 a week, subject to publisher Philip Graham's approval. Later that night, his sister (who then worked for *Vogue*) called to tell him she had found him a job at *Life* for $150 a week. The job was in the South, a region of the country Bradlee didn't know and found intimidating. "Well, hell, I gave my word to the *Post,*" said Bradlee, explaining to his sister that he could not go to *Life.*

At the *Post,* he found a place that suited his temperament: a crusading paper that went after gambling joints and misbehaving cops and to whom being noticed was as important as it was to Bradlee himself. Far from the prestigious publication it would eventually become, the *Post* had been auctioned only a decade and a half earlier at a bankruptcy sale.

Founded in 1877 by Stilson Hutchins, a former editor of the *Des Moines Telegraph* and an activist in Democratic party politics, the *Post* had started as an intensely partisan paper but eventually shifted toward middle ground. When sold in 1889 to partners Frank Hatton (a Republican) and Beriah Wilkins (a Democrat), the paper was profitable, respectable, and solidly conservative. In 1905, after both Hatton and Wilkins had died, a new editor and part-owner came aboard: John R. McLean, a former Democratic candidate for governor of Ohio and owner of the *Cincinnati Enquirer.* Eventually McLean obtained majority control. He also instituted banner headlines and sensationalized coverage, and the *Post* continued to prosper. Under his son, Edward Beale McLean, who inherited the publication in 1916, the good times screeched to a halt, leaving the *Post* in last place in a five-newspaper town.

The spoiled son of a rich, powerful businessman, the younger McLean never really learned the newspaper business; nor, as it turned out, did he learn sound judgment. A close friend of President Warren Harding, McLean lied to protect Harding's interior secretary from Teapot Dome investigators. The lie backfired; and McLean, who had claimed he had loaned money to Secretary Albert Fall, was forced to admit in court in

1924 that Fall's sudden wealth had come from elsewhere. That year, the *Post* (which had profitably coasted along despite McLean's neglect) went into the red for the first time. McLean was ill equipped to turn it around; and by the time the Depression arrived, the paper's financial sickness seemed terminal. Meanwhile, relations soured between McLean and his wife, Evalyn, who in 1932 sued for separate maintenance and McLean's removal as publisher.

In 1933, when the daily went on the block, it was $500,000 in debt and losing $300,000 a year. Eugene Meyer, a wealthy financier who had held high government posts in several administrations, bought the *Post* for $825,000. Thirteen years later, he turned it over to his son-in-law, Philip Graham.

Meyer had invested millions in the *Post,* finally putting it in the black during World War II; but its hold on profitability remained precarious. Profits for the wartime years of 1942–45 totaled $240,000. And though circulation had climbed impressively, the *Post* was still behind the *Evening Star* and the *Times-Herald.* Army Air Corps veteran Graham, desiring to keep costs down while improving the paper, hired James Russell Wiggins from the *New York Times* as managing editor and encouraged him to pursue aggressive local coverage.

After little more than two years on Graham's feisty publication, Bradlee became restless. He wanted to leave the world of rape and petty crime and break into a big-league reporting beat—maybe Capitol Hill or the White House. But "there were just too many people ahead of me." So he looked beyond the paper itself.

He asked the publisher to support his application for a Nieman Fellowship for a year of study at Harvard. As Bradlee remembers the conversation, Graham said, "Fuck you, you've already been to Harvard." And Bradlee, unwilling to sit still and despairing of rising at the *Post* anytime soon, took advantage of the French he had always spoken and signed up as a press officer with the foreign service in Paris. Graham, having taken a liking to the impatient young charmer, wrote letters of introduction to such notables as French economist and statesman Jean Monnet and American ambassador David Bruce.

Bradlee immediately discovered that the bureaucracy was not for him. The pace didn't suit his temperament; diplomatic tact didn't match his style; anonymity couldn't satisfy his ego.

Yet he loved being in Paris. He looked for a job that would keep him there and finally latched on to *Newsweek.*

Landing the position was a little like finding heaven. As European correspondent, Bradlee covered a territory that stretched from the Sahara to the English Channel, from Portugal to Israel. He saw himself as one man against the *Time* and *Life* hordes and he relished the competition, knowing that in the end he and they would be judged solely by the twenty-five hundred words that made it into their respective magazines.

In 1956, he was served with an expulsion order (later rescinded) from France—for "journalistic initiative," as *Newsweek* described it—after trying to contact the North African rebels while covering the uprising in Algeria. The showdown between *Newsweek* and the French government made news around the world and was Bradlee's first flirtation with celebrity.

Yet he was being tugged back to the States. His first marriage had collapsed and divorce was imminent. He was raising a child who didn't speak English and preparing to marry a woman who couldn't keep her four children abroad indefinitely.

He returned to Washington in 1957, and he was "scared to death." Having become a big fish in the small pond of American correspondents abroad, he was unsure of comparable success at home. So he compensated as he always had, by trying to outhustle the competition. And two years after his homecoming, Bradlee was assigned to John F. Kennedy.

Meanwhile, a series of events began that would catapult Bradlee to the leadership of the *Washington Post.* Vincent Astor, who owned *Newsweek,* died in 1959. The magazine, along with the bulk of his assets, went to the Vincent Astor Foundation. Bradlee was worried that the foundation would sell the magazine without considering the wishes of the staff. Osborn Elliott, then *Newsweek*'s number-three editor, was also troubled. He and Bradlee forged an alliance to try to keep the magazine in hands they could trust.

Bradlee knew Joseph Pulitzer, who had gone to St. Mark's, and Marshall Field, the publisher in Chicago, but he finally focused on Phil Graham, his old patron, as the most likely savior. One night near eleven o'clock, he called Graham on impulse and, to his surprise, was summoned to Graham's Georgetown home. After six hours of intense conversation, Graham commanded, "Go home and write about the people. Who are the people at *Newsweek?*" Bradlee raced to his typewriter. He appeared at Graham's residence at 9:00 A.M. that morning with a fifty-page document that recommended, among other things, that Elliott be made editor. Eighteen days later, Graham owned *Newsweek.*

The financing was inspired. Though the selling price was fifteen million dollars, only seventy-five thousand in cash was required. Bradlee, to his astonishment, got a generous finder's fee for his matchmaking.

Cupid could not have done better. The acquisition broadened Bradlee's career horizons and expanded the company's potential. It gave the Post Company a real stake in global journalism and provided *Newsweek* with an owner who wanted to make the magazine into something more than a refuge for "drunks, incompetents, and hacks," as described by Elliott, who became editor. It also set the stage for Frederick S. "Fritz" Beebe—who until then had served as outside counsel to Graham—to become chairman of the Washington Post. More than any other single individual, Beebe held the company together as Phil Graham, his manic depression worsening, drifted in and out of lucidity.

To Bradlee, however, Graham seemed a knight in silver armor on his way to greatness: "I mean he wasn't Henry Luce, but by God they were in there." And Bradlee was relieved the magazine finally belonged to someone he believed in, unlike Astor, whom he took to be "an asshole . . . who was a drunk," and unlike the other prospective bidders (including Doubleday, the book publisher, and S. I. Newhouse, the newspaper magnate) who he felt might milk the magazine and change it for the worse.

Yet even as *Newsweek* began its ascent and the *Washington Post* consolidated its position, Phil Graham was self-destructing.

Graham was over six feet tall and handsome, with a manner that, says Bradlee, "would charm the glasses right off your nose." Tenth in his class at Harvard Law School, president of the Harvard Law Review, clerk for Supreme Court justices Stanley Reed and Felix Frankfurter, confidant of Lyndon Johnson and John F. Kennedy, power player in Democratic politics—Graham had accomplishments that stretched on virtually forever.

The *Post* editorial page described him as one who "invested the full capacity of his mind and heart in anything that deeply moved and interested him. He was not a person given to qualified commitments to his country, his enterprise or his friends. It was a quality that precipitated the illness that led to his death." By all accounts, he was a brilliant, impressive, and charming man who put those close to him through hell as his illness gained control, and whose lieutenants tried desperately to protect the company from the excesses of their chief.

Graham's executives were likely to be fired on a whim, or to find themselves saddled with people Graham had hired on visits abroad. For Katharine Graham, the nightmare had begun in 1957, well before the *Post* vanquished the then dominant *Washington Star,* and it had deepened as her husband carried on an open affair with a *Newsweek* employee in Paris.

"In '57, just as we began to pull even [with the *Star*], Phil's illness . . . got to the point where he was absent for long periods of time," she recalls. And even when he was present and fully functional, he was much more interested in Democratic politics than in the management of his growing communications empire. Though the company's prospects were steadily improving, Phil Graham's erratic behavior was draining everyone, sapping energy that might better have been directed at charting a course for the corporation. Instead, recalls his widow, the year before his death was "taken up pretty much with chaos and trying to hold the company together."

Graham's death was the lead story in the *Post*'s Sunday, August 4, 1963 edition. Alone in a first-floor room of his farm near Marshall, Virginia, the publisher had killed himself with a .28-gauge shotgun. His wife and the servants were elsewhere in the house. Graham had just that day left Chestnut Lodge, a sanitarium in Rockville, Maryland.

Other stories told of the expected signing of the nuclear test ban treaty, FDA approval of an oral contraceptive, and of President Kennedy's refusal to predict the sex of the child Jacqueline was carrying, even though he had predicted the sex of John, Jr., in 1960. (Three days later Patrick Bouvier Kennedy was born prematurely and died after struggling for breath for nearly forty hours.)

No one was more distraught than Katharine Graham, a tall, thin, timid, dark-haired woman who had never envisioned herself running a corporation. Nevertheless, she appeared before her board. The impression she made lingers with *Newsweek*'s Osborn Elliott: "She had always until then sort of hung in the background . . . under the shadow of two very powerful parents and an extraordinarily dynamic, energetic, and attractive husband. And when Phil Graham killed himself, she was suddenly thrust center stage. . . . I think it was the day before his funeral when there was a meeting of the Washington Post board . . . and Kay, looking like a ghost, terribly upset, pulled herself together and said to the group, 'Look, I know there are a lot of rumors going around about this company. . . . I want you to know that no part of this company or the company itself is for sale. It's a family company and there's another generation coming along and I just wanted to reassure you that there are no such plans whatsoever.' "

She went on to thank those present for their professionalism and for coping with a most difficult year. Elliott thought the performance an awesome show of inner strength from a woman he sensed to be extremely insecure about stepping into a business dominated by men who knew so much more about it than she.

At the time, Katharine Graham had no idea that the *Post* could be a great international newspaper or that corporate management could be improved. She saw herself as something of a regent. Instead of actually running the company, she intended to oversee "sort of a holding operation until the boys grew up," relying on her managers to keep things going as Phil would have liked. In the meantime, she would learn as much as possible about the company just in case she had to make a major decision.

The status of women and her own conventional upbringing made it difficult for her to define her role differently. Yet selling the company or not participating in its operation was unthinkable.

So Graham, a product of the Madeira School for young ladies, Vassar, and the University of Chicago, and who had worked briefly for the *San Francisco News* and the family newspaper, found herself president of the Washington Post Company. And eventually, she began to see a *Post* beyond the one that Phil had built.

The change was sparked by her relationship with James Reston, columnist and former Washington bureau chief for the *New York Times.* A strong admirer of Reston, Graham had offered him a column at the *Post* and hinted that he might one day run the paper—though she never clearly promised him the editorship. Reston decided not to come, but during those conversations, he asked whether she wished to leave the paper a greater place than she had found it. For the first time, said Graham, "it occurred to me that *I could,* or that it might be possible, or that it was something I should do."

Others talked to her as well, including Robert Manning, a former *Time* writer and past assistant secretary of state for public affairs. Upon leaving government, he indicated to her in his oblique, State Department manner that he just might be available to become the *Post*'s editor. The job was not offered, but Manning's and Reston's critiques helped to persuade Graham that Alfred Friendly's newsroom was losing some of its zest.

In 1965, Friendly had been at the *Post* for more than a quarter of a century. He had been managing editor for a decade and assistant managing editor for several years before that. Phil Graham himself had guided Friendly's career, positioning him to eventually take over from James Russell Wiggins. Together, Graham, Wiggins, and Friendly had built the *Post* into a decent (though not great) newspaper. In convincing Katharine Graham that Friendly had finally run out of steam, Reston and the others forced her to confront Phil Graham's ghost, to consider the possibility of a leadership team and a vision different from those he had left.

Meanwhile, two senior editing jobs opened up at *Newsweek* in relatively quick succession, and Bradlee was asked to come to New York and get on the management ladder. Both times he refused. And that got Graham's attention.

She had no idea, however, what to make of his resistance. Certainly, he didn't want to be Washington bureau chief all his life. Yet he had given no indication of what he would like to be. She knew his bureau was filled with talented correspondents who were there largely because of him, that he was energetic enough to have impressed her late husband, and that he was just good-looking enough that television might lure him away. "So I thought I better talk to him and see what it is that he does want to do."

When she initially asked him what he wanted to do, Bradlee had no real answer. But when the subject of the *Post* arose Bradlee perked up and uttered, "Now that you've asked me, I'd give my left one to be managing editor of the *Washington Post.*" She found that "a rather surprising idea" and promised to think about it.

For Bradlee, editing the *Post* was more than a surprising idea; it was a calling. The chance to be at the helm of a vehicle that "can get someone out of jail in twenty-four hours and put someone in there damn near as fast" represented power unlike any he had held. A newspaper could get a hole filled, a tree planted, a wrongdoer indicted.

Graham, on the other hand, was not so sure about Bradlee. For though he had started in newspapers, he had really grown up at *Newsweek.* But all her advisers (Fritz Beebe, Walter Lippmann, and others) thought Bradlee a fine journalist—one with perhaps the spark the *Post* needed.

The idea grew on her, but she was too cautious to bring him in as managing editor or as editor-in-chief. She thought she might make him an assistant managing editor, let him mellow a couple of years, and then perhaps promote him. Bradlee, however, pushed for more. And on August 1, 1965, he started as deputy managing editor for national and foreign news: a man in a hurry about to turn forty-four.

Bradlee had many apprehensions, particularly given his ignorance of presses, production, and layout, but he felt he had one overwhelming advantage: "I had confidence that I was a good judge of horseflesh. . . . Above all, I thought I knew who was good. And I knew the *Washington Post* did not have the best people." Instead, the *Post* had a newsroom full of deadwood. And Friendly, with his diminishing energy and long absences from the paper, seemed incapable of or uninterested in pruning the staff.

Bradlee respected some *Post* writers, including Chalmers Roberts and Murrey Marder, but he referred to one senior reporter as "Black Sheet Jack," believing him to be a pilferer of stories from other reporters' carbons. Numerous others, including the White House correspondent, he judged to be hopelessly mediocre.

Though he lacked a grand vision, Bradlee felt one would emerge from his work: "Shit, I went to a little grade school once in Boston whose motto was 'Best today, better tomorrow.' And in a sort of funny way, I have a feeling that if you make your paper better this week than it was last, or today than it was yesterday, pretty soon you'll have something pretty good."

Despite Bradlee's persistent lobbying, Graham remained reluctant to give him a clear shot at the top job, and he didn't like waiting: "I had no timetable when I came here. I wanted one, but I didn't get one. And I said to Katharine that I'd give it a year. . . . It didn't seem worth it to come over here and just get lost in the woodwork."

Bradlee made no secret of his ambition. During a showdown in the managing editor's home, Bradlee told Friendly: "I want you to know that I will give you 110 percent. My life is filled with giving people 110 percent. I work hard as hell and I'm loyal as hell, but I don't think I ought to stay around more than a year." When Friendly told him a year was much too short, Bradlee replied that he thought a year was the outside limit.

Science writer Howard Simons barely knew Bradlee. He had met him once at a party and again when Bradlee, prior to joining the paper, had asked Simons to brief him on the *Post.* But by the time Bradlee appeared in the newsroom, Simons could predict the outcome.

"Clearly, he had the blessing of Mrs. Graham," says Simons. "Clearly, he was going to take over someday. Clearly, he knew what he wanted. . . . I don't think it was unclear to anybody."

William Raspberry, a beginning reporter at the *Post,* immediately realized that Bradlee represented something new: "Al Friendly was *professional.* [Executive editor] Russ Wiggins was *professional* . . . very dignified and all that. And here comes a guy who is by all accounts . . . a brilliant journalist and brilliant editor . . . but who is also brash and salty. . . . He brought a kind of glamor and spice to the newsroom that it hadn't had before." In three months' time, the brash newcomer had Friendly's job and Friendly was a globe-trotting correspondent.

In Bradlee's mind, the contest had been fair; he had given Friendly his 110 percent. And if things became "a little dicey around here," he had no apologies to make: "People said, 'Jesus Christ, you're . . . ruthless.' . . . I'm actually at peace with how I behaved."

He could not have ascended at a better time. For as Bradlee perceived it, Graham "was beginning to sort of come out from under her shell. . . . The paper was beginning to make some really good money." And glory seemed within his grasp.

In anticipation of Friendly's removal, Graham had frozen vacancies the previous April. So as Bradlee consolidated his power, he had plenty of maneuvering room. He quickly began assembling a constellation of stars—Ward Just, Hobart Rowen, Haynes Johnson, and others—journalists who not only knew Washington but could write with style.

Bradlee stopped by Simons's desk in 1966 and invited him to the cafeteria for a cup of coffee. "He asked me if I would be his assistant managing editor and we would make the revolution together," Simons recalls. "And I said, 'Absolutely.' "

Those lives touched most deeply by Bradlee, however, were not the established stars but the young reporters just starting their careers to whom Bradlee came to be a combination of big brother, boss, and minor god. Leonard Downie, Jr., and Robert Kaiser, both barely out of college, were two of many such journalists.

Kaiser had arrived with the first group of student interns in 1963; Downie during the summer of 1964; Kaiser from the Ivy League; Downie from the Big Ten; Kaiser via family influence; Downie via a fluke. Virtually all they had in common was their love of journalism and a desire to succeed.

Downie, an earnest young man from a minimally middle-class Cleveland household, came because a journalism professor at Ohio State University dreamed of starting a graduate branch in Washington. The professor had shared his aspiration and drinks with *Post* city editor Ben Gilbert and sent Downie to the *Post* as his first Washington trainee.

Gilbert barely remembered the conversation and was on the verge of sending the would-be reporter back home when Downie blurted out, "My god, I've got my wife and kid in an apartment . . . and I was expecting to spend the summer here and get a paycheck."

The benevolent Gilbert hired him and Downie became one of the stars of the summer. The next year, he became a full-fledged staff member, just as Bradlee was arriving. Shortly thereafter, Bradlee won the young reporter's heart by tossing out an advertiser who had complained about one of Downie's stories.

With his deep, resonant voice, well-tailored clothes, and confident manner, Kaiser was more typical of the young men who started at the *Post.* A product of Yale University and Loomis prep school, with a father who was resident minister at the American embassy in London, he had a sophistication the paper liked in its interns.

His love of newspapering had begun with a trip to New York with his father. The circulation manager of the *New York Times* had invited them to see the newsroom meet its deadline and, after dinner at Sardi's, to watch the first edition come off the presses.

That evening was for Kaiser an intensely sensual experience, with paper shuffling everywhere, foreign correspondents calling in by radio, and journalists rushing about.

After graduating from Yale in 1964 and spending the summer at the *Post,* Kaiser left for the London School of Economics, where he could both avoid the draft and pick up the education he had neglected while devoting his time to the Yale *Daily News.*

London was very much in the news. The Beatles had invaded the United States and British pop culture was in vogue. At managing editor Al Friendly's suggestion, Kaiser began writing occasional pieces from London and was soon getting complimentary notes from Bradlee. In 1966, Ben Gilbert (then assistant managing editor for local news) appeared in London with a message: Bradlee loved Kaiser's work and wanted to hire him for the national staff in Washington. But Gilbert had no intention of letting that happen; a new reporter like Kaiser, he insisted, belonged on local, getting a feel for the city, not hobnobbing with politicians on Capitol Hill.

Kaiser's first assignment on returning was to cover the District of Columbia government. Washington, previously governed by the U.S. Congress, was undergoing a transition to home rule. Gilbert was intensely protective of the city and its new administration, enough so that he would suppress news of incidents that might heighten racial tensions. Nevertheless, such incidents regularly occurred. Typically, the police would accost a black teenager, a crowd would gather, and tempers would flare.

After Kaiser covered one such episode, Gilbert tried to kill the story and Kaiser turned to Bradlee for help. A shouting match ensued between Bradlee and Gilbert and Bradlee finally decreed that the story would run. From that moment forward, Kaiser was a disciple, "one of the many people around here who would walk off a [plank] for him."

Kaiser realized, at that point, just how much the *Post* was changing. He realized as well that he had unwittingly become a bit player in a drama: the clashing of the *Post* old guard with the new. Bradlee did not share Gilbert's enthusiasm for boosterism. He wanted to make the *Post* belligerently independent. Nor did he share Gilbert's obsession with local Washington; Bradlee was more intrigued by Washington's national and international aspects—and intended for the paper to reflect that.

By then, new (and by *Post* standards) unusual journalists were regularly appearing in the newsroom. Robert C. Maynard, of Barbadian descent, with his scruffy beard, minister's voice, and Harvard vocabulary, was one.

While still in high school, Maynard had written for the *New York Age-Defender,* one of the oldest black newspapers in the country. He would check in with his home room, leave before his first class, and rush to the courthouse to find a story—which would always appear under a pseudonym, lest his parents realize he was working instead of attending classes. By the time they finally did catch on, he was no longer qualified to graduate. So when offered a full-time job at the *Baltimore Afro-American,* he accepted.

Before long, however, Maynard was fantasizing about working in the mainstream daily press with editors who had not been stifled by discrimination. In the mid-1950s that was not easy for a black reporter to do, but after sending out more than three hundred applications, Maynard was hired by a small paper in York, Pennsylvania. The accomplishment so thrilled him that Maynard suffered a nosebleed on being shown his typewriter and desk.

Much later, during a year of study on a Nieman Fellowship at Harvard, Maynard encountered Bradlee, who was visiting the Nieman class.

"Mr. Bradlee, how do you respond to those who say that the *Washington Post* is nothing more than a four-color press release for the State Department's policies in Vietnam?" Maynard asked, in a tone calculated to stir things up rather than elicit a serious response.

Afterward, Bradlee snapped, "I really like smartasses like

you. You got all the criticisms, but you don't have any solutions. . . . You don't offer to help."

Maynard was surprised that the bristly editor with the mile-high chip on his shoulder seemed to be reaching out, that he actually appeared to be seeking reporters who would challenge him and conventional thought. Later, Maynard went to see Bradlee about a job. He had already interviewed with the *New York Times* and found distasteful their seemingly rigid program of three years here, three years there, and four years somewhere else before he could get an important beat. "Do you have a program like that," he asked, "a ten-year program?"

Bradlee told him, "Hell, no, for all I know you'll get your ass thrown out of here in the first six months, or on the other hand, in six years you might be associate editor." Maynard liked the answer and signed up.

Maynard's employment was based more on intuition than on careful assessment, but like so many of Bradlee's hires, it proved a good one. Maynard was to go on to a distinguished career, eventually becoming editor and publisher of his own newspaper. But in the fall of 1967, the *Post* was where he wanted to be. For the paper had belatedly realized that it was in a majority black city at a time when black outrage was demanding a voice.

In September of his first year, in a seven-part series based on visits to five urban slums, Maynard tried to explain why the nation's cities were aflame.

> An angry and violent mood is nearing the explosion point in the black communities of America's largest cities. . . .
>
> This is a result of a strong conviction among Negroes that white Americans are bent on destroying black Americans. It could erupt into racial war, going beyond the recent summers of discontent. . . .
>
> The dream deferred too long has revealed the fury at last. The streets are hostile now, the tension is almost electric, the hatred of "the man" is out in the open.

Before long, racial problems would also surface at the *Post;* but for the moment the most notable tensions were in the streets, feeding Bradlee's kind of journalism: stories that demanded attention and hit with all the subtlety of a baseball bat to the head.

Meanwhile, Bradlee was hiring established pros along with the young hotshots. Political analyst David Broder and social commentator Nicholas von Hoffman were among the most prominent. And other changes were occurring. Katharine Graham lured Philip L. Geyelin from the *Wall Street Journal* in 1967, with the understanding he would be groomed to take over the editorial page when J. Russell Wiggins retired.

The following year, Geyelin hired Meg Greenfield, a fragile-looking, dark-haired woman who had graduated summa cum laude from Smith College and made something of a splash in the *Reporter* magazine with her first published article. The piece analyzed Richard M. Nixon's practice of advocating and opposing the same things in the same speech.

The editorial page was not part of Bradlee's turf, but Greenfield felt very much a part of the new order that Bradlee symbolized. Geyelin, it seemed, would do for the editorial page what Bradlee had done in news. He would bring in young people with a fresh outlook. He would also repudiate Wiggins's passionate support of the war in Vietnam.

Wiggins retired in late 1968 to become United Nations ambassador. Bradlee assumed his title of executive editor and Geyelin took over his editorial page, both reporting directly to Katharine Graham. Eugene Patterson, a Pulitzer Prize winner formerly of the *Atlanta Constitution,* replaced Bradlee as managing editor. Gilbert moved to the editorial page before leaving the paper in 1970.

That year the *Post* discovered Roger Wilkins, a soft-spoken, self-assured former U.S. assistant attorney general. Wilkins, an executive with the Ford Foundation, was invited by Nick Kotz, a Pulitzer Prize–winning *Post* reporter, to attend the Gridiron Club dinner—a lavish, annual ritual for Washington's political and press elite.

About a week later, he got a call from Meg Greenfield, who, while dining at Kotz's home, had heard that the Gridiron dinner had left Wilkins angry and depressed. Would he be willing to write about it?

Wilkins produced a biting, anguished piece, which took up nearly two full columns on the editorial page:

> The first impression was stunning: almost every passing face was a familiar one. . . . There were Richard Helms and

> Walter Mondale and Henry Kissinger and George McGovern and Joel Broyhill and Tom Wicker and William Westmoreland and John Mitchell and Tom Clark . . . and Robert Finch and Ralph Nader, and of course, the President of the United States.
>
> One thing quickly became clear about those faces. Apart from Walter Washington—who, I suppose, as Mayor had to be invited—mine was the only face in a crowd of 500 that was not white. There were no Indians, there were no Asians, there were no Puerto Ricans, there were no Mexican Americans. There was just the mayor and me. . . .
>
> There is something about an atmosphere like that that is hard to define, but excruciatingly easy for a black man to feel. It is the heavy, almost tangible, clearly visible broad assumption that in places where it counts, America is a white country. . . . This night in that room, less than three miles from my home in the nation's capital, a 60 percent black city, I felt out of place in America. . . .
>
> And when it came to an end, the President and the Vice President of the United States, in an act which they had consciously worked up, put on a Mr. Bones routine about the Southern strategy with the biggest boffo coming as the Vice President affected a deep Southern accent. And then they played their duets—the President playing his songs, the Vice President playing "Dixie," the whole thing climaxed by "God Bless America" and "Auld Lang Syne." The crowd ate it up. They roared. As they roared I thought that after our black decade of imploring, suing, marching, lobbying, singing, rebelling, praying and dying we had come to this: a Vice Presidential Dixie with the President as his straight man.

The article drew blood. The Gridiron Club gave up its all-white ways and the *Post* editorial page decided to do the same. Wilkins was offered a position but declined, feeling he owed the Ford Foundation more time. A year later, he took a salary cut and joined the page—his hiring yet another sign that the old ways would no longer do.

"In the early days [Bradlee] was . . . fighting an institution that didn't want to change. Gradually over a period of time, he took control of it," says David Laventhol, hired as night managing editor in 1966.

But something else was happening as well. Bradlee was altering the personality of the newsroom. After Bradlee's father-in-law died, leaving him a London-tailored houndstooth suit that required him to wear suspenders, notes Kaiser, "within a few months, there were half a dozen people in the newsroom wearing suspenders."

Noticeable though his fashion statement may have been, Bradlee's decision to promote Laurence Stern was even more so. Stern was a veteran *Post* reporter, one of the few of the old gang Bradlee genuinely respected. Stern was also a maverick, "always fighting with Gilbert and always on the outs with the [Graham] family," recalls Kaiser. "And suddenly Bradlee's here and [Stern is] the national editor. And they're fighting all these clowns who were clogging the system."

Despite the conflicts—or because of them—creativity was blossoming, particularly in the reshaped women's section, which became one of Bradlee's biggest headaches.

Responsibility for redoing that section fell to Laventhol, a native of Philadelphia whose father had also been a journalist and who had come to the *Post* by way of Yale and the *St. Petersburg Times.*

He was first hired by the *Post* in 1963 but stayed only a few months. In those pre-Bradlee years, the most exciting newspaper town was not Washington but New York, where a glamorous editor, James Bellows, was enlivening the *Herald Tribune.* Bellows had offered Laventhol a job and Laventhol could not say no.

When the *Herald Tribune* folded in 1966, Bradlee invited him back. And Laventhol, after revamping the newspaper's format, turned his attention to what was to become the "Style" section.

Bradlee's news magazine background had introduced him to the concept of the "back of the book," which combined fashion, entertainment, social trends, commentary, and books as one package. A broader version of that, he concluded, might breathe some life into the women's pages.

He told Laventhol to go to Chicago, Detroit, and Los Angeles and return with ideas. Laventhol came back with a design that incorporated much of what his old boss, Bellows, was doing with the *Los Angeles Times.* The new section was to include consumer listings and reports on relationships, life-styles, and virtually anything of interest that was not hard news or sports; and it would adopt a witty, irreverent manner that would encourage pompous Washington society to poke fun at itself. The proposal was taken to Graham and received her enthusiastic approval.

When launched in 1969, "Style" shocked official Washington, including Katharine Graham, who found it quite different from the concept she had endorsed.

"It was a tremendous change from the teacups, parties, and women's clubs and stuff," she notes, and that was fine. But it indulged in overkill. "We had page-long book reviews and then we'd have reviews of the reviewers." "Style" would also "carve people up," particularly those who attended society parties. "It was just very offensive to a lot of people and I was taking the heat. . . . There was no more fashion. . . . Home design, forget it. It was all out."

So she complained, often and loudly. "She was *nudzhing* me to death about 'Style,' " Bradlee recalls. "All her buddies were saying, 'Good God, what is this that you've started here?' "

She finally drove Bradlee to such distraction that he barked, "Get your finger out of my eye," and added that if she still didn't like "Style" in six months, he would change it.

Bradlee's words shocked her: "He had never said anything that frontal in all our relationship and . . . I stopped . . . because I realized it was serious and that he had never been that serious."

"Style" was Bradlee's most visible innovation up to that time, and he felt strongly enough about it to risk rupturing his relationship with his boss.

"Style" took considerably longer than six months to find itself. The search consumed a succession of editors and created a great deal of confusion. But eventually it became one of Bradlee's biggest successes—and a showcase for the woman who would become his third wife.

Washington Post

Donald and Katharine Graham

Katharine Graham with former President Richard Nixon at 1986 convention of the American Newspaper Publishers Association

© THE WASHINGTON POST

Milton Coleman

Bob Kaiser

© FRANK JOHNSTON, *THE WASHINGTON POST*

© FRANK JOHNSTON, *THE WASHINGTON POST*

Len Downie (left) and Ben Bradlee at *Washington Post* editorial budget meeting

Ben Bradlee

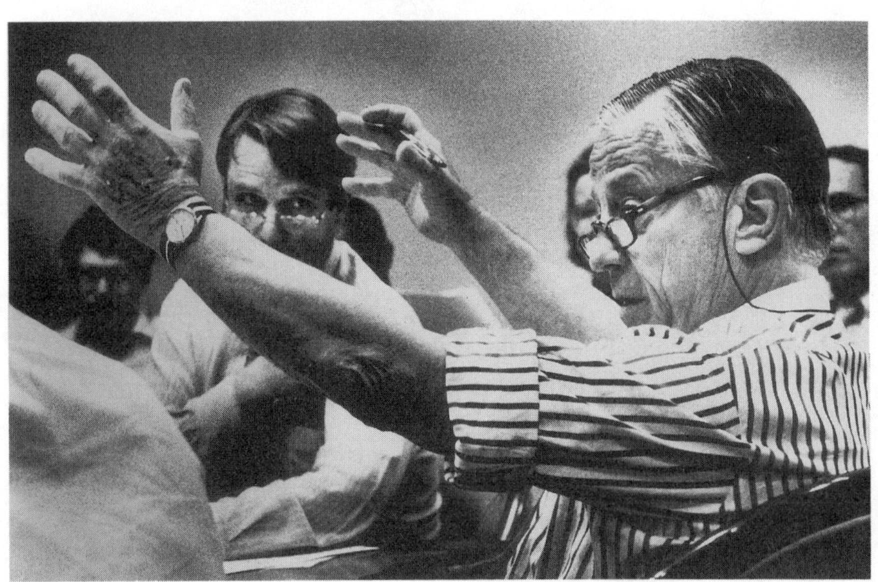

© FRANK JOHNSTON, *THE WASHINGTON POST*

Bob Woodward

Robert Maynard

Donald Graham

CHAPTER 2

MOVING INTO THE MAJOR LEAGUE

The 1970s were to bring the *Post* the Pentagon Papers and Watergate and force Katharine Graham to confront questions (of finance, politics, and ultimately of faith) that went to the very heart of what her paper and company were to be.

Privately held since incorporating in 1947, the Post was desperately strapped for cash. It could get that cash by borrowing, selling assets, or issuing stock. To borrow would create even greater future demands. To sell assets would diminish the company's foundation. But to sell stock would be to invite Wall Street to share in (and help shape) the future of the Post. Katharine Graham could keep the Post (at its peril) a family concern or take a deep breath and put the business on the Street.

Philip Graham had begun giving stock to valued executives in 1952, which the company redeemed when they left. The shares (valued every year by Price Waterhouse) had increased in worth more than twenty times. As managers retired, the company needed increasingly large amounts of money to buy them out.

Also under Philip Graham, the company had bought television stations WTOP in Washington and WJXT in Jacksonville, Florida, and it had purchased (and merged the *Post* with) the *Washington Times-Herald.* The 1954 merger had added 180,000 readers to the *Post*'s existing 200,000—making the *Post* Washington's largest newspaper. The television stations, however, were not yet making big money. And though *Post* advertising had grown, it had not kept pace with the company's needs.

Bradlee's budget, for instance, had increased from five million dollars when he took over to more than seven million by 1970. And *Newsweek*'s editorial costs had tripled since Graham acquired it.

Meanwhile, debt had piled up from the new headquarters under construction and from the purchase of a television station in Miami—renamed WPLG in honor of Phil Graham.

The Post generated revenues of nearly $65 million in 1965 and after-tax profits of $5.9 million. By 1970, revenues had risen above $178 million but profits had decreased to less than $5 million. The following year, company chairman Fritz Beebe told Katharine Graham that the need for cash had become so great that the company would either have to sell its Jacksonville television station or go public.

Times Mirror, Gannett, the New York Times, and others had already turned to Wall Street. The New York Times had done so in a particularly interesting way, issuing limited voting stock to the public while keeping control (and the majority of those shares with full voting rights) in family hands. The New York Stock Exchange wouldn't list the second-class stock, but the American Stock Exchange would. With the New York Times model in mind, the Post proceeded.

A stock offering was prepared and the announcements were made, and then the *New York Times* dropped the bomb that came to be known as the Pentagon Papers.

On Sunday, June 13, 1971, the *Times* published the first installment of the U.S. government study that documented the duplicity that had prolonged the Vietnam War. The U.S. Justice Department sued, stopping publication after the third day.

A day later, *Post* national editor Ben Bagdikian secretly met in Boston with Daniel Ellsberg, the *Times'* source. Bagdikian and Ellsberg knew each other since both had worked at the Rand Corporation—though on different projects—and Ellsberg gave Bagdikian the papers. Bagdikian brought the papers to Bradlee's Georgetown home, where reporters, editors, and lawyers had assembled. And that Thursday evening they fought over the company's soul.

The lawyers argued that the papers shouldn't be published,

that it was foolhardy to take on the government. The journalists contended that they had to be published and worked feverishly to get them ready.

Katharine Graham was at her Georgetown residence, giving a party for retiring business manager Harry Gladstein, and awaiting the outcome of the Bradlee discussions. "We called them at the time of the first edition and they said they weren't ready," recalls Graham. "So we just set the first edition with . . . promotion ads. . . . And then came time for the second edition . . . the big run."

Graham was on the lawn preparing to toast Gladstein when *Post* president Paul Ignatius tugged on her sleeve. "They want you on the phone," he said. "I'll be finished in a minute," she replied. "They want you *now,*" he insisted.

She finished the toast, picked up the phone, and listened. First, board chairman Fritz Beebe told her the decision would have to be hers. Then, Bradlee, Chalmers Roberts, and a succession of editors and writers said it was vital that the *Post* publish. Finally Beebe came on the line again and Graham sighed: "Well, the *Times* took two or three months to decide. Why do we have to decide in a minute?"

Ignatius, next to her, kept saying, "Take your time. Take your time." Finally, she asked Beebe what he would do, and he told her he probably would not publish.

The minutes ticked away. She weighed the advice of the lawyers, all urging caution. And she thought about the Post stock, wondering whether the company could even legally sell stock if it were criminally enjoined. Beebe had left her hanging—*her decision*—with only the slightest nudge in the direction of prudence. Yet "he didn't say, 'You're going to wreck the company' or 'Let's not.' He didn't close the door."

Still, Beebe's words unnerved her. For though a lawyer, Beebe identified with journalists and tried to see the world through their eyes. Never once had she ignored his advice. Yet all her editors were convinced that morale on the fifth floor would crumble if she said no.

Graham gave the go-ahead, the presses started, and the *Post* was one with the *Times.* Within twenty-four hours the *Post* too was enjoined. (The stock offering went ahead and was oversubscribed at the twenty-six-dollars-per-common-share asking price.) A week later, the case was before the Supreme Court. And by month's end, both newspapers had won the right to publish.

Howard Simons, who became managing editor later that year, believes that at the moment the case went to court, the *Post* stepped into a new league. A decade earlier, when he had joined it, the *Post* had had only one business reporter and one foreign correspondent—who was shared with the Post television station. The *New York Times,* with sources *Post* reporters could only dream of, looked down on the pushy, hometown paper. The Pentagon Papers, says Simons, began to turn that around: "It was the *Washington Post* and the *New York Times* that went to the Supreme Court, not just the *New York Times.*"

For Bradlee, the Pentagon Papers rivaled Watergate in importance: "Until the Pentagon Papers, the *Post* hadn't made some kind of ultimate commitment to go super first class . . . to take on everybody. . . . It very much was the greening of Katharine in that sense and the greening of Bradlee."

Few recently widowed women, believes Bradlee, could have matched Katharine Graham's toughness. Indeed, an urgent cease-publication request from the U.S. attorney general would have given virtually anyone pause. Yet if Graham had caved in, he insists, that "would have cost us all the momentum we had built up and it would have cost us a lot of staff. . . . There were no hard decisions in Watergate. *None.* Because the decisions had been made. . . . And the trust between her and me was total."

After the Supreme Court ruling, managing editor Eugene Patterson leaped on a desk to proclaim victory. But even as his paper was winning in court, Patterson was losing at work. Though Bradlee had hired him, his formal style seemed out of sync with Bradlee's newsroom. Also, the other editors, nominally his subordinates, noting that Bradlee didn't give Patterson real authority, chose not to give him respect.

"The trouble was that I did not give Gene the responsibilities that I should have," acknowledges Bradlee. "I stayed managing editor. . . . He was tough and he was everything that he should have been, except that I didn't let him be what I learned to allow Simons to be."

Leonard Downie, then a reporter on the metro staff, sensed the friction between Bradlee and Patterson but felt that Patterson's problems extended beyond Bradlee. Patterson was "too much the southern gentleman" for a rough-and-tumble place like the *Post.* Moreover, "the newsroom was going through its hippie period. . . . We were covering the counterculture more than a lot of newspapers, just as we covered civil rights more than a lot of other newspapers. . . . We all had long hair."

Unable to fit in, Patterson left; and Howard Simons moved up.

Thin, quick, and intense, Simons had none of Patterson's formality and was as good a political infighter as any at the *Post.* A nurturing editor attentive enough to soften the effects of Bradlee's hard edges, he was also, in one colleague's description, one who saw plots within plots and was a master at creating intrigue where none existed.

He had been born in Albany, New York, four months before the crash of 1929. After his parent's baby store went out of business following the economic collapse, his father had been unable to find a job for three years. During that period, his mother, working as a clerk, provided for both her family and her sister's—an object lesson in selflessness and support that Simons took to heart.

Simons's bunkmate in the army had worked for a small science news agency in Washington, D.C., where Simons (with a master's degree in journalism from Columbia University) subsequently got a job. That led to a Nieman Fellowship at Harvard, later to a brief career as a free-lance writer, and ultimately to a job offer from the *Post.*

Less than a year after becoming managing editor, Simons received a phone call that—with the help of Carl Bernstein, Bob Woodward, and city editor Barry Sussman—launched what the *Post* later came to see as its "holy shit" era.

The call—alerting him to a break-in at the Democratic National Committee (DNC) headquarters—came from Joseph Califano, general counsel to the DNC and a member of the new law firm selected by the *Post* in the aftermath of the Pentagon Papers. Simons immediately contacted metropolitan editor Harry Rosenfeld, who called city editor Sussman, who roused Bob Woodward at home and ordered him in to do the story.

Woodward, who had been at the *Post* only nine months, was dispatched to the preliminary hearing of the five men captured at 2:30 A.M. He fixed on one: tall, balding James W. McCord, Jr., who described his occupation as "security consultant." As reported in a book later written by Woodward and Bernstein, the judge asked McCord's place of employment.

> McCord, in a soft drawl, said that he had recently retired from government service. Woodward moved to the front row and leaned forward.
>
> "Where in government?" asked the Judge.
>
> "CIA," McCord whispered.

"Holy shit," Woodward said to himself, "CIA." The story, he realized, was far from routine. But neither Woodward nor anyone else at the *Post* had any real sense of what he had stumbled into. He certainly had no notion that the men before him were links in a chain that led to the president of the United States and would ultimately yank him out of office. Next day's story, which Simons ordered onto the front page (a team effort involving eight reporters and carrying Alfred E. Lewis's by-line), merely described an elaborate plot to bug Democratic headquarters.

Within days, however, Woodward and Bernstein realized that they had stumbled into the biggest story of their careers. With that realization came a professional marriage between a most unlikely pair—Bernstein, a former *Post* copyboy who had never finished college, and Woodward, shaped by Yale—whose personalities were as disparate as their backgrounds.

Bernstein, a thin, long-haired rebel who seemed a refugee from the counterculture, had the temperament of a poet and the imagination of a mystery writer.

Tom Wilkinson, a metro desk editor, lived in the same building as Bernstein and sometimes drove him to work. One morning, as the Watergate investigation was beginning, he turned to Bernstein and asked him where the story would lead. Bernstein spun out an elaborate scenario: well, since the break-in involved President Nixon's reelection committee, then it had to involve John Mitchell, and if it involved Mitchell it had to. . . . The speculations went on, linking one tenuous supposition to another, creating a latticework of unproven facts.

"I wasn't sure I believed him at the time," said Wilkinson, "but the possibilities were quite intriguing." It was a typical Bernstein performance from a reporter who early on (after his editors had decided to take him off) forced his way back into the

Watergate story by fashioning a memo consisting of speculations (never substantiated) linking an anonymous White House aide to the Watergate bugging.

Bernstein took great pride in his skill as a writer and would work fanatically on anything that caught his fancy, but when he didn't want to do something, he could become petulant.

Woodward was considerably more consistent; he would accept any story, sink in his teeth like a hungry pit bull, and hold on until he had squeezed it dry.

Whereas Bernstein was something of a hippie, Woodward—neatly dressed and unfailingly polite—was very much the proper midwesterner. Born in Geneva, Illinois, he'd gone to Yale on a ROTC scholarship and graduated in 1965, just in time for the Vietnam War. He'd deliberately avoided the fighting by getting assigned to a destroyer, but couldn't avoid Lyndon Johnson's order extending his four-year hitch to five. Originally he had thought of going to law school, but by the time he left the navy his marriage had fallen apart and Woodward wanted to get his life in order quickly.

The *Post*—which he had discovered while on duty in the Pentagon—was nearby. So he dropped in and, despite repeated rebuffs, kept coming back. The *Post* editors got him a job on the nearby Montgomery County *Sentinel,* but he refused to leave them alone, even showing up during the week of the Supreme Court's Pentagon Papers decision.

A friend who clerked for the court told Woodward the decision two days before its release. Woodward rushed to the *Post* to tell the editors—thinking that perhaps in their gratitude they would give him a job. Instead, they reacted with total disbelief; but he kept returning and finally wore them down.

Shortly after starting, Woodward, along with other new reporters, was invited to lunch with Bradlee. "Which one's Woodward?" asked Bradlee. Woodward, who had been working fanatically to generate stories, identified himself. "You're all over the paper," growled Bradlee, "and that's what I like."

Some three weeks after the Watergate break-in, Woodward again lunched with Bradlee—this time alone at Chez Camille, a restaurant near the *Post.* After groping for points of contact, talking about the navy and destroyers, they eventually got down to business. Woodward was trying to interest Bradlee in a story on drug dealers. Bradlee, who had heard the *Washington Star* was about to be sold, seemed obsessed with confirming his information, getting it into the paper, and catching the *Star* off guard. They talked past each other for most of the lunch. Yet Woodward left feeling that he understood Bradlee much better than before. Bradlee, he realized, delighted in yanking the covers from an adversary and showing him naked before the world. Whether that adversary was the *Star* or Nixon, Bradlee's attitude would be much the same.

Despite an initial mutual dislike, Woodward and Bernstein drew on each other. "Bob Woodward was not born a writer and Carl Bernstein, who could write, was not born judicious," observed Leonard Downie, who, having become deputy metropolitan editor, often oversaw their work. Yet in combination they made one super reporter: Woodward restraining or rechanneling Bernstein's wilder flights of fancy; Bernstein reshaping Woodward's clumsy prose.

Simons made them the permanent Watergate team that August, recognizing not only the symbiosis of the relationship but that the story had grown too big to be covered in any routine way.

Watergate carried Woodstein (as the team was called) from one end of the country to the other, sifting through canceled checks in the state's attorney's office in Dade County, Florida, trailing dirty trickster Donald Segretti to Marina del Rey, California, cornering the U.S. attorney general in a New York hotel, poring through purloined credit card records, tracking secret funds, investigating espionage and political sabotage. They ran into one dead end after another. They also persuaded scores of federal employees to talk—the most famous being Deep Throat, whom Woodward would signal with a flag on a balcony to set up meetings in an underground garage.

All the while, the *Post* lived in fear of making mistakes. And as the evidence pointing to President Nixon became compellingly clear, *Post* editors were overwhelmed at the prospect. "It never really seemed fun at the time," said Downie. "It was exciting, in the sense that when you're doing something death-defying it gets very exciting."

As Watergate heated up, Nixon's allies struck back, challenging Post television licenses in Jacksonville and Miami, and depressing the price of Post stock. The *Post* never blinked. Harrowing though the license challenges and White House threats were, Post executives knew the company was safe from a hostile takeover. By keeping control in family hands, Katharine Graham had seen to that. There was no watching the stock price with one eye and the front page with the other and fearing that the reporters would write the Grahams out of the family business.

President Richard Nixon resigned on August 4, 1974—two years after the first Watergate story. The following year, Hollywood came to the *Post.* Dustin Hoffman and Robert Redford casually wandered in and out soaking up atmosphere for the movie *All the President's Men,* the accompanying commotion making the *Post* a strikingly strange place to work.

The movie premiered at the Kennedy Center in April 1976 and the *Post*'s critic groused that it was not celebratory enough. "It might have seemed a little corny to end the film on a scene of triumph," wrote Gary Arnold, "but as a matter of fact there were such scenes. . . . A truthful rendering of one or more of them would not have violated reality." Most of the Kennedy Center crowd, however, thought the movie was just fine.

In the afterglow of Watergate, *Post* people puffed out their chests, confident they were a breed apart and belonged to the best and toughest muckraking paper in the world.

For Katharine Graham, Watergate was yet another confirmation of the *Post*'s increasing importance. Previously, the *Washington Post* had been relatively unknown abroad; after Watergate and *All the President's Men,* it was known worldwide.

Yet for some made prominent by Watergate, fame seemed a mixed blessing.

Bradlee, whose second marriage had ended, learned firsthand that celebrity breeds gossip. He bristled at Washington's constant whisperings about his live-in relationship with Sally Quinn—the attractive blond daughter of a general and the "Style" section's star writer. In 1978, he married Quinn, demolishing—as Bradlee saw it—one reason for rumors. But the paradox of celebrity stayed: "You can't say that some of it isn't fun, because it is, but, Jesus, you have to watch what you say. And I've made a pretty good living out of saying what I think."

Carl Bernstein left the *Post* in late 1976, after he and Woodward wrote *The Final Days,* their second book. With a name nearly as big as the *Post*'s, he seemed destined for stardom as an independent author—an expectation he has not yet fulfilled.

Woodward stayed behind, unable to imagine a life without reporting or apart from an institution; eventually he began to believe that he might one day get Bradlee's job.

Even those not quite so prominent felt the pressure of Watergate fame. Roger Wilkins, who wrote most *Post* Watergate editorials and was cited in the public service Pulitzer for the coverage, saw his boss, editorial page editor Phil Geyelin, undergo a shocking transformation. The pleasant, polished, gracious man became, said Wilkins, "possessive and petty and jealous . . . in his behavior toward me."

Wilkins felt that Bradlee was Geyelin's real target, but Bradlee was beyond his reach. So Wilkins endured Geyelin's nasty comments until he could take no more; then he left for the *New York Times.*

Wilkins's friend Nick Kotz also left, in part because he felt the paper was becoming colder and less interested in the social issues he thought important.

Bob Maynard, then *Post* ombudsman (or internal critic), took Wilkins's place. After a few years, Maynard resigned, not because of Geyelin—whom he also found abusive and "pretty goddamn awful"—but because after Watergate, the editorial page was boring. "I remember sitting there one afternoon and I was writing my two hundred forty-third piece on what was wrong with the food stamp program. . . . Not only did I not feel challenged, I didn't think I'd ever feel challenged . . . there."

Still, for every writer who departed, thousands seemed ready to join.

One was Milton Coleman, an athletic juggernaut of a man who had grown up in public housing in Milwaukee and who arrived at the *Post* (by way of the black press and the *Minneapolis Star Tribune*) in 1976, two years after completing a Ford Foundation–funded training program.

From his first day at the *Post* "he was like a steamroller," said Alice Bonner, the *Post* reporter who had directed him to the Summer Program for Minority Journalists. They both covered the bloody takeover of three Washington buildings by an armed group of Hanafi Muslims; and though Bonner beat Coleman to the site, the story quickly became his. The same thing happened with social services stories on her beat, leaving the gentle Bonner thoroughly frustrated. "I decided after three or four experiences that I had my way of reporting and he had his and, friend or not, I did not want to be on assignment with Milton."

Larry Kramer was also part of the post-Watergate wave. A native of Hackensack, New Jersey, he'd earned an MBA at Harvard, spent three years at the *San Francisco Examiner,* and dreamed of becoming the Woodstein of international finance. He quickly got his wish, complete with encounters in unlikely Amsterdam bars with sources (*à la* Deep Throat) terrified of talking to a reporter on their own turf.

Kramer found, as did Coleman—as Downie and Kaiser had found earlier—that Bradlee loved high-wire journalism and that when *Post* revelations brought howls from the powers that be, Bradlee always stood with his reporters.

The attitude inevitably encouraged muckraking even where no muck existed. Sally Quinn once reported—erroneously, as it turned out—that President Carter's national security adviser, Zbigniew Brzezinski, had unzipped his fly in front of a female reporter and then sent her a photograph of "this unusual expression of playfulness." The *Post* retracted the item the following day.

An item later popped up in a gossip column hinting that President Carter had bugged the official residence for White House guests while Nancy Reagan stayed there. "And at least one tattler in the Carter tribe has described listening to the Tape itself," reported "The Ear" column. Carter threatened to sue and the *Post* responded with a curious editorial that argued the paper was merely reporting gossip, not saying it was true: "It is one thing . . . to read that item to say that such a tale is circulating and being given currency by estimable public figures who repeat it—and quite another to conclude from this that the place was in fact bugged and that the Carters did in fact perpetrate such a scheme. We weren't there." The *Post* eventually retracted that item as well.

CHAPTER 3

A NEW GRAHAM, A LAST STRIKE

Wrenching as the Pentagon and Watergate battles were for the *Post,* another showdown loomed that would be even more traumatic. That contest would pit production workers against white-collar workers and the Grahams against a union they felt had violated their trust. In a way Watergate could not be, the labor dispute was a fight over the future of the paper—and of the company. Whereas Watergate raised constitutional and governmental issues, the struggle with the pressmen's union raised the most fundamental corporate question of all: Who was to control the means of production?

As the Pentagon Papers incident had been a rite of passage for Katharine Graham, the pressmen's strike would be one for her son, Donald, on whose shoulders ultimately would rest full responsibility for the *Post.*

A tall, athletic figure with dark hair and a ready smile, Donald Graham had presided over the Harvard *Crimson* as Bradlee had settled in at the *Post.* Though his mother had always assumed he would end up at the paper, Don was not so sure.

In his history of the *Washington Post,* Chalmers Roberts reports that when the Post bought the *Times-Herald,* Donald Graham's grandfather remarked, "The real significance of this event is that it makes the paper safe for Donnie."

Graham first heard Eugene Meyer's comment some twenty

years after it was supposedly uttered, from *Post* editorial writer Merlo Pusey, who was then working on a biography of Meyer. He was stunned. For though he had known he was expected to do something of consequence, he had supposed that he (like his older sister and two younger brothers) had the option of saying no to the *Post.*

Katharine Graham never explicitly told Don to make a career of the *Post,* but she had always assumed that one of her boys ("and I did think in terms of boys then") would eventually take over: "And I supposed it would be Don because of his love of newspapers and because the others were so much younger."

Don had run the paper at St. Albans (an Episcopal preparatory school for boys that stresses community service) and had joined the *Crimson* his freshman year. He had spent summers while in college newspapering, once in Winston-Salem and once with James Reston of the *New York Times.* Yet only after a long and tortured journey would he answer the call of the *Post.*

Herbert Denton—Harvard class of 1965, a year ahead of Don, with roots a world apart—would make part of that journey with him.

Denton, the son of an elementary school teacher in Little Rock, was born a year too late to be a part of the so-called Little Rock Nine who integrated Central High in 1957. But the young racial pioneers lived in his neighborhood. And along with the rest of the nation, he watched the 101st Airborne Division take over his hometown to ensure that the black students could go to school. The studious Herbert, sickened by the racial frenzy whipped up by Governor Orval Faubus, wanted out.

His chance to leave came serendipitously. The summer following the integration crisis, Denton went to a summer science program at Howard University sponsored by the National Science Foundation. There he befriended a fifteen-year-old whose father was a professor at Howard and who attended the Windsor Mountain School in Lenox, Massachusetts. To Denton, raised in a Jim Crow system where black schools lacked the most basic equipment, Windsor Mountain sounded like an enchanted place.

His new friend not only got Denton admitted into the boarding school but got him a scholarship, setting him on a path that led far from the South and directly into Donald Graham's world at Harvard.

Denton, who encountered Graham at the *Crimson,* recalls him as a leader of a "solemn and serious" group. Robert Maynard, who met Graham during his Nieman Fellowship year, remembers Graham, along with several others of the *Crimson* staff, putting out a daily while the Boston papers were on strike. The strike paper was no great success, but Graham impressed him: "Donnie was never interested in everybody else's obvious answer . . . never interested in the simple or the lazy or the easy answer."

After Harvard, Denton had gone to Washington, where he joined the staff of the National Student Organization as an editor with the *American Student.* He was chagrined to find out later that the organization, set up to represent student governments, was subsidized by two hundred thousand dollars a year from the CIA. By that time, however, he was already with the *Post,* a beneficiary of the feeling at the newspaper in early 1966 that a race riot would inevitably come to Washington and blacks would be needed to cover it.

Graham, uncomfortable with pursuing the outs easily available to a Harvard man of his family status and connections, tried to arrive at a principled decision regarding the draft and the Vietnam War.

He completed his studies in 1966. By the end of that year the number of troops in Vietnam had risen to 375,000, up from 25,000 the previous year. Young men were beginning publicly to burn their draft cards as the antiwar movement picked up steam. A black revolt swept the cities and the nation was deeply confused.

Many of Graham's closest friends opposed the war. Yet, for him, the proper course was unclear. He read every book on Vietnam that he could find and his ambivalence remained.

"When I graduated, I did not feel the United States should pull all its troops out of Vietnam. So I let myself be drafted," he says, having found, in his quest for answers, no reason to shirk responsibility.

Denton's approach was less methodical; he was not so much interested in working through abstract issues of right and wrong as in seeing, firsthand, what Vietnam was all about. As he tells it, "I was curious enough to allow myself to be drafted."

The two men met at the induction center, neither having expected to see the other. Graham, in blue jeans, found it funny that Denton had worn a suit. They went through basic training together and then went their separate ways, reuniting several months later as information specialists in the First Air Cavalry Division in Vietnam, an elite division styled after the old Horse Cavalry, except the horses were helicopters.

The war up close was infinitely different from the war in Graham's books. "It felt different than any description I had seen." And, in the end, it felt futile.

Some "grisly incidents" occurred shortly after they arrived, recalls Denton. In one instance, American troops and Vietnamese police swept a village and shot a woman. Those responsible said she had refused to talk. An investigation revealed the woman to be deaf. Such occurrences made Denton realize that those shaping strategy "had very little understanding of what we were into."

Graham never set foot in any Vietnamese city and was generally far from civilians. He spent much time with infantry companies, interviewing, taking pictures, and publishing a division newspaper and quarterly magazine (which to Denton looked a lot like *Newsweek*). He and Denton also were assigned to write press releases, escort American correspondents, and periodically dispose of excrement by burning it in a big oil-filled drum.

Graham received a Bronze Star. And for a brief while, says Denton, "I think he achieved something he had always wanted . . . anonymity." Upon Denton's arrival, Graham had pulled him aside and whispered, "Please don't tell anybody who my mother is." To the other troops, he was simply PFC Graham—until Senator Ted Kennedy visited Vietnam and sent PFC Graham a message.

After that, the major in charge, concluding that his own future depended on keeping Kennedy's sidekick safe, refused Graham permission to go out with the troops. Graham, conspiring with others, got around the special treatment.

When Martin Luther King was assassinated in April 1968, a shaken Graham broke the news to his friend. Denton had just returned from the fighting in Khe Sanh, the big story of the day, to find that battle upstaged by the latest casualty from "the war back home."

Denton read a piece in the *Village Voice* one day by a fellow Harvard graduate advocating victory for the North Vietnamese. "He was our friend, and he was saying he hoped the guys who were shooting us would win. . . . That's hard to digest," recalled Denton.

Fragging incidents and some of the other uglier aspects of the war were foreign to Graham's experience. For the most part, the soldiers he knew served well and professionally, despite not wanting to be in Vietnam.

By the time he left, Graham was more troubled than ever. "I was terribly confused about Vietnam at the time," says Graham, "and I still am." Denton remembers his commenting, once back home, that he felt particularly bad for those soldiers who would follow; the futility of their effort was too clear to ignore.

Graham returned in July 1968 to his wife and *Crimson* sweetheart, the former Mary Wissler, and to a city (rocked by riots after Dr. King's death) that he barely knew.

He had grown up in Georgetown, gone to a private school, then headed for Harvard and Vietnam. "I hoped I could come to the *Post,* hoped to spend the rest of my life here, and I thought before that I ought to see if I could do something to learn about the city."

He spent several months sorting through his options, part of the time working for a college professor writing a book on IBM. He considered joining the poverty program and teaching, but found himself increasingly drawn to police work. The police had become controversial in some communities, and Graham wished to understand their job better. The police department, desperate for people, was actively recruiting recently discharged veterans. Initially suspicious, the department accepted Graham into the academy in January 1969.

For a year and a half he patrolled Near Northeast Washington, a section as different from Georgetown as Watts is from Beverly Hills, taking twenty or so calls a shift. Family fights, landlord disputes, burglary victims, the mentally disturbed, the offerings of a troubled city occupied his nights.

He left the force with a deeper knowledge of Washington and glad to have served near the bottom of a couple of organizations.

A private spends "a lot of time thinking about the effectiveness of different kinds of sergeants and lieutenants," noted Graham.

In time, he would build his own team of sergeants and lieutenants with the firm hand of one who knew what he wanted. But before taking his place in the family business, he desired to spend time with his wife, who had just finished law school. When Graham finally came home to the *Post* in January 1971, the paper was at the gateway to greatness.

In five years, Graham went from D.C. cop to assistant general manager of the family newspaper. He apprenticed in every major department—accounting, circulation, promotion, advertising, and editorial—and at *Newsweek.* Everywhere his quiet, intellectual intensity and fanatical devotion to work marked him as something more than just the publisher's kid. As sports editor, his first real management job, he knocked out a wall separating his staff from the newsroom and pushed the section to showcase good writing.

For him, the newspaper was a thing of wonder—with advertising people sending down ads from one floor, editors sending down copy from another, and all of it coming together in a composing room where pages were assembled from which plates would be made. The plates would be attached to rows of presses and newspapers would almost magically emerge; then the papers would be assembled and dispatched by trucks as the cycle began again. Graham loved the pace and delighted in turning out a new product every day. He had difficulty believing that anyone could work in such a wonderfully energizing place and not feel affection for it. Consequently, he found the behavior of the *Post* pressmen incomprehensible.

Since the late 1960s, *Post* production had been throttled by the pressmen. They regularly disrupted the production schedule to wring concessions from the company or stretched out their work to get overtime. Graham saw the actions as a form of guerrilla warfare that made delivering the paper on time impossible.

In Ben Bradlee's view, "the word negotiations with the union was a joke. You didn't negotiate, you bluffed the union. And when they wanted to call your bluff, you caved. You had to cave. You were in a highly competitive race with the *Star* and you couldn't afford to stop, and you couldn't print without them. . . . Ultimately, the business side would agree to anything."

Management was eager for change. In 1972, the *Post* began sending executives to a facility in Oklahoma City to learn how to put out the paper during a strike. The next year, the newspaper hired a tough new labor relations director who had a printer fired for participating in a work slowdown. The pressmen refused to run the presses until the printer was rehired. The company backed down.

Robert Kaiser, formerly a *Post* labor reporter, believes the company's retreat helped to convince the union that intimidation worked.

Shortly after 4:00 A.M., October 1, 1975, following the midnight expiration of the current contract between the pressmen and the *Post,* the quiet war came out into the open. Aware of the training *Post* executives had undergone, the pressmen apparently believed that only by rendering the presses inoperable could they prevent the paper from being published. A small group held a screwdriver to the throat of a foreman as others systematically vandalized the presses, ripping out wires, stripping parts from the machines, wrecking air hoses, and setting one press aflame.

The *Post* estimated they did more than a quarter of a million dollars of damage before setting up a picket line outside. The foreman, badly beaten and covered with blood from a cut above his eye, stumbled into the office of general manager Mark Meagher. Twelve stitches were required to close the gash.

Years later, many in management would see that strike and the violence that accompanied it in the way veterans see a great war, as an event that shaped nearly everything that followed. In the beginning, however, the *Post* was a reluctant combatant; for it seemed the paper had more to lose than to gain.

Joe Allbritton, a Texas millionaire determined to give the *Post* a run for its money, had recently bought the *Star.* "We really felt that our first priority should be to keep our competitive position," said Don Graham, "and that meant sustaining publication. . . . We agreed that we shouldn't take a strike at that point." When the strike came anyway, it fell to Graham to keep the presses going.

Until the very end, the *Post* team thought the negotiations would work out. The night the contract expired, management saw no reason for alarm. As the deadline approached, the *Post* got a written statement from the union indicating that work and negotiations would continue.

Graham went home well after midnight, but was awakened by a predawn phone call telling him of the destruction at the

Post. He leapt out of bed, got dressed, and grabbed a taxi, stopping to pick up Don Rice, the paper's recently hired assistant to the general manager. They were greeted by chaos: angry pressmen, a growing army of policemen, fire trucks. Then they went to the pressroom and glumly viewed the devastation.

So began a period for Graham, Rice, and many other *Post* employees when nights and days became as one, leaving time for neither respite nor reflection. Many slept on cots, rarely leaving the building, sustained by little more than willpower, camaraderie, and the feeling that they were fighting the good fight.

Bradlee took ads on the phone. Howard Simons handled plates in the pressroom. Katharine Graham worked in the mail room. The effort so destroyed Don Rice's home life that it indirectly led to a divorce.

Nearly all involved agreed with Frank Manzon, a circulation executive who said, "I have never been that tired. I mean tired, tired."

The dispute forced the Newspaper Guild to make a painful choice. Many of the members were reporters who identified much more with the *Post* than with the pressmen. Yet to refuse support to the pressmen would be tantamount to shattering the already weak ties between the Guild and craft unions.

In a meeting filled with tension and recriminations, the Guild voted to cross the pressmen's picket line. Uncomfortable as many journalists were with crossing that line, they were even less comfortable with supporting a group that would wreck a press.

The Guild (which included not only reporters and photographers but telephone operators, sales personnel, data processors, and others) was the only union that did not support the strike. Yet repeatedly, each time after agonizing debate, the majority voted to cross the picket lines. Rather than do so, more than two hundred members stayed home.

The national office threatened sanctions against the *Post* local, whose members responded by taking steps to form another union and nearly succeeded in ousting the Guild.

As the Guild debated, *Post* executives escorted television reporters through the wreck of a pressroom. Others called nearby papers and eventually got six to agree to print the *Post.* Helicopters were hired to shuttle photographs of the pages from which plates would be made.

On October 3, a twenty-four-page version of the *Post* appeared, the paper having missed only one day of publication. An editorial in that edition assailed the saboteurs, comparing them to book burners and political assassins. The *Post* was publishing, it announced, as a matter of principle: "That principle is the duty of all citizens, including those who put out newspapers, to reject physical violence and calculated sabotage as a way to settle an argument."

Telephone threats were received, employees were beaten, and an editor's window was shot out. "It was a long, difficult, hard slog for many of us who . . . were taken by van in the back alley to drop-off points away from the building so we wouldn't be beaten up," said Simons.

For no one, however, was the slog harder than for Katharine Graham, who knew that the world was judging her and who also was judging herself. All the while, she worried about the safety of the people in the building and about whether the *Post* was doing the right thing.

By October 6, the *Post* presses were repaired and a ragtag crew of employees was put together to run them. Don Graham, who presided over the operation, watched in amazement as the inexperienced team began to click. Almost immediately, the substitute pressmen demanded to produce something more complicated than the forty-page paper they were doing. Concerned about their safety around the huge unfamiliar presses, Graham denied the request. But gradually, he became a believer and gave in. By late October, the *Post* was 148 pages (of which 84 were printed inside) and by mid-November the paper was 160 pages (of which 96 were done by *Post* workers and the rest outside).

The workers' enthusiasm greatly impressed Don Graham. Loyce Best, a credit department employee who crossed the picket line, noted years later that Graham remained acutely aware of those people who "had been loyal" during the strike and seemed to take a particular interest in their careers.

In early December, the *Post* began hiring replacements for the pressmen. By then, no one was in a mood to retreat. The *Post* continued to reject hiring any of those who had damaged the presses and one union official carried a sign past the *Post* building reading: "Phil shot the wrong Graham."

In short order, the unions that had walked out with the pressmen, most notably the printers and the mailers, came back to work. By February, the pressmen were alone. When twenty-six of them sat in at AFL-CIO headquarters in Washington, D.C., to demand support, they were thrown out by the police.

"Looking back on it, I'm still at this distance very, very sad that we ever had an episode here where a couple of hundred people lost jobs," said Don Graham. Yet a confrontation had been inevitable; the violence and the hardening of attitudes by the *Post* and the pressmen simply made it come sooner rather than later.

In replacing the pressmen, the newspaper hired people who in most cases had never worked in pressrooms. The work force was, in Don Graham's eyes, not only different but better—no longer intent on wrecking his paper, no longer all white and all male at the journeyman level. "Today . . . the superintendent of this plant is black," said Graham in 1987, noting that under the old regime the man would never have had a chance to work even as a journeyman pressman. Presses once run with up to twenty-two people now require eight.

The impact of the strike went far beyond the *Post.* Don Rice, who was eventually promoted to operations director, believes it showed the industry that control of production could be taken back. "It's not that the unions are whipped or anything, and we're not trying to get rid of the unions; it's just that they really lost all of that threat. . . . And so they seem less relevant as time goes by."

Kaiser summed up the matter more succinctly: "In a way no other big-city daily paper had dared try, the *Post* defied its craft unions and prospered without them."

By then, Kaiser had been at the *Post* for more than a decade. His reporting career had taken him far from home, to the paper's bureaus in Vietnam, Moscow, and Europe. He had returned barely in time to cover the strike, the biggest labor story Washington had seen in years. And as he immersed himself in Washington and in labor at the *Post,* he began to realize that the paper being formed in the crucible of the strike was very different from the *Post* he had known. The Graham outlook, so benevolent in the past, was tougher.

Kaiser had bought stock when the company went public, but

had sold it to buy a house and had not given much thought to buying more. Covering the strike forced him to think about that stock and about where the company he had grown up in was headed. He concluded that the company had finally become serious about its future. And he bought one hundred shares of stock, certain that they eventually would be worth a great deal.

CHAPTER 4

CHOOSING A TEAM

Don Graham performed well enough during the pressmen's strike to be made *Post* general manager shortly thereafter. The job (ranking just below publisher) put him in charge of all business operations and forced on him responsibility for solving a paralyzing managerial crisis.

Problems had been building at least since 1969, when John Sweeterman retired as business-side boss, leaving no trained successor. He was followed by Paul Ignatius, a former secretary of the navy with no newspaper background. Widely viewed as a disaster, Ignatius lasted less than two years. John Prescott, an experienced newspaper executive, did not last much longer and was replaced by Mark Meagher shortly before the pressmen's strike. In short order, Meagher was promoted to president of the corporation, scarcely having had time to begin reinvigorating the paper.

The turnover at the top led to turnover in the middle, which meant a thinning of management talent throughout an organization that had never paid much attention to leadership development—partly because many executives were insecure in their own status and resisted training potential rivals. Also, the production unions, which dominated the *Post,* had no interest in strong managers emerging.

Over time, the paper's production schedule had become so slapdash that circulation, which had shot up like a rocket during the 1960s, had become stagnant. (Daily circulation was 523,000 in 1972; 534,000 in 1973; 533,000 in 1974; 535,000 in 1975; 524,000 in 1976.) During the mid-1970s, the classified advertising department was so slow in answering its phones that one of every eight callers finally hung up in frustration. Computer equipment was inadequate. Bills were generated by hand.

Happily for the *Post,* the paper at least was making money. Post company revenues were $309 million in 1975, $376 million in 1976, $436 million in 1977, $520 million in 1978, $593 million in 1979, and $660 million in 1980. Pretax profits climbed as well, from under 9 percent in 1975 to nearly 17 percent in 1978, and then dipped as the nation struggled through a recession.

Newspaper division figures improved after the pressmen were replaced. Between 1975 and 1980, the division's profits never broke 16 percent; but some newspaper firms consistently earned more than 20 percent and the Post broadcast division functioned like a money machine, with profits that climbed up to 33 percent.

Don Graham—named publisher in January 1979—found little comfort in those figures. The *Post* newspaper, the part of the company he loved most, was barely carrying its own weight. Over the next several years, the major share of his efforts would be devoted to changing that—though one of his first appointments following his promotion was on the editorial side.

Phil Geyelin's team had consciously pulled the editorial page back from the hawkish jeremiads of the Russ Wiggins days; but some *Post* editors felt that the page had gone soft, that it was too predictable, too fuzzy, too polite, and that Geyelin himself was no longer an energetic and effective leader.

Graham replaced editor Geyelin with Meg Greenfield, who intended to make the page livelier and turn up the noise level while tilting away from its knee-jerk support of the Left. She also hoped to make the op-ed page a center of intellectual debate. Graham, who respected Greenfield's mind and liked her interest in people, never considered anyone else for the job.

Graham's other major appointment his first year as publisher was of his top lieutenant for the business side. He wanted someone intensely competitive to help in the battle with the *Washington Star,* which had been bought in 1978 by Time Incorporated—a marketing powerhouse that conceivably could make the paper a real threat. And he found that person in

Thomas Ferguson, a handsome, silver-haired, wisecracking New Yorker given to white shirts, dark suits, and martinis after work.

In many respects, Ferguson was Graham's opposite—brash and irreverent, the apotheosis of Madison Avenue. Ferguson, nine years older than Graham, was an outsider, not only to the paper but, in many respects, to the industry.

Yet the *Post*'s revolving-door reputation made many newspaper executives nervous. And no candidate loomed in-house. Graham fixed on Ferguson early—sensing that underlying their disparate styles and backgrounds lay a chemistry that could work.

Ferguson's parents had come to New York from Ireland in the midst of the Depression. His father had been a welder and school custodian and his mother a part-time cleaning woman. His family could not afford to send Tom to college, but a basketball scholarship took him to St. John's University in New York. Instead of graduating, however, Tom fell in love, dropped out of school, and got married.

His first job was in the marketing department of American Tobacco Company, and as children began to arrive, he held two more jobs on the side—one washing dishes in a local restaurant and the other working weekends at a race track. During his free evenings, he went to school and dreamed of success in the marketing world.

He got his wish, leaping from American Tobacco to Eagle Pencil, and then to American Cyanamid, which owned Breck shampoo. Parade Publications lured him away with a vice-president, marketing job, the first rung in a ladder that led to the presidency of the company.

He met Graham during a visit undertaken to persuade the *Post* to keep *Parade.* Their lunch, as Ferguson remembers it, did not go very well, but he achieved his objective.

Nearly two years later, in January 1979, the *Post* again was considering dropping *Parade.* Ferguson's phone rang and he turned to his circulation manager and snapped, "Sit right there. Don't move. This is Graham, and I know goddamn well he's going to throw *Parade* out of the *Post.*"

Graham had something else on his mind: "Look, I'd like to talk to you. A couple of significant things have happened in my life. Number one, my mother has made me publisher of the newspaper. Number two, Time Inc. has bought the *Washington*

Star. . . . I need a president–general manager to help me run this place. . . . I'd like to come talk to you."

Ferguson was stunned, but quickly agreed to Graham's visit. The *Post* job was less than tempting. Nonetheless, time with Graham could cement the relationship between the *Post* and *Parade.* Graham, however, had his own agenda, and over several meetings he patiently drew Ferguson into his web.

At one point, Ferguson explained that he loved his current job and the autonomy of managing a company whose owner only showed up once a week or so. How could he possibly give that up to play second fiddle to an intense, hands-on manager like Graham in a company that treated presidents and general managers like temporary workers? Graham acknowledged the *Post* had made mistakes in the past, but his eyes were now on the future—which he and Ferguson could shape together.

That April, Ferguson learned that his teenaged son had leukemia. Devastated, he wrote Graham a note explaining that their conversations must end. The best doctors, he pointed out, were in New York; and his child, it went without saying, would have no less. Though somber, he felt a surge of satisfaction, realizing, as he completed the note, that over the past few months he and Graham had become friends.

A month later, Graham called, inquired about his son, learned he was making good progress, and then mentioned that he wanted to see Ferguson again.

Ferguson made a reservation at the 21 Club. (Only later, after he came to know Graham much better, did he realize Graham "would have been happier in a diner.") Before Ferguson could bring his martini to his lips, Graham suggested that he come to Washington and get to know Graham and his family.

Ferguson tried to change the subject, but Graham kept returning to it. Finally, nearly worn out, Ferguson said, "Don, look, there are a lot of good people in business, a lot of good people I'm sure in the communications business. I don't know them all that well. . . . Let me use the analogy of love. Why don't you date a lot of people and if after dating a lot of people you feel we ought to get together, then let's talk some more."

So ended the lunch and, so Ferguson thought, the conversation. Then he heard from friends that Graham was calling around town checking him out, talking to people Ferguson had worked with ten or fifteen years earlier. Finally Graham virtually ordered Ferguson to report to Washington for a day or two.

They dined in Graham's home, along with Ben Bradlee and Sally Quinn, a couple whose company Ferguson thoroughly enjoyed, and as the time crept toward 11:00 P.M., Graham insisted Ferguson accompany him to the newspaper. They tromped through the plant with its presses running, Graham greeting everyone they passed by name. Afterward, they went to Graham's seventh-floor office and talked newspaper economics. Ferguson, feeling weary, thirsty, and closed in, insisted they go across the street to the Madison Hotel bar for a beer. Graham, not normally given to frequenting bars, went along.

The next morning, Ferguson flew back to New York and discussed the *Post* with his wife and six children. They talked late into the evening; and it became clear that the family, which had always lived in New York, thought Washington would be a great adventure. Ferguson called the *Post* switchboard, was connected to Graham at his Virginia farm, and accepted the job—never once having discussed salary.

By then, pay was almost irrelevant. Graham had gotten him to buy into a dream; together they would recreate the *Washington Post.* The money would work itself out. Graham, he was convinced, would see to that.

Ferguson's faith in Graham's fundamental decency was not unusual. Graham's behavior made thinking of him as anything other than a good guy virtually impossible. One afternoon, for instance, during a driving rain, reporter Eleanor Randolph huddled in an alcove three blocks from the *Post.* Graham appeared and asked whether she was returning to the office. She said yes, grateful to share his umbrella. "Well, I'm not going to be back for another hour and a half," he replied. "Here, take this." He thrust the umbrella into her hand and walked off, water pouring down on his unprotected head. She stood dumfounded for several seconds and finally made her way back to the building, later sending back his umbrella with a package of vitamin C.

Thomas Might fell under Graham's spell during the winter of 1977, his first year at Harvard Business School. The *Post* was interviewing business school candidates for summer internships and some of the most promising had been invited to dine with

Graham. Might, along with five others, was seated at Graham's table. A slight, soft-spoken student who had briefly studied for the ministry, the reflective Might felt out of place among the extroverts at the table. But Graham, who had memorized everyone's resume, got him to talk about his army days in Germany and his student days at Georgia Tech. By the end of the dinner, Might was thoroughly relaxed and filled with admiration for the man who had taken the time to learn so much about him and his peers.

Might was hired to work in the publisher's suite. Over the summer, Graham and Mark Meagher lavished attention on him all out of proportion, he thought, to his very junior status. Later, they told him that upon graduation a job awaited him at the *Post* as Graham's aide. Grateful though he was, Might saw no logic in an engineer with an MBA going into newspapering. Traditional manufacturing made more sense. But as graduation neared, he realized that in a manufacturing company he would be one of hundreds, whereas at the *Post* he would be something special, assistant to the heir apparent and a charter member of a team charged with taking the company into the modern age. That April, he stopped by Graham's office on his way from an interview with Lockheed and said: "I give up. I take the job."

Other team members quickly followed.

Boisfeuillet Jones, Jr., a St. Albans' classmate and *Crimson* colleague of Graham's, left a Boston law firm in 1980 to join his old friend as general counsel to the *Post.*

Theodore C. Lutz came from government service. A former official with the federal Office of Management and Budget (OMB), Lutz had also served as general manager of the Washington Transit Authority and head of the Urban Mass Transit Administration. After President Carter left office in January 1981, Lutz was looking for work. Graham needed someone to revamp his budget review process and OMB veteran Lutz seemed made for the job.

That same year, John Kuhns, from the law firm of Williams and Connolly, took a newly created job as director of business planning. He was to think about new businesses the *Post* might go into and oversee development of the national weekly edition already in the works.

Nicholas Cannistraro came a year later, from a string of

successes as marketing vice-president at Bristol Myers—where he had successfully launched Comtrex.

Ferguson and Graham recruited talent wherever they could find it. And if their recruits were generally green to the newspaper world, they were well schooled in the disciplines of management, marketing, and finance. Their charge from Graham was to reshape an organization whose technology was virtually obsolete, whose major divisions didn't communicate, and whose profit margins were slim. And just as they were beginning to sort things out, the *Washington Star* hit them with a twenty-megaton surprise—an announcement on July 23, 1981, that it would soon cease publication.

Few in Washington, least of all the *Post,* were prepared for the collapse. The *Post* had built a new three-press plant in Springfield, Virginia, that was expected to handle all printing needs through the end of the century. But the key assumption, said Tom Might, who oversaw its construction and operation, was that the *Star* would continue to publish.

Suddenly the *Star*'s three hundred thousand readers were up for grabs, and Graham was ordering his team to seize them. Even after eliminating the roughly half who had taken both papers, the *Post* faced a major expansion. And as quickly became clear, the company didn't have the press capacity to handle it.

Ferguson grew increasingly nervous. To order and install new presses would take two to three years. The *Star* had presses, but local investors had already expressed interest in resuscitating the paper. *Post* lawyers warned Ferguson that to obstruct that effort would be to flirt with an antitrust action.

Nearly two months after the *Star*'s announcement, the attempts to revive it were going nowhere. Finally, in frustration, Ferguson called the Time Incorporated manager in charge of disposing of the plant. Mindful of the lawyers' warnings, he expressed interest in the property without asking for any details or indicating a desire to buy it. The man, however, had frustrations of his own. "We can't give the goddamn thing away," he confided, despite the pressure Time's president was putting on him to unload the plant and despite his own desire to go home. Ferguson, suddenly beside himself with excitement, began working on an offer. Within weeks, the plant belonged to the *Post* and two of its five presses were running five nights a week, just enough to get the paper through the crunch caused by the *Star*'s demise.

By 1982, *Post* circulation was 736,000 daily and 979,000 on Sunday, roughly 150,000 more a day than before the *Star* folded. Graham had achieved his objective. Virtually every *Star* reader not already taking the *Post* had been brought into the fold. And in seeing Graham through his first crisis as publisher, the new management team had bonded.

Still the episode underlined what Graham already knew—that the *Post* planning process was ragged. Ferguson's initiative notwithstanding, the purchase of the *Star*'s plant depended on luck. "That guy could have been cool," acknowledges Ferguson, and the sale might never have been made. And without the presses, adds Might, "we would have gone back to being very late and lost a lot of customers."

Even as it was, the new customers were hard to retain. Frank Manzon, who became circulation director in 1982, needed two years to find a solid circulation base.

Advertising also presented difficulties. Margaret "Peggy" Schiff, the budget manager who came from Price Waterhouse following the 1975 strike and later became controller, recalls that for years the *Post* had told advertisers that the only readers worth reaching took the *Post.* "And now," she recalls, "we were confronted with . . . saying, 'Well, you need to pay a lot higher rates because we've got all the extra *Star* circulation,' which we had told them was never worth anything to begin with."

Might, who went from overseeing the construction of one plant to determining how best to print a paper among three, quickly moved on to an even more consuming project—figuring out how to whittle down production labor expenses.

Indeed, with senior managers the pursuit of higher profits took on the characteristics of a quest: a major change from the days of Eugene Meyer, who ran the paper almost like a private charity—pumping millions in to keep it going and never expecting much in return. Such an attitude was not possible in 1982; public shareholders and Graham would never stand for it.

Since the 1973 death of guiding light and chairman Frederick S. Beebe, the parent company had lacked stable leadership. Larry Israel, who took over many of Beebe's responsibilities, left in 1977. Mark Meagher, its president since 1977, resigned at the end of 1980—in pursuit, he claimed, of undefined new challenges.

During those years, the company had been unable to maintain a clear strategic focus. At one time, the Post had considered becoming a major newspaper chain, purchasing the *Trenton Times* in 1974 and the *Everett Herald* (some thirty miles north of Seattle, Washington) four years later. Both papers, however, became major management headaches, and the Post was hesitant to obtain more.

Post television stations were doing well, but those holdings had not grown since 1974, when the company added a fourth—WTIC in Hartford, Connecticut—and immediately renamed it WFSB in honor of Beebe.

(After the U.S. Supreme Court upheld a Federal Communications Commission rule barring newspaper owners from owning a radio or television property in the same market in 1978, the Post unloaded its Washington stations. Having acquired them before the 1975 rule, the Post could have kept them, but acted in anticipation of possible future regulatory problems. The company sold WTOP-AM radio outright, gave WTOP-FM radio to Howard University, and swapped WTOP television—plus two million dollars in cash—for WWJ television in Detroit.)

The Post had successfully started specially targeted "demographic editions" of *Newsweek,* but its efforts to launch a totally new magazine, *Inside Sports,* were foundering.

During Meagher's last year, the Post had run aground of a recession and earnings dipped, from eighty million dollars in 1979 to less than sixty-six million in 1980. A new president, Richard Simmons, took office in September 1981 after losing a battle to move up from president to chairman of Dunn and Bradstreet Corporation. He was a tough, competitive, bottom-line executive with no emotional attachment to the Post's past mistakes. Within sixty days, the *Trenton Times* was sold.

Since its purchase, the *Times* had confounded the Post. Seeing it as a miniature *Post,* editors had descended from Washington in the manner of missionaries—"propagating the Faith to the heathen," as described by author Howard Bray.

Post deputy managing editor Richard Harwood was the first. He soon discovered that small-town journalism was markedly different from that practiced in the nation's capital. In Trenton, the paper was a part of the family, not a grand dispenser of truth. The lesson, however, took a while to sink in.

Though by Washington standards the *Times* improved, circulation remained sickly (never going much above seventy-four thousand daily) and staff turnover mounted. Finally, Larry Kramer, the Harvard MBA from Hackensack, was asked to give up reporting and go to Trenton as metropolitan editor.

Kramer, who knew a few reporters in Trenton, had already concluded that the paper was without direction, without local roots, without any sense of how to compete in a small ethnic northeastern city. "I don't think your problems are going to be solved with a new metro editor," he told Katharine Graham. What the paper really needed, he said, was a good editor at the top. And that job, he knew, was beyond his experience.

After further urging by Bradlee and Howard Simons, he agreed to go to Trenton in January 1980, intending to spend a month or so analyzing the paper and then report back on what he had learned. Within weeks, publisher Edward Padilla offered to make him managing editor. By then Kramer had become fascinated with the paper and grown attached to the young, driven reporters on the staff.

Shortly thereafter the executive editor left and Kramer, who had just turned thirty, moved into the job. He tried to make the paper folksier and boost employee morale—even as he oversaw a staff reduction ordered by company headquarters. He speeded up the editing process so stories that formerly had languished were quickly edited and readied for publication; and he encouraged reporters who previously had been neglected.

In early 1982, two years into his tenure, the mailroom was the object of a teamster organizing drive. One evening as Kramer approached the parking lot in his company-issue Omni, he was surrounded by a mob that—taking him for a scab driver—started rocking his car. A lug nut crashed through the windshield, missing his head by about an inch. Fearing for his life, he gunned the engine and made it inside the gate. The publisher had the teamsters enjoined from interfering with delivery during the strike and the paper continued to publish.

By then Kramer was a vice-president of the *Times* and dreaming of a turnaround. The paper's tough handling of its labor problems, he thought, had cemented his relationship with Katharine Graham. She herself had dropped in and had seen how morale had risen. In a few years the *Times* should be solidly on top—and profits would soar.

Kramer, however, was not to have a few years. Post president Richard Simmons wanted results, not dreams, and the paper had not turned a profit since 1978. Shortly after the teamster organizing effort, Kramer found himself in a *Newsweek* office, looking at Padilla, Simmons, and Katharine Graham, alone in arguing for holding on to the *Times.* He knew, even as he talked, that his arguments were soft, and knew as well that he was losing. But he went on because he thought his superiors should see what he saw—that the *Post* should have a place like Trenton to send its executives for seasoning, where they could experience real competition and manage inadequate resources. The arguments came from his heart, not his calculator. Because he knew that they had no chance, he was surprised when Simmons called the next day to discuss the paper further. Nevertheless, Simmons decided the *Times* had to be sold. That same week Kramer's wife miscarried with their first child.

Bradlee suggested Kramer take some time off and offered to send him to a fancy resort in St. Martin. But after so many months of begging for resources for his newsroom and always hearing money was in short supply, Kramer refused to spend *Post* funds on a resort costing several hundred dollars a night. Instead, he and his wife went to Hawaii, where they visited a friend. Later, he explored jobs at Times Mirror newspapers in Denver and Dallas and at Knight-Ridder in Miami, finally returning home to the *Post.*

Richard Simmons had known little about media companies before getting a call from a search firm about the Post. He hadn't even known the Post owned *Newsweek.* But the more he learned, the more excited he became about the chance to move the Post into management's major leagues.

His vision of the company mirrored Don Graham's vision of the newspaper. If he could form a partnership with Katharine Graham, concluded Simmons, they could turn the business operation around. "Consistency in earning growth was not something the Post company was known for in the early 1980s," observed Simmons.

Katharine Graham supported his recommendation to sell the *Trenton Times* and (later) *Inside Sports.* The magazine, launched in April 1980 with a guaranteed circulation base of five hundred thousand, was sold in January 1982. In Simmons's book, it was losing far too much money and had no reasonable hope of success.

In addition to cutting losses, Simmons also sought reasonable avenues for growth. To that end, he hired financial whiz kid Alan Spoon, a graduate of Harvard Law School, the Sloan School of Management, and Massachusetts Institute of Technology. A science nut whose father was a small commercial developer in Michigan, Spoon had selected MIT in part because of the sailboat on the brochure. He regarded competitive sailing as "kind of like playing chess on the water."

Uninterested in practicing law, Spoon had joined the prestigious Boston Consulting Group—largely for the challenge of analyzing some of the world's great companies and figuring out how to make them work better.

Simmons was a client. So when Spoon returned from summer vacation in 1981 and found on his desk a clipping of Simmons's appointment and a message that Simmons had called, he assumed he would be consulting for the Post.

Simmons quickly corrected that impression and, over the next several months, spelled out what the Post could mean for a bright, ambitious man like Spoon, who would become part of a cadre of exceptionally talented people rebuilding a company that produced something of consequence.

Spoon joined as a corporate vice-president in early 1982. He was thirty years old and eager to hit the ground running. Almost immediately, he got involved in programming strategy for Post stations and pricing plans for *Newsweek,* but his biggest early project was cellular radio—a new type of radiotelephone service that facilitated calls from cars and briefcases.

After noticing that Metromedia was investing in related areas, Spoon called investment bankers he knew to try to find out why. Cellular radio, they told him, was worth looking into. After reading all the literature available on the technology, he concluded that it was well suited to the Post portfolio. The operating costs were low, the capital investment was modest, the economics were easily mastered, the technology was similar to that used by Post broadcast concerns. Moreover, the Post was respected by the Federal Communications Commission (which would license only one nontelephone company to provide the service in each area). The Post formed partnerships with other prospective bidders and ended up with substantial stakes in six markets.

Meanwhile, the one other newspaper owned by the Post was barely limping along.

Christopher Little, previously vice-president and general counsel of the *Post,* had become president and publisher of the *Herald* in 1979. His mandate was to lift editorial quality and launch a Sunday paper.

Mindful of the mistakes made in Trenton, Little—a balding Yale graduate with wire-rimmed glasses—vowed not to repeat them. He took no *Post* editors with him and no preconceived notions about ministering to the heathens.

Shortly after Little arrived, the economy collapsed. Within two years, Boeing Aircraft went from eighteen thousand employees in the city to eight thousand. Several major paper mills shut down. Even with a new Sunday edition, total advertising dropped. Little froze pay for two years and reopened labor contracts to scale down already-agreed-to increases—and weathered the crisis without layoffs.

The *Herald* became profitable, but even its relative success only highlighted the company's failure to develop into a national newspaper presence.

During the late 1960s and early 1970s, when Times Mirror and Gannett were buying newspapers, the Post had not had the resources to compete. Later, when resources were available, the company lacked knowledge of how best to expand. "And by the time I learned," says Katharine Graham, "it was sort of too late to buy small newspapers and rather hard to buy big ones unless you wanted to pay greater prices than we probably were capable of paying."

If only the Post had been in the newspaper acquisitions game ten, twenty years ago, "newspapers could have been bought for a bargain," lamented Boisfeuillet Jones, *Post* counsel and childhood friend of Donald Graham.

Like Katharine Graham, Spoon argues that in recent times newspapers have become simply too expensive.

"We have been looking at newspapers very actively from the first day I got here and we've been at lots of tables where we made offers that could have been accepted for hundreds of millions of dollars—to television station owners and to newspaper owners and to cable owners—but we have a very rigid sense of self-discipline as to how much we're willing to pay for a property. And we lost the auction . . . more often than we might have expected," said Spoon.

"I've been there. I've uttered the phrases. I've written the letters and been told, 'If you raise your price you might get it'—to which I've responded, 'That's our price. That's our bid. If we don't get it, we don't get it.' "

Spoon compares the process to bidding for a beautiful diamond: "If you pay a high price for this diamond ring, which is, let's say, a really highly esteemed media property, and you really go overboard . . . to buy this diamond ring, and the next thing you do to unburden yourself is to hock the diamond to pay for the ring, then what you've got left ain't what you bought."

Frustrated in acquiring newspapers, the company looked elsewhere—paying particular attention to properties that had economic characteristics similar to newspapers and television stations: businesses that generate significant amounts of cash, don't require huge amounts of capital, and allow some measure of control over price.

The strategy was an indisputable financial success; but some employees, particularly those within the *Post* newsroom, wondered whether, in so adapting, the company was somehow becoming less pure.

CHAPTER 5

A NEWSROOM IN TRANSITION

On September 28, 1980, the *Post* featured a drawing of a wide-eyed youngster watching a needle about to plunge into his arm. The accompanying text began: "Jimmy is 8 years old and a third-generation heroin addict, a precocious little boy with sandy hair, velvety brown eyes and needle marks freckling the baby-smooth skin of his thin brown arms."

The front-page account of reporter Janet Cooke's foray into Jimmy's world of fast money, drugs, and dreams of the good life was riveting. Jimmy had been hooked on heroin supplied by the lover of his approving mother. He went to school only to study math, in order to count money from drugs he would one day sell. Or so reported Cooke. And it was all a lie. But that was not to be discovered for months.

Readers demanded that the child be saved. And the police, determined to find him, combed the streets for seventeen days—threatening in their frustration to subpoena Cooke and her editors. The mayor, pressured for results, announced that the child had been identified but was in hiding with his mother. Through it all, the *Post*—unwilling to violate its promise of confidentiality—refused to name the child.

Managing editor Howard Simons was on vacation when the story was completed: but upon returning, he told Cooke to take her editor, find the mother, and get her to seek help for her child. Cooke responded with a memo saying she had gone to the house and the child had been moved. Her life would be in danger, she hinted, if she tried to find out more. There the matter dropped.

Six months later, "Jimmy's World" won a Pulitzer Prize; and the announcement set off a series of events that exposed the story as phony and Janet Cooke as a fraud.

In the biographical information submitted with the Pulitzer nomination, Cooke had claimed a master's degree from the University of Toledo and a baccalaureate from Vassar—neither of which she had. (She also claimed to speak several languages—none of which she spoke.) When reporters peppered the *Post* with inquiries attempting to verify the information, her story began to unravel. After a tense interrogation that lasted late into the night, the weeping writer confessed her lies. Shortly thereafter she resigned. The episode was one of the saddest in *Post* history, and one of the most revealing.

Nearly a year later on national television, Cooke told Phil Donahue that she made up "Jimmy" because she felt compelled to account for her time working on the story. She fell victim, she said, to pressure in the *Post* newsroom "to be first, to be flashiest, to be sensational."

The incident provoked one of the most in-depth public confessions ever seen in American journalism. The report, by *Post* ombudsman Bill Green, published the Sunday after the Pulitzers were announced, was based on forty-seven interviews and pieced together everything Green could find out. So thorough was Green's investigation that Bradlee could say several years later, "Nothing about that case was ever learned from any source other than the *Washington Post.* We came totally clean."

The episode also provoked some serious self-examination by the *Post* editors who had pushed the story through—particularly the two most intimately involved: city editor Milton Coleman, the "steamroller" who had come to the *Post* prepared to make a splash; and his superior, Bob Woodward, the Watergate legend and metropolitan editor. What was missing in them, they wondered, that they had not seen the truth? And what about Janet Cooke made them so eager to believe her lies?

A strikingly attractive black woman with designer clothes, burning ambitions, and flair, Cooke was interviewed by the *Post* in mid-1979. She was a twenty-five-year-old reporter with two years' experience at the *Toledo Blade.* Herbert Denton, then city editor, questioned whether she was tough enough for the *Post.*

His colleagues, dazzled by her education and charm, decided she would do fine. She started in January 1980, writing for a "zoned" section that circulated within the city limits.

After several months of solid work, Cooke was assigned to investigate a new kind of heroin being sold on the streets. She never found the heroin, but eventually she found "Jimmy," a story too big for her zoned section but perfect for the *Post* front page. That meant she would write for Coleman, who had replaced his mentor Herbert Denton as city editor.

Doubts about the veracity of the article surfaced soon after its publication. Courtland Milloy, a streetwise black reporter, went with Cooke to do a follow-up piece and came back convinced that she didn't know the neighborhood where "Jimmy" supposedly lived. Cooke's investigation, he told Coleman, didn't add up. Vivian Aplin-Browlee, also black and Cooke's first editor at the *Post,* likewise told Coleman the story seemed false. Coleman brushed off the objections as professional jealousy.

Woodward later came to see "Jimmy's World" as the biggest mistake the paper had ever made; and he blamed himself, wondering how he—the "resident skeptic"—could have failed so horribly as a journalist and as a human being.

"What was going through my head?" asks Woodward. "It's as if a reporter came to me now and said, 'Gee. I've got this great story. There's a kid whose parents are torturing him. He's eight years old and they're hanging him by his thumbs in the closet and we can't name him, but we'll write this story about child abuse.' "

Woodward believes his reaction now would be substantially more compassionate than with "Jimmy." He would demand to know the child's location, call a doctor who knows something about drug abuse, and say, "There's a kid who's a drug addict at this address, and he's eight years old. Save him, rescue him." If he had followed that course with Cooke, Woodward laments, "Jimmy's World" never would have been published.

His voice becomes slightly muffled as he adds, "I just don't understand what kind of roller coaster we thought we were on that we could say the hell with the kid."

For Coleman, who had zoomed through the *Post* like a shooting star, the unraveling of Janet Cooke's story was a brutal shock—"kind of like body blows."

He had come so far, from public housing in Milwaukee to the

city editorship of the *Washington Post.* And he had done it by willing himself ahead, one step at a time. Years before, when an injured knee had ended his dreams of a football scholarship, he had not given up but had won an academic scholarship instead. And though he had been forced to live at home and work to make ends meet, he had finished college. He had made himself into a star at the *Post.* And now he had brought disgrace on his paper and embarrassed those black colleagues who saw him as a symbol of achievement—and who thought that he, who knew the streets so much better than Cooke, should have seen straight through her.

Only his superiors' strong support saved him from despair. "If you decide to run in the fast lane," said Bradlee, "you're going to stumble." So Coleman tried to take his misfortune in stride and swore to protect himself, as best he could, from ever being manipulated so easily again.

Bradlee remains furious at Cooke. And he remains perplexed about why she blew it: "Jesus, she came so close. She had it all. She was bright. She was well spoken. She was pretty. She wrote well."

Over time, Bradlee got to know Janet's father, Stratman Cooke, a forty-year employee of Toledo Edison who retired as corporate secretary. "Once I met him," says Bradlee, "I knew more about her." Cooke was a very dark-skinned man; yet, thought Bradlee, "he looked . . . in the mirror and . . . saw somebody who was white." He had paid an awful price, Bradlee concluded, to succeed in the white world; and his daughter had paid a price as well.

Bradlee sees no overarching lessons in the affair. What protection is there, he asks, from a reporter who lies to you? And even if Cooke had told him her sources, what was he to do with the information? "A fuckin' lot of good it would have done if I had known her source was Big Red, or something like that. . . . Shit, I'm not going to get in and out of [that neighborhood] alive."

Cooke had never associated much with other black reporters, seeming to operate largely in a world of her own. And yet, recalls features writer Jacqueline Trescott, blacks at the *Post* initially felt "that we were all going to be punished in some way—which, to a lot of people's credit, didn't happen."

Following the episode, the *Post* began checking applicants' references and records more closely. "As a matter of course, we now check where everybody graduates from school," says assistant managing editor Tom Wilkinson.

Less than a year after the Cooke affair, Woodward talked at length with Don Graham. Woodward had several job offers and was seriously considering his options.

"I don't want you to leave. I'll do just about anything to keep you from leaving," said Graham. "But you're not going to be the editor of the paper. You know that. I know that. We might as well say it."

That conversation was the beginning, as Woodward sees it, of his real friendship with Graham, and the beginning of his truly accepting the view that he shouldn't be editor, that his temperament, his interests, and his background made him unsuitable for the job. Janet Cooke, he thinks, helped that conversation along, or at least helped Graham decide that Woodward, the premier investigative reporter at the *Post,* would never take Bradlee's place.

While not rejecting the "holy shit" journalism Woodward personified—demonstrated at its best in Watergate and at its worst in "Jimmy's World"—Graham was indicating that the next editor of the *Washington Post* had to bring more to the table than the instincts to uncover some future Watergate. Woodward's star appeal notwithstanding, on the news side, as on the business side, Graham's emphasis would be on the basics.

Following his conversation with Graham, Woodward left the metro desk and became assistant managing editor of investigations. In that position, he could write books, set his own hours, and lead a small group of investigative reporters. He would leave the headaches of administering a large staff and jockeying for Bradlee's position to others.

For a time, the metro desk (with its more than one hundred employees covering Washington and its suburbs) was run by Woodward's former deputy, David Maraniss. But dissatisfaction with his management skills led to his replacement by Larry Kramer, who had served briefly as Bradlee's assistant following the sale of the *Trenton Times.*

City editor Milton Coleman, who didn't like Kramer, was not inclined to educate a third boss on how to cover Washington. Believing that Kramer was "kind of cheapening the news," he was eyeing the national desk as a way of getting out from under him.

Several years earlier, while a metro/city reporter, Coleman had been offered a transfer to the more prestigious national staff. But Herbert Denton, then city editor, had asked Coleman to say no to the assignment and remain to help upgrade local coverage.

Coleman had agreed. He was in no great hurry to play second fiddle to such national staff heavyweights as star political reporter David Broder. He, instead, would be the David Broder of metro. In return, Coleman had exacted two promises from Denton. One was that Denton himself stay around for at least two years and the other that the national desk option stay open for Coleman to exercise at another time.

In 1983, that time came. Denton had become a national correspondent and then a Beirut-based reporter. Coleman, who had become city editor after Denton, worried that he might not be replaced with another black but decided to follow his heart anyway. He told Howard Simons that he was cashing in his chit and was transferred to national.

Coleman was assigned minorities and immigration, but was quickly swept up by politics. He spent several months covering Chicago's mayoral election as Harold Washington became the city's first black chief executive. And he spent months after that examining the role of blacks in the Reagan administration. By then, the 1984 political campaign had begun and he became the main reporter assigned to Jesse Jackson, eventually covering other candidates as well.

In February, he contributed to a story revealing that Jesse Jackson had privately referred to Jews as "Hymie" and New York as "Hymietown."

The article led to Coleman being threatened by Jackson associate Louis Farrakhan, a minister of the Nation of Islam (known as the Black Muslims). And it triggered debate among black reporters around the country on whether Coleman had betrayed blacks by informing on Jackson or violated journalistic ethics by reporting "off the record" remarks.

The period was one of the hardest of Coleman's life. Strangers called his home with threats. Friends were harassed and told they were traitors for supporting him. Coleman prayed that the experience not make him bitter. And as the storm raged, he felt compelled to write a long Sunday column, an explanation and a justification for what he had done.

> There were only 18 words, a single sentence that appeared two-thirds of the way down in a long story published Feb. 13 in the Washington Post. The subject of the article was the strain in relations between Jesse Jackson, the Democratic presidential candidate, and American Jews.
>
> "In private conversations with reporters, Jackson has referred to Jews as 'Hymie' and to New York as 'Hymietown.' "
>
> The controversy sparked by those words is now more than seven weeks old. It has variously been a sideshow, a backdrop or a main event in the campaign for the Democratic nomination. It has been cited as the cause of heightened tensions between blacks and Jews and of embarrassment, disillusion and infighting among blacks. It has forged divisions among journalists, black and white. It has brought strident threats of harassment, punishment, humiliation and death against me and my family.
>
> The accuracy of that sentence is not in question. Jackson acknowledged six weeks ago that the statement is true. . . .
>
> Even in context, even in "private" among reporters, even "off the record," the remarks suggested . . . insensitivity. . . .
>
> At the time I was aware of one similar situation. Earl Butz, as secretary of agriculture in the Ford administration, had, in the private company of a reporter on assignment, told a joke that demeaned blacks. The reporter reported it, and Butz was forced to resign. Jackson's remarks, I decided, were in the same general category. . . .
>
> There are some reporters who pull punches to curry favor with those they cover. Those people should not be categorized as white racist reporters protecting white candidates. Those are bad reporters. They come in all colors.

The controversy did not end with the article but swirled around Coleman and Jackson for months. "It made me really understand the price you pay if you're black and decide to be a certain kind of reporter," said Coleman. Yet he could choose no other way; for to treat black public figures more gently than whites would be to accept racist standards he had always opposed.

Coleman came to see the Jesse Jackson and Janet Cooke episodes as crosses he would have to bear. Throughout his career, concluded Coleman, critics would always attribute his advancement at the *Post* to his having "done in Jesse." And they would attribute any setbacks to his failure with Janet Cooke.

As Coleman considered the next step in his career, the *Post* pondered the conclusion of Bradlee's. The executive editor would turn sixty-three in 1984 and the newsroom anticipated the naming of a successor.

With Woodward no longer in contention, speculation focused on Len Downie, Larry Kramer, and former "Style" editor Shelby Coffey.

Downie had been in London on a journalism fellowship when Watergate broke, with plans to return and develop an urban affairs beat. Instead, he was asked to become deputy metropolitan editor. He subsequently took over the metropolitan desk, overseeing the last of the Watergate coverage.

After Watergate, he supervised other investigations (including a series of reports on corruption that led to the conviction of Maryland governor Marvin Mandel) and beefed up coverage of Washington's quickly growing suburbs. He went to London in 1979 as the *Post*'s correspondent. Bradlee and Simons saw the assignment as an opportunity for Downie to broaden his perspective and get the overseas reporting credential that would enhance his stature at the *Post.*

When he returned as national editor three years later, Downie's ambivalence about editing was gone. He had stretched his writing talents as far as he could in London, yet he felt something was lacking. His stories should have been better than they were: "The editor in me could sense that and the reporter and writer in me couldn't carry it out." Time had come, he concluded, to put reporting aside.

Managing editor Howard Simons was likewise contemplating his future. He had been at the *Post* for twenty-three years, would be fifty-five in June 1984, and could not imagine Bradlee leaving anytime soon. He wanted to write books. He also felt it time that he, one of Katharine Graham's people, step aside to make room for one of Don's. He left in the summer of

1984 to become curator of the Nieman Foundation at Harvard University.

Downie replaced him as managing editor, becoming the leading candidate (over Kramer and Shelby Coffey) for Bradlee's throne.

Like Downie, Coffey had spent his entire career at the *Post.* He started writing for the *Post* magazine while still in college and joined the staff as a sportswriter in 1968 after graduating from the University of Virginia. He was transferred to the magazine and subsequently became its editor, leaving that job in 1976 to head up the "Style" section.

Coffey had spent most of his childhood in Lookout Mountain, Tennessee, but he was a Washington native and his maternal grandfather was a U.S. senator. He felt at home in Washington's swirl of society and politics and loved working with writers and shaping their copy.

Slender and elegant, he looked the part of a *Washington Post* editor; but his lack of hard news experience was a colossal deficit. Bradlee, wishing to elevate Coffey "to the role of contender," made him deputy managing editor in 1982. After Downie became managing editor, Coffey replaced him as head of the national desk. Within a few months Coffey was gone, having accepted a job as editor of *U.S. News and World Report.*

Unlike the rest of the newsroom, "Shelby understood . . . that Don had really already made his choice of a successor to Bradlee when he made Len managing editor," said Bob Kaiser, who succeeded Coffey as national editor.

The following year, Larry Kramer, feeling his management skills underappreciated, left to become editor of the *San Francisco Examiner.*

When Harvard MBA Kramer had taken over as metro editor, he had a reputation as a wunderkind and potential that seemed unlimited. Though the metro desk had chewed up a succession of editors, including Woodward, Kramer believed that he would be different: "I really thought it was a management problem, and I had the skills to deal with it and . . . they didn't."

He expanded suburban coverage by transferring some two dozen reporters from downtown, and instituted a performance-appraisal-feedback process that was sometimes brutal. He also delegated substantial authority to his editing staff, becoming less involved in nuts-and-bolts editing than his predecessors.

When staff members rebelled against his innovations and management style, Kramer's bosses responded with criticism of him. "I expected a little bit more support from above," he said.

In San Francisco, where his friend William Hearst III had become publisher, Kramer knew management would be solidly in his corner.

A short time after Downie was promoted, John Kuhns, formerly director of business planning at the *Post,* was sent to the newsroom as a deputy managing editor. The newsroom then had close to six hundred people and a budget approaching fifty million dollars a year. Kuhns was charged with making sense of budgeting, accounting, planning, and other management functions—his appointment serving as yet another indication of a new age dawning at the *Post.*

As the *Post* evolved, Kaiser—who remembered "that tiger of a managing editor we all fell in love with" during the 1960s—saw a new Bradlee emerge. He no longer read everything before it went into the paper, nor did he generally dictate what went on the front page. The night of the Challenger shuttle disaster, Bradlee approached Kaiser and Downie around 10:00 P.M. and said, "You guys have got this thing under control. I'm going home." Downie was being brought along; Bradlee was stepping back from involvement in details that had once consumed him.

The process was not to be confused with retirement; Bradlee remained very much in charge. "When am I going to go? I don't know," said Bradlee in 1987. "I've got about five people—nobody but me knows their identity—out in the city room who have promised to tell me when they think I have lost a step. And they'll tell me and I'll get out. And I won't go upstairs."

CHAPTER 6

MATTERS OF RACE

Following Larry Kramer's departure for San Francisco, Milton Coleman was named metropolitan editor; but first, Coleman completed a major reporting assignment. Though it did not generate the drama of the Janet Cooke and Jesse Jackson controversies, like them, it raised sensitive issues of conscience and race and provoked acute soul-searching at the *Post.*

The catalyst for Coleman's investigation was the resignation of a longtime employee—the very woman who originally had directed him to the paper.

National reporter Alice Bonner had left Washington in 1978 to accompany her husband, Leon Dash, to Africa—where he was to open a news bureau for the *Post.* She returned in 1980, following the breakup of her marriage, and worked as a metro reporter—regaining her "newsroom legs"—before moving on to a variety of editing assignments.

She enjoyed editing, particularly the nurturing and shaping of young reporters. But she grew concerned—especially after Howard Simons left—that *Post* management wasn't sufficiently attentive to the human side of editing and had created an environment in which paranoia flourished. She thought she could change that if given formal responsibility for career guidance at the *Post.*

She also wished to escape the supervision of metro editor Larry Kramer, who appeared to resent her four-days-a-week, ten-hours-a-day schedule. The arrangement had resulted from Bonner's desire to spend time at home with her young daughter, who had cerebral palsy.

Over lunch, she explained her career development idea to Robert Signer, a former deputy metro editor then handling personnel matters, who she thought would be sympathetic. He listened respectfully and replied that he would carry the suggestion upstairs but doubted it would be approved. The *Post* was not ready, he suspected, to have a black person in such a job. Later he told Bonner his fears had been confirmed.

Feeling battered and unappreciated, she accepted a job with Gannett. When she told Bradlee, she was astonished to find him genuinely disappointed. She saw that Downie was heartsick as well and realized that neither had ever heard her proposal—that she, in effect, had been seeking Signer's job. By then, she had tendered her resignation and felt she could not turn back.

Bonner was only one of several experienced blacks who left the *Post* around that time. Alarmed, Bradlee asked Coleman that December, "If I gave you a couple of hours at Pugwash [the *Post* editors' annual retreat] to talk about affirmative action in our paper and about why we only seem to do well by accident . . . what would you do?"

Coleman replied that he would survey all blacks on staff, review the *Post*'s past ten years, and make a set of recommendations that he expected to be followed. "Do it," said Bradlee, and the project eventually grew into an examination of attitudes held by all newsroom professionals.

The survey, designed with the help of the *Post* pollster, revealed that blacks felt especially left out, but that whites also thought favoritism and poor communication to be serious problems at the *Post.* "I don't think the *Post* has a problem with the way it treats minorities—it has a problem with the way it treats people," wrote one unidentified respondent.

As a result of the report, Tom Wilkinson, assistant managing editor in charge of newsroom personnel, was mandated to hire more blacks and to pay attention to staff development. Two professionals were added to his domain, including Jeanne Fox-Alston, a black former graphics editor who was given jurisdiction over newsroom recruitment.

The survey also ignited rumors that Coleman was about to

become "assistant managing editor for blacks." The speculation was fueled by a questionnaire item asking whether a high-ranking editor should be appointed "among whose principal duties would be providing advice and assistance to blacks." Both blacks and whites, fearing ghettoization of the staff, soundly rejected the concept.

Many of the issues raised by Coleman's survey were not exactly new to the *Post.* They had been simmering ever since the paper hired its first black reporter in 1925, and had flared up repeatedly since the newsroom began aggressively recruiting blacks in the 1960s.

Dorothy Gilliam, a minister's daughter raised in Louisville, was one of three black reporters when she was hired fresh out of Columbia University's Graduate School of Journalism in 1961. She found Washington a cold, polarized place where she was hassled by doormen, ignored by taxi drivers, and snubbed by many of her white colleagues. Though city editor Ben Gilbert welcomed her, some *Post* reporters would turn away upon encountering her on the street.

William Raspberry, the son of two teachers in Okolona, Mississippi, came to the *Post* a year later, following army service in Washington, D.C. "As far as the *Post* was concerned, I had zero experience," discovered Raspberry, despite his four years with a black weekly in Indianapolis. He passed himself off as a teletype operator, figuring, once in, he could "arrange to be discovered."

Within months, he became a reporter and by 1965 was working as an assignments editor. In August of that year, Watts, California, erupted in a riot that left thirty-four dead.

Having started a joint news service with the *Los Angeles Times,* the *Post* initially depended on the *Times* for coverage, but the *Times* had no black writers. "The reports we were getting back here were sort of like the riots as seen from police helicopters," recalls Raspberry, who was yanked off the assignment desk and sent to California.

The Watts riot was a warning to the *Post,* which resolved not to be caught short as the *Times* had been. Suddenly the door was open for black aspirants. The *Post,* however, made no real effort to advance black reporters once they were taken on. Consequently, many felt stifled; and none was angrier about it than Leon Dash, a handsome, husky activist with a deep, booming voice, who was a product of the age of black awareness.

Dash was eleven years old when Rosa Parks triggered the Montgomery bus boycott by refusing to stand so a white man could sit. He was fourteen when four blacks from North Carolina Agricultural and Technical College launched the sit-in movement at F. W. Woolworth. He was eighteen when Martin Luther King, Jr., challenged the nation with his ringing "I have a dream" oration.

In 1965, midway through college, Dash switched from Lincoln University to Howard University to study African history. Short of cash, he got a job steam-cleaning buildings at night. But as winter approached, the work fell off.

Dash discovered the *Washington Post* had an opening for a copyboy (or clerk) on the 8:00 P.M. to 4:00 A.M. shift. The hours suited his class schedule and he applied for and got the job. Though a diligent worker, Dash was too proud to respond when editors summoned clerks—as was the custom—by shouting "boy." Boy, he felt, was not an appropriate designation for a black man in 1965.

Some months after he had started work, a white *Post* reporter told him her editors feared a riot would erupt that summer. Their anxiety, she suggested, might get Dash promoted. She spoke to the city editor on Dash's behalf and he was accepted into the reporting internship program—and was subsequently given full reporter status though still attending classes at Howard.

Dash covered a variety of race-related stories, including the aftermath of Dr. King's assassination in 1968, but he grew increasingly irritated at the *Post*'s limits on black opportunity. Shortly after King's death, he went to Kenya as a Peace Corps volunteer to teach in a rural high school.

Upon returning in 1971, he became outraged over the condition of blacks at the *Post:* "It was very obvious to me that nothing had changed. . . . A lot of promises had been made . . . but nothing had been done. . . . Things were still operating in the same plantation style."

That most of his black colleagues seemed complacent surprised him nearly as much. Dash took some of them aside and argued for bold action. Otherwise, as he saw it, the *Post* would continue to freeze blacks out of significant management positions and reporting assignments.

By early 1972, he had forged a coalition, a group of black reporters on the metropolitan staff that came to be known as the Metro Nine. They presented Bradlee with a list of specific complaints and demanded to know why the *Post* discriminated against blacks. They also insisted that the paper develop an aggressive antidiscrimination program. Bradlee promised to try to be responsive but would not agree to the dissidents' specific demands.

One meeting led to other meetings and to increasingly frayed feelings on either side. A religious Metro Nine member dropped out, telling his colleagues he would wage his battle through God, and the group became the Metro Eight. Nonetheless, momentum grew. Other blacks in the newsroom signed a letter of support drafted by the two most prominent on the editorial staff: Robert Maynard (then on leave of absence), who had become a national staff star, and Roger Wilkins, the editorial writer.

Free legal advice was provided by Clifford Alexander, Jr., a former chairman of the Equal Employment Opportunities Commission, who was with the prestigious law firm of Arnold and Porter.

Demands were laid on the table: 35 percent black hires, the promotion of a set percentage of blacks to assignment editors. Bradlee would not agree to quotas and countered with proposals that seemed token in comparison. Dash became increasingly agitated.

Months earlier, he had confronted Don Graham over drinks one evening in Graham's Capitol Hill home, accusing the young heir of inheriting his position and coasting on his name. How could Graham possibly understand what Dash was going through? "So don't tell me anything about what blacks should do and what blacks should not do," Dash had railed.

The attack had drawn blood and left Graham with no real answer. Given Graham's acute awareness of his privileges, and given his persistent attempts to overcome them, Dash's words couldn't have been more calculated to hurt.

A similar face-off ensued with Bradlee. While out on assignment one night, Dash called Bradlee at home and suggested that they talk. Bradlee invited him over. Dash, who had a serious drinking problem at the time, showed up near midnight. "No gloves," he said upon walking in. "Bare knuckles," meaning that he wanted to get to the root of their problems and that nothing would be couched in polite, diplomatic language.

Bradlee produced two water glasses and a bucket of ice and they went into his study. Dash drank Scotch. Bradlee drank bourbon. And ultimately Dash lost control. "I called him everything but a son of God," Dash recalled. And in the process, or so Bradlee later told him, he awakened Bradlee's wife and children, who wondered, as Dash raved on, whether Bradlee was in danger. Something in Dash's way of speaking, his manner of letting his voice drop so Bradlee could respond, convinced Antoinette "Tony" Bradlee that her husband was safe. The conversation, however, settled nothing. And the black reporters eventually filed a complaint with the Equal Employment Opportunities Commission and held a press conference to tell about it. Herbert Denton pulled out, reducing the group to the Metro Seven.

Denton did not feel "the same depth of grievance" as the others. He is not precisely sure why. Maybe, he mused, his boarding school experience had made him more comfortable around whites. Maybe he was treated differently because of his well-known friendship with Graham. Maybe his reporting was good enough that he got better breaks. Maybe there were other reasons, obscure even to him. The certainty, however, was that he would not close ranks with the outside world against the *Post.*

The EEOC found in the Metro Seven's favor. But the *Post* lawyers, citing mistakes in the EEOC report, demanded it be withdrawn, after which the EEOC decided not to prosecute. The Metro Seven considered going to court, but the law firm would no longer represent them for free. The protest fizzled out—but not before encouraging *Post* women to file a sex discrimination complaint of their own.

Dorothy Gilliam had gone on maternity leave in 1965, planning never to return. She was invited back as an assistant editor in the "Style" section in 1972 (and later became a *Post* columnist). The reason, she thinks, had a lot to do with the Metro Seven.

Several years later, another protest rocked the *Post.* And though it too was instigated by suspicions of racism, the complaints came not from *Post* employees but readers—outraged over a new *Post* magazine that they felt was promoting stereotypes anathema to many blacks.

The premier issue (on September 7, 1986) featured a breathless account of a twenty-year-old black rap artist called "Justice" (or Just Ice) whose father once beat him with a baseball bat, who dreamed of making it big with his rap poems, and who had been accused of shooting a man in the head and chest in a dispute over drug money.

"If one thing is for certain," wrote author John Ed Bradley, "it is that in Justice's world, people are born poor and quickly learn to do without, and they pass their days using whomever and whatever they can to make the ride easier."

The piece, titled "Murder, Drugs and the Rap Star," was preceded in the magazine by a Richard Cohen column that presented a defense for New York subway shooter Bernhard Goetz and an argument for locking young black men out of Washington boutiques.

"Especially in cities like Washington and New York, the menace comes from young black males," wrote Cohen. "Both blacks and whites believe those young black males are the ones most likely to bop them over the head."

The juxtaposition of the Cohen column and the Bradley article astounded and angered many black readers. Local radio personality and owner (WOL-AM) Cathy Hughes remembers feeling ill after reading a few pages of the magazine. "By the time I got to Richard Cohen's article, I said, 'Oh my God, the *Washington Post* has declared war.' " The next morning, her station's forty-two telephone lines were jammed with callers complaining about the publication. The protest grew from there—ultimately gaining support from the Washington Urban League, church groups, labor organizations, and others.

Hundreds of demonstrators, led by Hughes and including Walter Fauntroy (Washington's nonvoting delegate to Congress), massed in front of the *Post,* dumped copies of the magazine, and demanded an end to its publication.

Post ombudsman Joseph Laitin wrote, "Never have there been so many readers' calls about a single story as there were this past week about the cover article in the first issue of the new Sunday magazine."

Cohen wrote a second column explaining that his original

article "was attempting to point out . . . that what seems like racism—the refusal to admit or serve young blacks—is often more complicated than that."

Ben Bradlee wrote an apology and urged readers not to judge the weekly solely by its first issue.

William Raspberry sided with the outraged readers, asserting in his column that *Post* editors had failed to consider the impact of publishing a magazine that "was, in the minds of thousands of black readers, an indictment of young black men."

The editor, Jay Lovinger, was new to Washington and to the *Post.* Formerly a senior editor at *People,* Lovinger had hoped his premier edition would let Washington know that his magazine would be something special; it would not pander to Georgetown yuppies or Washington politicians but deal with important subjects in an emotionally powerful way. When a profile of George Bush, a possibility for the first issue, had been delayed, Lovinger had not been overly concerned. In "Justice" he had thought he had something even better.

To Lovinger, the "Justice" story had seemed sensitive and insightful. He later concluded that the adverse reaction stemmed largely from the Cohen column and the overpowering graphics that illustrated the cover story.

Don Graham was horrified at the uproar; but instead of blaming Lovinger—who was kept on the job—Graham blamed himself for letting the offending articles appear. He and Bradlee spent hours meeting with black community representatives. Graham also appeared several times on Hughes's radio program to explain the *Post* and agreed to return periodically to continue the discussion. He refused to suspend the magazine's publication and ultimately the commotion died down.

Afterward, Graham concluded that the community reaction probably had more to do with the newspaper overall than with the magazine, that it was a cry for fair and balanced coverage of black Washington, and that the *Post* would have to do better.

CHAPTER 7

FACING THE FUTURE

That offensive articles in its magazine could mobilize a community was a sign of how important the *Post* had become. No longer was it a pauper crying for attention, but a power in its own right. Presidents cringed when needled in its gossip columns. Corporate moguls fumed when dissected in its news sections. And sometimes they doggedly counterattacked, determined to vanquish an institution that, in its maturity, had come to represent the might of the press.

One such episode began in 1979 after the *Post* published a story by reporter Patrick Tyler. The article claimed that the president of Mobil Oil Corporation had set up his son in a shipping business and helped him get Mobil contracts.

It was a hard-hitting, carefully researched piece that *Post* editors and lawyers thought took all proper precautions. Nevertheless, the year after publication, Mobil president William Tavoulareas filed a fifty-million-dollar libel suit against the *Post.*

The trial opened in the summer of 1982 with Tavoulareas's lawyers accusing the *Post* of "reckless . . . unrestrained investigative reporting." A six-member federal court jury agreed, awarding Tavoulareas $2.05 million in damages (on the same day that Bradlee's infant son, Quinn, born with a hole in his heart, underwent successful open heart surgery).

A U.S. district judge overturned the decision the following year, but he was overruled by a three-judge panel of the U.S.

Court of Appeals. The ruling, which attacked the very craft of investigative journalism, enraged editors across the nation.

In 1987, the full U.S. Court of Appeals decided that the story was substantially true and that the *Post* therefore could not be guilty of libel. The U.S. Supreme Court refused to review the decision. The case drained everyone involved in it—the editors and reporters who spent days on the stand, the lawyers who spent years fighting it, the company, which spent well over a million dollars defending itself. Some feared that the real price would be even higher, that it would make the *Post* and other newspapers a little more timid than before.

"Pat Tyler comes to me now and says, 'I've got a good story; it's going to cost you a million and a half to run,' " snorted Bradlee. "He can go piss up a rope."

That Bradlee could joke about such a sum said much about how wealthy the Post company had become. The corporation, with profits of less than $5 million in 1970, earned $132 million (after taxes) in 1987—plus $54 million from the sale of cellular telephone and cable interests.

In the early Bradlee years, the firm's major possessions were the *Post, Newsweek,* some television stations, and a significant interest in the *International Herald Tribune.* By 1988, the company had added a New York–based business that prepared students for college admissions tests and a Washington-based company that provided (via computer) the full text of congressional bills and resolutions. It had acquired and sold a cellular telephone business, launched the *Washington Post National Weekly Edition* (a sixty-thousand-circulation tabloid) and a Japanese-language version of *Newsweek,* as well as several demographically targeted editions of the magazine for the U.S. market. In 1985, for roughly $350 million in cash, the company had made its largest acquisition to date—purchasing fifty-three cable television systems from Capital Cities/ABC. The Post also held a substantial interest in the Cowles Media Company, which owned the *Minneapolis Star and Tribune.*

The Post, so cash-poor when Katharine Graham took over, was maturing into a cash machine. Between 1980 and 1987, company revenues roughly doubled and profits more than quintupled.

For the Grahams and the new Post team, the numbers—

anchored in some hard-nosed cost cutting—were as welcome as rain in a drought, a sign to their peers and to Wall Street that the Post had become as serious about its business as about its news.

The *Washington Post* remained the paramount property in the company—the foundation for its rejuvenation having been laid by the collapse of the pressmen's union and the *Washington Star.* In 1987, the newspaper contributed over $600 million to total corporate revenues of $1.3 billion. Newspaper division (pretax) profit margins were 22 percent.

From 1971 to 1986, composing-room man-hours required to assemble a page of the *Post* went from 27.7 to 8.4. Simultaneously, man-hours required to produce a ton of newspapers went from 4.28 to 2.66 and production costs as a percentage of revenue dropped from 20.8 to 9.3 cents. The savings went directly to the corporate bottom line. And though the most dramatic improvements had immediately followed the strike, progress had steadily continued.

The change in attitude among production workers was nearly as striking as the statistics. Following a visit in 1987 to the plant in Springfield, Virginia, *Post* president Thomas Ferguson commented, "For the first time, I felt like I was in the 1980s as opposed to the 1930s." The following year, the *Post* negotiated a contract with its mailers that guaranteed lifetime jobs and gave cash incentives in exchange for more efficient labor practices.

Some employees were ambivalent about the new *Post.* Loyce Best, manager of circulation systems, mourned the loss of family spirit. Although she knew Donald Graham cared deeply about his workers, she was unsure his senior management team felt likewise. She was mystified that "being profit-minded and business-driven can come so much from people under Don [when Graham] seems to be so different, so interested in the employees, so interested in people he knows are dedicated to getting a quality paper out."

And despite production workers' increased flexibility, labor relations at the *Post* remained turbulent. The Newspaper Guild accused the paper of discriminating against women, blacks, and those hired after the pressmen's strike. Union members were peeved as well that *Post* minimum contract salaries, which had ranked first among Guild newspapers in 1975, did not even rank in the top ten in 1987 (though many members were paid well above the minimum).

Several black female journalists (following a Guild analysis) wrote Downie a letter complaining that their salaries showed "black women are the least valued employees in the newsroom." Downie rejected the charge and promised to review each person's compensation individually.

In protesting a 1987 *New York Times* op-ed column critical of *Post* negotiating tactics, John Kuhns (vice-president, personnel) declared, "The *Post* is a staunch believer in collective bargaining." In response, Guild representative Sandra Polaski fired off a letter that recalled "the history of the *Post* as a pioneer in newspaper strike breaking" and accused the *Post* of purposefully thwarting negotiations. As recriminations flew, the feeling persisted in the newsroom that the future remained dismal for unions at the *Post.*

The outlook for the *Post* itself, however, could not have been brighter—though Don Graham was taking nothing for granted. In 1986, he had appointed production chief Tom Might to head up a committee of his business- and editorial-side peers to ponder the *Post*'s future. The committee was to make recommendations about a new printing plant that could cost upward of two hundred million dollars and that the *Post* would have to live with well into the twenty-first century. Before deciding what (and how many) presses to buy, the group had to determine how the *Post* would likely change with the times.

Might's team members studied newspapers in Los Angeles, Chicago, New York, and elsewhere and returned convinced that many major newspapers had let expansion opportunities slip away. The *Post,* they hoped, would make no such mistake. They would not concede the outer suburbs to the competition as New York's newspapers had done (allowing *Newsday* to flourish on Long Island and to launch an assault on Manhattan); or as the *Los Angeles Times* had done (allowing the *Orange County Register* to thrive).

Still, *Post* managers brooded over how—in Ferguson's words—to make the paper relevant to Washington readers as well as to "the person who is in the car at 6:30 in the morning in the exurbs . . . not headed to Washington, but to another suburb."

As Ferguson sees it, trying to reach those readers and advertisers will force the *Post* to create an increasing number of zoned sections tailored to specific population groups or advertising markets, even as the *Post* tries to retain its broad circulation base.

In many respects, the *Post* and its market are unique. The Washington area never really suffers a recession or seems to stop growing, and its residents are faithful newspaper readers. In 1987, some 54 percent of households in the *Post* circulation area took the paper daily; 73 percent took it on Sunday, giving the *Post* the highest household penetration by far of any major daily in the nation. The *Post* worked hard to keep that figure high: "Our sense of things has always been different here," said Graham; and (alluding to the period under the previous owner when the *Post* had nearly died) he added, "It's always derived from being a fifth paper in town . . . and really having a tremendous sense that every copy sold mattered."

Several years ago, a McKinsey and Company consultant suggested that perhaps the *Post* should consider getting rid of some of its poorer readers and concentrate on the more affluent, whom advertisers valued most. Katharine Graham's response was emphatic: "Look . . . we are a newspaper for all the people, period."

Don Graham is equally passionate. High market penetration "was our circulation strategy in 1957 and that's our strategy in 1987," he says. "The great thing about it is that if we ever change our minds . . . it will be real easy for us to lose circulation, but . . . nobody in recent years has [shown how to] rapidly regain the circulation you decided to slough off."

Even as it fights for readers in the Washington area, however, the *Post* has conceded the national newspaper market to others. Though many in the newsroom crave the prestige of a true national edition that could compete with the *New York Times* and the *Wall Street Journal,* Graham has no such plans.

"It makes no economic sense at all for us to publish the paper on a daily basis nationwide and never will that I can see," says Graham. Barring a change in strategy, the *Post* national publication efforts will be confined to the weekly, a tabloid that boils down the *Post* political coverage for an elite audience.

Some within the *Post* criticize the decision not to challenge the *New York Times* head-on, citing it as evidence that the paper has become too much the hostage of MBA types who cautiously look at every decision from the vantage point of financial return.

Such caution, they argue, has kept the Post from becoming a major newspaper chain. Graham dismisses the complaint. He acknowledges that the company missed some deals, but counters that, in the late 1970s, when many other companies were buying newspapers, the Post was buying back 20 percent of its outstanding stock. That stock, then going at between twenty and twenty-five dollars a share, increased more than eight times in value over the next decade. The investment was not particularly ego-gratifying, he says, but "no deal in the 1970s would have been better financially for the Post."

Still, some workers wonder whether the new *Post,* the comfortable, successful *Post,* is becoming too careful for its own good and losing some of the fire that made it such an exciting place to work. Those concerns generally come from reporters and editors who grew up under Bradlee and worry that some of the paper's passion will leave when he does.

Downie's fans insist that he will be a good newsroom leader. "He has Bradlee's journalistic values and Don Graham's human, managerial values," says Bob Woodward. Downie himself maintains that there will be no lessening of the *Post* passion for public accountability. Honesty, he says, "really drives me; it's always driven me as a reporter. . . . I get most excited by stories that have to do with accountability." In that regard, he does sound a bit like Bradlee. (Asked about the *Post* political coverage that helped drive Gary Hart out of the 1988 presidential contest, Bradlee responded, "I suppose that there's a growing interest in this paper . . . to catch lying early.") Yet Downie clearly does not have Bradlee's charisma, as he—well aware of the folly of trying to impersonate Bradlee—would be the first to agree. "I'm not a high-profile person," he readily admits. "I'm not an interesting personality."

"I don't know if anyone around here has the feeling they would walk off a cliff for Len . . . or any of the rest of us the way I would walk off a cliff for Bradlee," says Kaiser. "I don't think it's there. I don't think it *will* be there in exactly the same way."

"I have no doubt," said one editor, "that the paper will be more consistent under Downie than under Bradlee. I worry, however, that though the lows will not be as low, maybe the highs will not be as high."

Howard Simons, the former managing editor, has a similar worry, noting that the *Post* will have to force itself to continue "jumping off the high board occasionally."

"If you have everybody who thinks like the stereotypical MBA," says assistant managing editor Tom Wilkinson, "then you're going to get the stereotypical MBA paper. And . . . I don't think that's the hallmark of this paper. I think the hallmark of this paper is its willingness to take chances."

No one questions Downie's management ability, least of all Bradlee, who observes that in the nuts and bolts of management, "in the sense of getting the trains to run on time . . . [Downie is] very good at managing in a way that I'm not."

Neither does anyone question Downie's closeness to Graham. In personality and style, they are similar: low-key workhorses who tend to basics and are constantly trying to improve.

"I guess the most significant thing about me is . . . that I keep growing and changing as I go through life," says Downie. "I've changed a long way from where I started out, and there's a long way that I want to go . . . in maturation as a journalist and now as a manager and in my personal life."

On one level, the concerns within the *Post* newsroom are not about individuals—a Downie versus a Bradlee—or individual management styles. They are about whether a paper as successful as the *Post* will inevitably become complacent; whether approaching management more systematically will inevitably lead to stifling bureaucracy; whether emphasis on managerial success will translate into less tolerance for oddball people and oddball ideas that can sometimes make a publication great. For that reason, some found solace in the choice of Jay Lovinger, a disheveled hippie by current *Post* standards, to edit the *Post*'s new magazine.

Lovinger rejected the suggestion that his hiring was particularly significant in that regard: "Every company likes to think of itself as being more liberal than it is and it's really not unusual to find a company to hire one or two weirdos so that they feel they're not too rigid."

Fighting the potentially crippling effects of institutionalization is only one of several major challenges Don Graham and other Post company managers face. Another task will be deciding exactly what the corporation will grow to be. Having whittled costs and cut debt, the Post is primed to generate mountains of cash. "We are going to either have to create new products from within or go out and buy them on the outside," says Simmons. And even as the company makes its choices, Graham will have to make his.

Christopher Little, the former publisher in Everett who became president of *Newsweek* in 1986, voices the sentiments of many of those in the Post company when he says, "I can't imagine Don doing anything else other than being part of the Post company. . . . He's the right person to be in control of the company after Kay just as Kay is the right person now."

That is a prospect Graham (who is already a vice-president of the corporation and a member of its board) prefers not to discuss. He begins by saying that his future isn't strictly up to him and then adds, "I am totally comfortable with the current arrangement and suspect it's going to go on, with Kay as chairman and chief executive officer, for a number of years." Finally, he admits, "I guess I don't want to speculate about my own future down the line. The Post is really stocked with some very, very good people."

Yet, barring an act of fate, Don Graham is likely one day to run the company. His older sister and two younger brothers are not actively involved in Post management and his four children (the oldest of whom was born in December 1972) are years away from real responsibility. Even if Don Graham resists taking the title of chairman when his mother relinquishes it, whoever does take the title will have to solicit his counsel.

Graham has had no shortage of role models and tutors. And to the extent that a man can be defined by his heroes, the values that will guide Graham are not in question. The two men he most admires are James Reston, considered the premier journalist of his time, and Warren Buffet, one of America's shrewdest investors, a longtime adviser to Katharine Graham, and a former member of the Post company board of directors.

Yet even as Graham assumes broader corporate responsibility, he will not easily give up running the *Post.*

Katharine Graham suggests that one could act both as chairman of the company and publisher of the paper: "Warren Phillips [of the *Wall Street Journal*] does." But if Don Graham does move up, she adds, he will have to grow "out of that direct involvement" with the newspaper.

That may well be Don Graham's hardest lesson. For he cares deeply about the paper; and he thrives on seeing it respond to that care. Moreover, the mantle of power rests more comfortably than it once did on his shoulders; he smiles more easily and seems to worry less about his own worthiness, even as he worries more than ever about the city that he loves.

Graham thinks often of his days as a policeman, those days before coming to the *Post* when he drove his squad car through Northeast Washington. "I spent much of my time going into very poor people's homes and seeing that they lived in very tough circumstances, but there was a feeling in the country at that time, an expectation that there [would be] an improvement of conditions in those homes in another generation—or that conditions in the homes of the children would be better. . . . Washington's had consistent economic progress since then, but If I went back to those same neighborhoods tonight . . . the conditions in the homes haven't changed much."

Shortly after returning from Africa in 1984, Leon Dash did spend time in one such neighborhood. More mellow than in his early *Post* days, Dash had not touched alcohol in years and had apologized to those persons—including Graham—he had offended while drunk. He was encouraged by the presence of more blacks in the newsroom but bothered that none had become an assistant managing editor. (Milton Coleman had not yet been promoted.) But as he caught up with events in the United States, he heard something that troubled him even more.

Over half of the black children in the United States, he learned, were born to unmarried women and more than a third of those mothers were teenagers. The figures astounded him. In Africa, he had heard nothing of America's "black underclass" and had little immediate understanding of what the phrase meant. He began reading materials on poverty and pregnancy and asking friends why so many black teenagers were having kids. None of the reasons given made much sense. Finally, he asked his editors for time to investigate.

He had envisioned doing the story for the national desk; but Howard Simons, then managing editor, steered him to Bob Woodward's investigative unit, telling him: "If you go and do it with Bob, it will get done right. If you go and do it on the national desk . . . you will rush through it and we won't have anything significant."

Dash was reluctant. He thought of Woodward as someone "into spies and CIA and toppling presidents," while Dash cared about ordinary people and their problems. Also, Woodward's style made Dash uncomfortable: "He still wore a white shirt, so . . . that made me suspicious of him. . . . I saw him as a midwestern all-American boy who would not want to touch . . . black sexuality." To Dash's surprise, Woodward and his deputy, David Maraniss, passionately embraced the project.

Dash rented a one-bedroom apartment in a poor, black Washington neighborhood and began work. Woodward insisted that Dash return again and again to reinterview subjects he had interviewed numerous times already. By so doing, Dash slowly stripped away his sources' glib veneer. He emerged in January 1986 with a stunning portrait of a troubled community—and haunting images of young women having babies out of deep distress.

Sherita Dreher, an eighteen-year-old with a two-year-old son, originally told Dash she had surrendered to the advances of her then sixteen-year-old boyfriend believing she could not become pregnant. After countless recitations, her story changed—as would happen with so many others.

> Her pregnancy, she said, was no accident. She *wanted* to have that baby, *needed* to have it. She said she had tried to get pregnant, hoping that it might help her hold on to her boyfriend, William Wheeler, the same boyfriend who was her first sex partner—when she was 11 and he was 12.
>
> She was afraid of losing William, she said, and afraid that if she did, she would never get another boyfriend as handsome.

The depressing series offered no ready answers, but Dash resolved to do what he could. After some badgering, he got Sherita Dreher to agree to go to college.

Don Graham, with whom he had finally built a genuine rapport, was deeply affected by the articles and called them the most important journalism the *Post* had done that year. One day, as the two men discussed a Graham-sponsored scholarship program, Graham solicited Dash's views on providing self-help incentives for adolescents like those in Dash's stories. Dash took the opportunity to inform Graham that Dreher had been accepted at the University of the District of Columbia. He would like to help her, Dash explained, but he already had one daughter in college and another who was handicapped; the bulk of his money went for his two girls. Graham listened quietly and then agreed to pay Dreher's tuition and book bills as long as she stayed in school.

PART TWO

THE CONTENDER: TIMES MIRROR

CHAPTER 8

IN PURSUIT OF PERFECTION

Well before it became a fashionable concept of the 1980s, Otis Chandler had launched his own search for excellence. The only son of one of America's most prominent families, he could have coasted through life, his station guaranteed from birth, but he was driven by an insatiable urge to compete, a need to prove that he was every bit as good as his name. So he molded himself into an Olympic-level athlete and—in time—turned the family publication, the *Los Angeles Times,* into a world-class newspaper.

The Chandlers had a history of grand ambitions. They played a key role in molding Southern California and, in the process, built the *Times* into a wealthy enterprise. Otis Chandler, however, was less interested in building an empire than in improving the paper. That—in the end—he could do both was a tribute not only to his overpowering will but to the underlying strength of the organization he inherited.

Authors Robert Gottlieb and Irene Wolf described the Chandlers as "the single most powerful family in Southern California." David Halberstam was more emphatic: "No Easterner can understand what it has meant to California to be a Chandler, for no single family dominates any major region of this country as the Chandlers have dominated California."

Without question, patriarch Harrison Gray Otis and his son-in-law Harry Chandler were among the most dynamic and formidable men of their day. A big, blustering Civil War hero from Ohio, Otis moved to California in 1876 to edit the newly launched *Santa Barbara Press.* Unable to make the newspaper a success, he resigned in 1880. Two years later, after serving as U.S. Treasury agent for Alaska's Seal Islands, he was hired as editor of the *Los Angeles Daily Times.* The original owners, following several months of mounting losses, had turned the four-page daily over to its printers. Otis added staff (originally, the only editorial personnel were he and his wife), editorialized on the great promise of Southern California, and united the local merchants behind him. The paper flourished, and in 1884 Otis and an associate acquired it. Shortly thereafter, he bought out his partner, becoming sole owner of the parent company, incorporated as Times Mirror.

Otis, however, lacked the entrepreneurial vision and managerial talent to create a grand enterprise. Harry Chandler possessed both. A Dartmouth College student who had fallen ill out East, Chandler came to California to restore his health. Through harvesting and hauling fruit, he built himself into a hulk of a man and soon lost all interest in returning to Dartmouth.

Chandler plowed his earnings into *Times* delivery routes, which were so successful that eventually he came to Otis's attention; a warm relationship sprouted between the two men. Like Otis, Chandler was a dreamer and a builder, but whereas Otis was impulsive and combative, Chandler was deliberate and collegial; whereas Otis was fundamentally an editor, Chandler was first and foremost a businessman. Chandler's marriage to Otis's daughter, Marian, solidified the men's bond. And while Otis carried the editorial banner, vigorously attacking unionism and Democrats, Chandler became Southern California's leading real estate baron and back-room politician.

The two prevailed in virtually every dispute they entered. In the early 1900s, for instance, Southern California's agricultural and business development was threatened by a perennial water shortage. Otis, Chandler, and their associates endeavored to remedy the problem by diverting water from the Owens Valley (fed by the Owens River) nearly 240 miles to the northeast. By working with the federal Bureau of Land Reclamation and keeping Owens Valley residents ignorant of their true intentions, the Otis-Chandler interests pushed through construction of an aqueduct (completed in 1913) to deliver the water from up north. The project dehydrated the Owens Valley, fed the growth of Los Angeles, and substantially augmented the wealth of the Chandlers, who had invested heavily in the San Fernando Valley, into which the water flowed.

Harry Chandler was also a key player in the war to make the city an open-shop stronghold. In 1910, at the height of that struggle, union activists blew up the three-story *Times* building, but to little avail. By 1917, when Otis died, the *Times* had become the strongest and most influential newspaper in the region. It was also considered one of the least impartial.

At times the paper seemed little more than a tool in the service of Chandler's personal projects, one day boosting the career of a promising politician, the next day promoting the construction of a coliseum or some other gigantic public works scheme. Harry Chandler's interests went so far afield of the newspaper—to real estate, politics, and countless peripheral businesses—that when his son, Norman, took over the company upon his father's death in 1944, the new publisher resolved to pay closer attention to the paper and a little less to the role of kingmaker.

The *Times,* he felt, had suffered from his elder's scattered attention. Also, Norman seemed naturally less passionate than Harry—whose shadow the son never quite outgrew. Moreover, Los Angeles itself was changing; no one family could remain as influential as the Chandlers had been.

In 1957, *Time* magazine discussed the family's evolving role: " 'The difference between Harry and Norman,' says one old-time Angelino, 'is that Harry sat in his office and ruled this city like a king. Norman doesn't rule; he isn't interested in ruling. What he wants is to become an institution.' Yet in a town where the Times is one of the few enduring institutions, Norman Chandler knows better than to try to wield an overpowering political club. Today's Los Angeles is too amorphous for one man to rule, one newspaper to command, or even one political organization to anneal."

The article ended with an observation from Dorothy Buffum Chandler, Norman's stylish, strong-willed wife:

" 'I don't say Los Angeles is the most beautiful place on earth, or even the most desirable. I love San Francisco, for instance. But I could never live there, because everything that needed doing has long since been done. In Los Angeles, things will always need doing, things will always need to be made better. Los Angeles is a place for the kind of people who are willing to try something new. It's a place for people who want to build a new world.' "

Frank McCulloch, a sharp-tongued ex-marine, was *Time*'s Los Angeles bureau chief and the lead reporter on that story. In the course of his research, he got to know Norman and Buff Chandler well. And to his surprise, McCulloch found himself liking them. They were not the pampered Neanderthals McCulloch had been expecting. Nor were they lacking in desire to improve their parochially eccentric newspaper.

After the article came out, the Chandlers and McCulloch continued to talk, and McCulloch realized that Buff and Norman were searching for a way to turn their rich publication into a newspaper of stature. The *Los Angeles Times* was appearing on lists of the worst newspapers in the country, and the Chandlers hungered for the sort of prestige accorded the owners of the *New York Times.*

Norman Chandler was turning sixty in September 1959. Behind him in the succession line was his younger brother, Philip, the paper's general manager and a John Birch Republican. Norman feared that Philip would steadfastly resist any efforts to upgrade the paper. Only Otis, among those even nominally in the running, represented a real break with the past. And only he, in his early thirties, was young enough to reign until new ideas took root. Originally, his parents had thought that Otis might first take over the *Mirror*—an afternoon paper started by Norman in 1948 and a much lesser property than the *Times.* But by 1959, the *Mirror*'s days were clearly numbered. If Otis was to make the leap to publisher, it would have to be at the *Times.*

Such a stretch would have been daunting for virtually anyone of his age. Yet if someone had to be chosen to advance Chandler aspirations, Otis was practically perfect. Hollywood could not have created a more impressive hero than the young blond giant—well over six feet tall with massive shoulders and tree trunk arms—who dominated, by sheer physical presence, any room he entered.

Otis Chandler was born in November 1927, a time of unprecedented national prosperity. Los Angeles—with a population of 577,000 in 1920—was on its way to becoming a city of 1.24 million in 1930. Good times and growth seemed unlimited.

Chandler traces his thirst for achievement to the darker period that followed, when the country sank into a depression and an accident nearly took his life. At the age of eight, he was thrown by a horse and landed on his head; he lay motionless and silent, apparently dying, his horrified mother looking on. She scooped him up and rushed him to a hospital, where young Otis was pronounced dead. But Buff Chandler, refusing to accept the judgment, bundled him into the car and sped to another hospital. There she found a doctor who labored over the young body and eventually detected a heartbeat. Otis spent two months in the hospital and nine more recovering at home. When he returned to school, a year behind, something in him had changed.

"For some reason . . . when I got out of the hospital and [after] recovering at home . . . I began to be able to run faster and jump higher," he says. Chandler remains uncertain how the accident could have brought about the transformation. Yet he is sure that a connection exists.

Even more striking than his metamorphosis from average to outstanding athlete was Chandler's change in outlook. He developed an unquenchable craving for competition and for "excellence in personal development."

Though young Otis thought his parents lacked competitive spirit, competition became the very essence of his life. During his junior year, he transferred from an unchallenging local school to Phillips Academy in Andover, Massachusetts, lettering in track, soccer, and basketball shortly after arriving. He repeated the feat as a senior.

At Stanford University, which he entered in 1946, his immersion in sports continued. His roommate, Norm Nourse (with whom he had also roomed at Andover), convinced Chandler to follow a weight-lifting regimen. By the beginning of track season, Chandler had gained seventy pounds of muscle. Carrying between 215 and 220 pounds on his formerly slender frame, Chandler broke existing Stanford records for freshmen weight lifters and shot-putters and came close to breaking national records in his events. His senior year, Chandler was captain of the track team.

Shot putting and weight lifting had a special attraction for

Chandler. Unlike basketball or baseball, those sports required individual excellence: "Particularly when I got to Stanford, I wanted to prove that I could make it to the top on my own and not as a team member. . . . I wanted to achieve and have individual marks."

Chandler failed to make the Olympic team as a shot-putter in 1948, but when he graduated in 1950, he was ranked among the best in the world. He tossed the shot over fifty-seven feet and was consistently beaten only by Jim Fuchs of Yale. His Olympic dreams, however, were frustrated again; a sprained wrist a week before the 1952 Olympics (by then Chandler was co-captain of the U.S. Air Force track team) kept him off the field.

He left the air force in 1953, giving up his quest for Olympic gold. An athlete's training schedule and newspapering simply did not mesh. Yet the specter of the games would haunt him forever. "If the Olympics had been in '49, '50, '51, I would have made them," he would say.

As athletics moved from center stage, family and business filled the void. He had married (Marilyn "Missie" Brant) in 1951, had his first child (Norman) in 1952, and was preparing for a career in a company and a city where to be a Chandler was to command nearly incalculable power.

Chandler's training program took him through all the major departments of the *Times:* advertising, production, the truck garage, and the newsroom. The apprenticeship—designed not only to stretch and test the young heir, but to steep him in the enterprise and mold him into a leader—was very similar to the one devised for Donald Graham a generation later at the *Washington Post* and subsequently for Arthur Sulzberger, Jr., at the *New York Times.*

From the moment Chandler came to the *Times,* many there assumed he one day would be the boss. But only toward the end of the grooming process, when he was given real responsibility and handled it well, did Chandler himself believe he would.

Once empowered, Otis Chandler would transform the *Times* into a strong voice for moderation; but in the early 1950s, as political paranoia reigned in Los Angeles, he buried himself in his work. Meanwhile, California was requiring a loyalty oath of its employees; and the *Los Angeles Times*—which had campaigned for prison camps for Japanese-Americans during the war—

joined the chorus behind Joseph McCarthy, the red-baiting senator from Wisconsin.

In 1957, at his father's behest, Chandler became marketing director for the *Mirror-News*—the afternoon tabloid started by his father in 1948 to compete with the Hearst-owned *Herald-Express.* There he discovered his talent for management: "I had a sense after a while that I seemed to be doing okay in leading much older men, in leading a department and handling a deficit newspaper operation."

Chandler prayed the paper would prosper because his father so desperately wanted it to. He fought managers at the *Times* to ensure that the *Mirror*'s books didn't carry *Times* expenses and, for a while, fought his own growing conviction that the paper could not succeed. The red ink, however, would not go away, and Chandler saw no sign it ever would. And he finally advised his father that the *Mirror* would never be anything more than a noose around the neck of the *Times.*

Norman Chandler opted to try to keep the *Mirror* going, but made Otis marketing manager of the *Times.* While the afternoon *Mirror* wallowed in losses, the morning *Times* basked in wealth—which Otis was convinced could be radically increased. In 1957, the company earned $2,122,055 (after taxes) on revenues of $70,350,136. By 1960, profits had climbed to $5,196,539 on revenues of $112,560,118. Virtually all of the increase came from the *Times* and from Otis Chandler's success at marketing the paper.

As the dollars poured in, his confidence swelled: "I realized maybe I could be publisher someday because I did generate a lot of revenue." He realized as well that the paper he was selling was not worthy of his efforts. And he suspected that the advertisers and readers knew that too and that sooner or later the *Times'* ability to grow would be constrained by its mediocrity.

Cautious of overstepping his authority, Chandler told Nick Williams, the *Times'* relatively new editor, "We better get this paper out of the dark ages." Otherwise, said Chandler, he would be unable to continue meeting his own circulation and advertising goals.

Chandler began keeping a notebook of thoughts—later shared with Williams—on improvements for the paper. By making Williams an ally, Chandler hoped to coax the paper in the direction of respectability. The likelihood of having a more direct impact seemed slim. Norman Chandler did not believe in putting young people in charge. "And I didn't see that he was going to change that attitude," said Otis.

The company's success, however, ultimately left Norman Chandler little choice. Though not exactly gigantic, the corporation (consisting of the two papers, television station KTTV, a commercial printing operation, and part ownership of the Publishers Paper Company in Lake Oswego, Oregon) had become too big for one man to run. Also, with the lion's share of company revenues coming from one profitable newspaper, Times Mirror was poorly positioned to weather any serious economic threat.

Consultants from McKinsey and Company were urging diversification as a solution. America was on the verge of its "go-go" era, a time of seemingly limitless corporate growth through acquisitions. Newspaper companies had not yet jumped on the bandwagon, but McKinsey thought they should.

Because managing growth and diversification was a full-time job, Buff Chandler, McKinsey, and some members of the board recognized that Norman Chandler should not continue as publisher of the *Times.* Moreover, Norman and Buff knew that their day in the sun was ending; their greatest impact on the paper now would be selecting a successor.

Yet if Norman Chandler gave up his publishership, how was he to prevent brother Philip from succeeding him? McKinsey provided an out by recommending that the next publisher serve for at least fifteen years, effectively disqualifying Philip on account of age.

Thus the stage was set for Otis Chandler's ascension—which took place April 11, 1960, at the Biltmore Bowl auditorium at a luncheon for 725 prominent Californians. Norman Chandler's invitations had spurred an avalanche of rumors; for virtually no one summoned knew the purpose for the event. Norman Chandler played with the crowd's curiosity, waiting until several minutes into his speech before letting his bombshell drop: "I hereby appoint, effective as of this minute, Otis Chandler to the position of publisher of the *Los Angeles Times,* the fourth in its seventy-nine-year history."

Then he turned to his son and uttered, "Otis, as my successor, and as my son, I say to you—you are assuming a sacred trust and grave responsibilities. I have the utmost confidence that you will never falter in fulfilling these obligations. This trust is dearer than life itself."

Young Chandler—breathless—stepped to the podium and pronounced his first word as publisher of the *Times:* "Wow." Then, groping for a way to describe his feelings, he drew from the one area in which he already had shown that he measured up to the best in the world. He felt, said the flushed publisher-athlete, as if he could put the shot seventy feet or high jump eight. Then, with appropriate humility, he talked of the difficulty of living up to his father's accomplishments and of his intention to carry on his father's work. Next day, he elaborated on that promise in a front-page editorial accompanying the story of his "historic" elevation. "No changes are in the offing," wrote Chandler. And if the statement was not quite a lie, it was far from the truth. For the young man who had grunted, sweated, and willed himself into physical perfection was hoping to similarly reshape the *Times.*

The elder Chandlers had not believed in separating their politics from their reporting. So the political editor, with the quiet approval of the Chandlers, had developed into a Republican power broker—and played a major hand in shaping political careers, including the early phase of Richard Nixon's. The paper had one foreign bureau (in Paris) and only two reporters in Washington—neither of whom Otis judged to be very good. The city hall correspondent was more an ambassador and power broker than a reporter. The *Times,* thought Otis, deserved much better.

Both son and father realized the newspaper, encrusted in bad habits, could not be turned around easily. But they thought *Time* bureau chief Frank McCulloch had both the experience and the temperament to shake things up; he also had the confidence of editor Nick Williams. McCulloch came in as day managing editor shortly after Otis's elevation.

Lacking a detailed blueprint for change, Otis studied newspapers he admired and occasionally made suggestions to the editors. Though his high expectations were clear, he (in his early days) would generally defer to his elders. "I intend to sit in the corner of the room and listen to the graybeards," he once told them.

McCulloch, in contrast, wanted immediate action; he intended to hurl the *Times* into the twentieth century, even if that brought him into conflict with the Chandlers. He thought the paper's reporting was timid—at least in exploring the darker side of anything other than Democrats—and was hell-bent on changing that. He was also ready to take on right-wing zealots and organized crime and research the region's growing Chicano community.

Sometimes, he realized, he would push too far, perhaps needlessly alienating the powers that be. He depended on the more diplomatic Nick Williams to tell him when to ease up. Whenever Williams did so, McCulloch would try to determine the source of the heat—usually without success: "My impression was it never came from Otis. My impression was it came from the elder Chandlers."

Once during a dispute with Carlton Williams, the political operative and city hall reporter, Williams insisted that McCulloch back away from a pet reform. "We'll see," McCulloch grunted.

Both time and Otis Chandler were on McCulloch's side. Shortly after McCulloch's arrival, Carlton Williams and political editor Kyle Palmer retired and others of the old guard were quietly moved aside.

In January 1962, the Chandlers finally shut down the *Mirror-News.* The Hearst-owned morning *Examiner* closed the same day by prior agreement, leaving the *Times* with a morning monopoly.

"People look back today and say it was a great scheme on our part," says Otis Chandler. "Well, what we wanted to do was get rid of our money loser and we wanted them to get rid of their money loser. . . . We thought, up until the very end, that they would get rid of their afternoon paper and then there would be two morning papers." He surmises the Hearst organization shut down the *Examiner* to avoid continuing to compete head-on with the morning *Times.*

(Despite the agreement's apparent violation of antitrust statutes, the Justice Department looked the other way—reportedly because one of its own attorneys had suggested the collusion. Several years later, when the Justice Department prosecuted Times Mirror for monopoly and restraint of trade stemming from the purchase of the *Sun* newspapers of San Bernardino, the matter came up in court. Norman Chandler admitted foreknowledge of the *Examiner*'s closing, and still the matter was not pursued.)

The newsroom revolution continued. At McCulloch's urging, reporter Ruben Salazar did a series on the Mexican-American community and reporters Jack Tobin and Gene Blake wrote numerous articles linking a two-hundred-million-dollar Teamsters pension fund to organized crime. Those articles led to McCulloch's most serious conflict.

The Tobin and Blake stories intimated that the pension fund had become a gigantic laundry for mob money. McCulloch heard that the articles angered Attorney General Robert Kennedy, who feared they might ruin pending Justice Department cases against Teamster president James Hoffa. Nick Williams had another concern; he thought the stories were boring and told McCulloch so.

Bristling at what he perceived as an attempt to muzzle his reporters, McCulloch did not tell Williams that another pension fund article had just been edited. Instead, he simply put it into the paper. When Williams questioned him about it, McCulloch got angry and snapped, "If you want me to stop the series, you'd better give me an order." Williams gave the order.

Later—though McCulloch argued that newspaper magazines are second-rate and drain resources from the newsroom—the *Times* decided to publish a new magazine to be called *West.* Williams asked McCulloch to be responsible for it. McCulloch fumed, convinced that Williams was pushing him into a corner and threatening his journalistic integrity. When *Time* magazine publisher Henry Luce called, inviting McCulloch back to *Time* to sort out events in Saigon, McCulloch accepted, leaving in November 1963—to the chagrin of many in the newsroom who feared the *Times* would revert to its pre-McCulloch mediocrity.

The fears proved to be unfounded. Otis Chandler liked the direction in which the paper was moving; and he was beginning to say to himself, as he would later say publicly, that he wished to make the *Times* into the best paper in the country—perhaps the best in the world.

Events themselves forced the *Times* to broaden its coverage. The Watts riots erupted in August 1965, catching the paper flat-footed. With not one black reporter on staff and whites fearful of going into the black Watts community, the *Times* could report little more than what the police and assorted black spokesmen told them. Desperate for news, the editors upgraded a young black advertising salesman to reporter and sent him behind the lines. He produced sensationalistic nonsense of dubious journalistic merit. "I, too, learned to shout 'Burn, baby, burn' after several shots were fired at me," wrote Robert Richardson.

Following the riots, a team of reporters took a more serious look at Watts in a sympathetically written seven-part series. Nick Williams submitted the series, along with the paper's riot coverage and editorials, to the Pulitzer Prize committee, which awarded the *Times* a Pulitzer for public service—apparently less for the quality of its riot coverage than for its belated attempt to understand Watts.

In his Pulitzer nominating letter, Williams wrote of the newspaper's obligation to report "what those who lived in Watts thought about the rioting and about the rest of the community." The *Times* believed, he added, "that this city and this nation must come to grips with the vast and terrible problems of urbanization while there is still time."

Harry Chandler's *Times,* of course, would not have cared what black Angelinos thought; nor would it have wrestled with "the problems of urbanization." It would have denounced the rioters as scum and left the matter at that.

Less than a year after the Watts disturbance, another major story highlighted the growing difference between the new *Times* and the old. In June, James Meredith, a black man who four years earlier had desegregated the University of Mississippi, started marching from Memphis, Tennessee, to Jackson, Mississippi. The 220-mile walk, he said, was to encourage voter registration and combat black fear. Meredith was wounded some thirty miles south of Memphis by shots fired from behind. A relatively minor demonstration became a major civil rights event.

National news editor Ed Guthman and one of his assistants, George Cotliar, were on duty when news of the shotgun attack came in. Shortly thereafter, Cotliar, Guthman, and Atlanta bureau chief Jack Nelson held a three-way conversation on the story.

"How long will it take you to get there?" Guthman asked at one point, whereupon Nelson launched into a dissertation on plane schedules and lack of direct flights. "About four hours," he finally replied.

"Charter a plane," Guthman shot back. Cotliar nearly fell from his chair—the moment marking, for him, the point at which the *Times* entered its golden age.

Never, in his nearly ten years at the paper, had Cotliar heard of such a thing. Indeed, though responsible for the Sacramento bureau, Cotliar (as an economy measure) had been told to call the bureau no more than once a day. Throughout his shift, he would write himself notes, saving up all his questions for his one call.

"I went from . . . being able to call Sacramento once a day . . . to Guthman saying, 'The hell with the money. Cover the story,' " said Cotliar.

Even the hiring of Ed Guthman as national news editor had struck many as symbolic of a refreshing new spirit at the *Times.* Guthman had won a Pulitzer Prize at the *Seattle Times* and served as press secretary in Robert Kennedy's Justice Department. Not only was he a distinguished journalist but a Democrat—which in the old days would have made him automatically suspect.

While the *Times* was trying to redefine itself, the parent corporation was gobbling up one property after another.

By 1962, Times Mirror had become the largest commercial book binder west of the Mississippi, purchased one company that made air navigation charts and another that made road maps, atlases, and assorted travel materials. It had become a book publisher (acquiring the New American Library and an English paperback house) and purchased a newspaper serving Orange County, California. "Times Mirror is now constituted as a holding company," wrote Norman Chandler in the 1961 annual report. "It will provide financial control and growth planning to an international group of complementary operating units . . . concentrating in the related areas of communications, graphic arts, and education."

On May 27, 1964, the corporation became listed on the New York Stock Exchange. The step gave the company virtually unlimited access to capital for growth, but no guidance on how to grow.

McKinsey's consultants had warned against buying more

newspapers. If one had a bad year, McKinsey had argued, they likely all would have a bad year. Moreover, the future for newspapers looked gloomy and diversification was a perfect way to minimize risks. Wary of getting far afield from the company's expertise, Norman Chandler had concentrated on acquiring properties that had at least some relationship to newspapers. But as Times Mirror moved into the late 1960s, management was questioning the wisdom of McKinsey's advice.

Robert Erburu, a Ventura, California, native who had joined the company as general counsel and secretary in 1961, summed up management's attitude as, "Hell, the *Times* is doing very well; other newspapers are doing well. . . . We bought all these other companies. Why don't we get back to newspapering?"

The desire to own other newspapers had always been present. In 1962, despite McKinsey's advice, the company had acquired the *Orange Coast Daily Pilot;* and through the years, Norman Chandler had held discussions with the owners of the *San Bernardino Sun-Telegram* and the *Santa Barbara News Press.* Price was always a sticking point for the Santa Barbara paper, but in 1965 Times Mirror bought the *Sun-Telegram.*

The following year, the Justice Department sued for anticompetitive practices under the Clayton Antitrust Act. The action shocked Norman Chandler and Erburu, who thought the acquisition legally acceptable. Some executives concluded the suit was simply the Justice Department's way of redeeming itself for not acting when Times Mirror and Hearst simultaneously shut down their papers in 1962. Nevertheless, Norman Chandler took the proceeding seriously; so much so that while the suit was in litigation the company hesitated to buy any other newspapers lest the Justice Department take offense. Ultimately Times Mirror was ordered to divest and sold the *Sun-Telegram* to Gannett in 1968.

No longer under the sword of the Justice Department, the company started looking at newspapers again. Negotiations started with the owners of the *Dallas Times Herald* in 1969. The next year that deal was completed, along with the purchase of *Newsday,* a feisty daily on Long Island.

By then, Otis Chandler had run the *Times* for a decade; he had been vice-president of the newspaper division for nine years and a member of the board for eight. Increasingly, he oversaw not only *Times* affairs but activities of the parent company. Members of his father's generation were stepping aside; and as slots opened up within the fast-growing corporation, Otis was moving his own people along. Both the *Times* and the company were huge financial successes; despite the expensive acquisitions in Dallas and Long Island, Times Mirror earned more than thirty million dollars (after taxes) in 1970 on revenues of nearly half a billion. By any standard, the *Times* was an infinitely better newspaper than when he had taken over. Yet Chandler remained unsatisfied. He routinely ran into other publishers of consequence and knew he could hold his own against any of them, but something about those encounters stuck in his craw. Though the *Times* was becoming a great newspaper, his publisher colleagues didn't seem to realize it. "I would go East to the conventions and I would sense that people there still looked down on the West, that they still looked down on Los Angeles and that they still looked down on the *Los Angeles Times*. . . . And . . . that bothered me."

Chandler resolved to make the *Times* even better, to show the snobs out East that they had gravely underestimated the thirst for greatness in the West.

CHAPTER 9

KINDRED SPIRITS

As *Times* editor Nick Williams approached retirement, Otis Chandler contemplated his replacement. He started out with a bias toward a big name, someone whose appointment would command attention and respect back East. Ideally, that man—and there was never any doubt that the next editor would be a man—would also have the strength and grace to work with the family and the board.

Early on, Otis thought of Frank McCulloch, the former *Times* managing editor who had fearlessly taken on the old guard before stalking away from the fight. The impending retirement of a featured columnist gave Chandler the opportunity to invite McCulloch back. In the course of a long conversation in Los Angeles, McCulloch—then *Life*'s bureau chief in Washington—was offered a column in the *Times.* Chandler never said it explicitly, but McCulloch took his real message to be that—if all progressed as expected—McCulloch would end up editing the paper. McCulloch accepted his old friend's offer and, as he ambled through the building, ran into a few former colleagues who thought themselves in line for Nick Williams's job. On the flight back to Washington, McCulloch thought a great deal about the prospect of having those men edit his column for two years while he waited for Williams to retire. The more he thought, the more uncomfortable he became. Those editors inevitably would view him as a threat and might do anything to sabotage him. Two years was a long time to work under the knives of rivals. McCulloch called Chandler and backed out, clearing the way for a candidate from inside.

The two most whispered about in the newsroom were national editor Ed Guthman and metropolitan editor William Thomas—a long-standing *Times* employee whose first newspaper job had been in Buffalo. One day, Dennis Britton, a young editor under Guthman, chanced upon Chandler's secretary and asked who was to be named editor of the *Times.* She replied, "Well, if you bet on Thomas or Guthman, you bet wrong." Britton was stunned but kept the conversation to himself and eventually the secretary's meaning became clear.

In the early 1970s, Washington bureau chief Robert Donovan was the brightest star in the *Times* firmament. A charming, low-key sophisticate whose national reputation had accompanied him from the *New York Herald Tribune,* Donovan wished to stay in Washington. But at Chandler's behest, he came to Los Angeles as associate editor, a waiting position until Williams retired.

Before long, signs began to appear that Donovan might be a bit too eastern, too genteel, and too disorganized for the job. He had not worked out of a newsroom in years and had never managed a large staff. When George Cotliar would see Donovan walking around the building with a copy of the *New York Times,* he would think—but never had the nerve to say—"Bob, don't carry the *New York Times.* Carry the *L.A. Times.*"

Others also sensed that Donovan was unsuitable, that, though a great reporter, he simply could not manage the *Times.* Eventually Chandler came to share that feeling and let Donovan keep his title but sent him back to Washington to write.

In the end, Donovan's many partisans felt their man had been abused; that he had been lured into a game he did not want to play and then tossed out in humiliation. Yet Chandler could not entrust his most precious possession to a man in whom he no longer believed.

Perhaps, decided Chandler, an editor's prestige was not the most important attribute after all. The *Times* of 1971 had already made a name for itself. Its circulation hovered at just under one million a day; its pages carried more advertising than any other newspaper in the nation. It had easily withstood the launch (and possibly hastened the death) of a West Coast edition of the *New*

York Times. The paper had installed correspondents across the globe and set up a news service in cooperation with the *Washington Post;* it had established a reputation as a serious publication and had generated momentum that could carry it a good deal further. The problems, in short, were less pressing than when Nick Williams—pushed from below by McCulloch and coaxed from above by Chandler—had taken an elephant of an institution and turned it around. The current need was for a leader who could hold the paper on course while helping to correct its remaining defects.

Chandler had watched Bill Thomas climb through the ranks at the *Mirror-News* and the *Times* and had been impressed with his management and editing skills. He was also personally comfortable with Thomas who (unlike the older Donovan) was a contemporary, and who (though a midwesterner by birth) had been a Californian long enough to identify with Chandler's eastward-directed resentments.

Thomas had noticed the Williams-Donovan transition wasn't working; but like virtually everyone else, he had assumed that Donovan would be made editor anyway. He was dumfounded when Chandler summoned him in 1971 to tell him the job was his.

In retrospect, the choice was all but inevitable. The son of a Bay City, Michigan, banker, Thomas had a low-key insider's style that would endear him to the board; and his vision of the *Times* as a writers' newspaper with a sophisticated, literate personality boded well for Chandler's courtship of affluent, well-educated readers.

Thomas's classy journalism was beyond the ability of much of the staff. Many reporters did not even write their own stories, but simply gave their notes to rewrite people. Thomas proposed to get rid of those reporters—even as he chipped away at the baronies warring in the newsroom.

As things stood, a national reporter following a presidential candidate turned the story over to the metro desk the minute the politician crossed the state line—resulting in the story acquiring a new reporter, a new editor, and probably a new angle. The features, metro, and business desks would all send writers to the same event. Weekend editors would assign stories that daily editors had already assigned or killed. The Washington bureau would constantly get conflicting demands. "Everyone was just charging ahead, and no one was saying, 'These are the tracks; let's stay on them,' " recalls George Cotliar, Thomas's managing editor.

Years would pass before Thomas had a team he felt was really his own. For he was not one to move precipitately. Indeed, critics would complain that he moved too cautiously and that his direction was too unclear, leaving problems to fester in the third-floor newsroom as he sat in his office on the second floor.

But those criticisms belonged to the future. The present seemed infinitely sunny—for Thomas, for the newspaper, and for the parent company, whose revenues would top half a billion dollars in 1971.

A portion of those revenues were impressively displayed at a new headquarters building in Times Mirror Square. The company also pumped resources into the *Dallas Times Herald* and *Newsday*—of which Dave Laventhol was made editor.

Much of *Newsday*'s staff had grown up with the paper, but Laventhol had arrived from the *Washington Post* in late 1969, only months before Times Mirror. His future had been limited at the *Post;* Ben Bradlee was the editor and apparently always would be. *Newsday* offered an opportunity for advancement. Though Laventhol was as shocked as the rest of the staff when Times Mirror showed up, he was optimistic. Instead of viewing the company as an alien invader, he saw it as an old acquaintance, having become familiar with it while at the *Post* working with the *Times-Post* news service.

Laventhol knew the new owners would change *Newsday*'s folksy front-page culture; he welcomed that. For Times Mirror represented undreamed-of resources—money to launch a Sunday paper and a magazine; to expand national, international, and cultural coverage; to get new presses, a new building; to go from being a decent local newspaper to being an outstanding national publication.

Like Thomas in Los Angeles, Laventhol abhorred the practice of editors writing (or redoing) reporters' stories—and leaving reporters feeling alienated from their own work. Times Mirror's presence provided an opening for reform, an opportunity to tear down the walls dividing editors and reporters. And if the price of progress was that the independent, one-time underdog publication became part of a larger machine, so be it. The discipline and controls that Los Angeles would impose symbolized less a loss of independence than a gateway to a grander destiny.

Newsday and the *Times Herald* were conspicuous ornaments to Norman Chandler's expansion strategy; but Norman Chandler himself was easing into the background. He was nearly seventy when he retired as chairman of the board in 1968 to take the less demanding position of chairman of the executive committee. Though strongly involved in corporate matters, Otis had balked at becoming chairman; he wished to continue running the *Los Angeles Times.* Frank Murphy, chancellor of UCLA, became corporate chairman and Otis Chandler was named vice-chairman while remaining publisher of the *Times.*

Even as power flowed to Otis Chandler, it was also being dispersed—not only to Murphy but to other managers who had joined the company with no previous ties to the family.

Robert Erburu, a graduate of Harvard Law School, was among the first of that group. He had been hired as secretary and general counsel in 1961 and appointed to the board in 1968.

Other Harvard-trained recruits followed. Al Casey, a business school graduate, joined the company in 1963 and was made president three years later. Phillip Williams, another Harvard MBA, signed up as a vice-president in 1969 to help the corporation develop its cable television operation.

Almost invariably, the recruits shared Otis Chandler's craving for greatness for Times Mirror and the *Times.* But none would share the vision quite so completely or identify with it quite so intimately as Wyatt Thomas Johnson, a passionate, unfailingly courteous striver, with dark hair, glasses, and boundless enthusiasm, who was not only from another generation than Chandler but from a completely different background, and who eventually would succeed him as the first nonfamily publisher of the *Times.*

Johnson was born in Macon, Georgia, in September 1941—several weeks before the attack at Pearl Harbor plunged the United States into World War II. Too young to fight in that contest, Tom Johnson found one a good deal closer to home: a struggle against his family's marginal existence.

At various times, his father, although white, worked as a laundry route man and peddler of watermelons and wood in

Macon's black community, but never regularly enough or remuneratively enough to lift the family into the middle class. Though his mother worked (endlessly, it seemed) as a clerk in his uncle's store, money was always in short supply. And Tom felt an obligation at age fourteen to go to work and help ease the load.

He uncovered two job prospects: one at a filling station owned by his uncle, the other as high school sports correspondent for the *Macon Telegraph and News*—a position recommended by his ninth-grade English and journalism teacher.

Tom presented himself and got the newspaper position—because no one else really wanted it, he later suspected. But he attacked his after-school job (which paid fifteen cents per column inch of sports news) with all the energy young ambition could generate. His productivity and attitude were such that before long he was noticed by the city editor, the editor, and ultimately the publisher—who found enough to admire in his bright, driven employee to watch over him as he might a favorite son. The pattern was to be repeated often in Johnson's life. Unable to identify with his own father, he had an uncanny ability to bring out the fatherly instinct in others, particularly in powerful, persistently determined men, who no doubt saw—or thought they saw—in Johnson a younger reflection of themselves.

Johnson's duties soon expanded into general news and he began to think of newspapering as a possible career. Journalism's pace, prestige, and involvement with people made it more satisfying than any other field he could imagine; and Johnson's first "champion," *Telegraph* publisher Peyton Anderson, became a role model.

Johnson lacked money for college, so Anderson volunteered to pay the bills. Johnson went to the University of Georgia, largely because the *Telegraph*'s editor had gone there.

During his college years, Johnson never left the paper's employ, working summers and weekends in a variety of reporting and editing assignments and even covering the desegregation of his university. He also edited the school paper.

In spring of Johnson's senior year, Anderson called in his protégé and asked him what he intended to do with his life. Unsure exactly how to respond, Johnson said he wanted a job like Anderson's, that he would one day like to be a publisher.

Anderson, taking him at his word, replied that in that case Johnson would need some broadening. That summer, he assigned Tom to the circulation department. He also advised him to go to what he saw as America's one great business school and added, "If you can get accepted, I will pay the way."

The application deadline had passed, but the *Telegraph*'s editor called Harvard Business School and told the admissions office about the Macon kid destined to be a publisher. Harvard reviewed the application and waved Johnson into the school.

He had virtually no background in math, accounting, finance, or marketing and had to struggle to keep up, but he absorbed Harvard's lessons and hungered for more. He heard about a new White House Fellows program and decided it might give a nice polish to his education. A journalist, after all, should understand government; and what better university than the White House? He got Anderson's blessing and applied.

David Rockefeller chaired the selection committee. John Oakes, editorial page editor of the *New York Times,* was a member. They listened as Johnson verbalized his aspirations, after which Oakes sized him up and said, "One day you may just become editor of a paper . . . in the South."

Johnson was not offended. His ambitions had not yet crossed the Mason-Dixon line; his fate, he figured, was bound to the region of his birth.

Once in the White House, Tom was assigned to Bill Moyers, President Lyndon Johnson's press secretary. Tom felt a special kinship with the brilliant young Moyers, a sense of shared values with a politically progressive southerner. But even without Moyers, the White House would have been stimulating. Vietnam and civil rights were commanding the nation's attention, and the White House had become a center of controversy.

When Moyers asked Tom—on the president's behalf—to stay beyond his fellowship year, he was tempted but also torn; he felt a strong sense of obligation to Anderson in Macon. The next morning, Tom was given a copy of a letter written by President Johnson.

> Dear Peyton:
>
> Last Saturday I had what I considered a very successful trip through three states of the Midwest. Your Tom Johnson set up

the whole thing for the Press Office. I don't think one man has ever done so much work in such a short period of time. But it was a flawless effort and greatly impressed the press and me.

Before he left to advance that trip, I had Tom sitting in on my highly confidential meetings with the Congressional leadership and the National Security Council. His notes were lucid, thorough and accurate.

Mrs. Johnson asked Tom to help out with some of the press problems attached to the wedding. He has been of immense help, and Luci and Pat in particular have come to have a deep appreciation for what he has done.

I don't know of anyone who is held in higher esteem by the working members of the regular White House Press Corps than Tom. He has become an invaluable pillar of the Press Office and one of the most popular members of the staff.

All of which is to say: I need Tom Johnson. Can you spare him?

Tom feels a strong moral commitment to return to Macon because of everything you have done for him. His conscience won't let him walk away from that commitment. I am proud of the way he feels and of his integrity, but I also believe he has a great opportunity here to make a significant contribution and to continue to grow. This place has a way of stretching one's capacities, especially if he is young and eager like Tom. . . .

If you feel you can spare Tom Johnson, his country and his President need him.

Anderson replied in the only manner possible. He could not refuse his president, nor could he offer experiences comparable to those available in Washington. He wrote back, releasing the young journalist.

By taking splendid advantage of all that had been offered, Tom had already repaid him, wrote Anderson. And even though many of Anderson's plans had been made in anticipation of Johnson's return, he recognized it would be "extremely difficult to face day to day problems in a small area when the world has been your field of operation." He wished Tom well and encouraged him to remain with the president—who was under sustained attack for escalating the war in Vietnam.

LBJ's credibility was crumbling, and a disheartened press office headed by an increasingly distressed Moyers was trying to shore it up. Meanwhile, Moyers's brother committed suicide, leaving him with two families to support on one White House salary. So when Moyers was asked to become publisher of *Newsday,* he said yes. "Bill sort of handed me off in a way," recalls Tom, transferring to Tom the trust LBJ had reposed in Moyers. The president never forgave Moyers for abandoning him. Years later, when gravely ill, LBJ adamantly refused to see him. But he gratefully accepted the gift of Tom, using him first in the press office and later as one of eight special assistants.

With more than half a million troops in Vietnam in 1968, college protests were growing ugly, as was sentiment toward LBJ. Senator Eugene McCarthy of Minnesota came close to defeating Johnson in the March 12 New Hampshire Democratic primary. Senator Robert F. Kennedy entered the presidential race.

Ghosts of the recently departed haunted LBJ; not only Moyers, but aide Jack Valenti, Defense Secretary Robert McNamara, HEW Secretary John Gardner, National Security Adviser McGeorge Bundy.

With his support collapsing—particularly after the Tet offensive in early 1968—the president threw himself on his sword. On March 31, he announced that he would neither seek nor accept his party's nomination.

Calm did not soon return to the world. Days after Johnson withdrew, Martin Luther King, Jr., was slain in Memphis. Shortly thereafter, Robert Kennedy was killed in Los Angeles. Riots again swept the nation's cities and protests raged across its campuses.

As LBJ's White House years were ending, Tom once more felt the tug of Macon, and—as before—he was torn. LBJ asked Tom to stay for the transition; Anderson wanted him in Georgia.

His aging patron came to Washington and met Tom for breakfast in the White House mess. Theirs was a difficult conversation. With LBJ's presidency ending, Anderson was no longer competing against the White House, but against another man like himself who needed a younger man to lean on. He had made plans for Johnson in Macon and wanted to see them carried out. The decision was painful, but in the end Tom had to go with LBJ. Virtually everyone else had abandoned him.

LBJ returned to Austin, Texas, in 1969, carried by the same Boeing 707 in which he had taken his oath of office. Anderson went back to Macon and eventually sold his paper to Knight-Ridder.

In Austin, Tom worked on LBJ's presidential library and book projects, and also as a general executive with his broadcasting company. His relationship with the former president had never been better; yet as he watched LBJ's health fade, he knew that his chief would not be in charge much longer. In all likelihood, the company would be run by Chuck Robb and Pat Nugent, the former president's sons-in-law, neither of whom he was extremely close to. Tom knew he would have to move on.

On January 22, 1973, Lyndon B. Johnson died. Tom made the announcement.

Already another key relationship was forming. The previous year, Tom and Otis Chandler had met when a Times Mirror team came to Austin to look over Johnson family television station KTBC.

Having sold a radio station acquired with the *Dallas Times Herald,* Times Mirror needed to invest in another broadcast property to avoid paying taxes on the proceeds. The Johnsons, prodded by federal regulators to divest one of their properties, were interested in selling.

Jack Valenti, who knew Times Mirror president Al Casey from Harvard Business School and LBJ from working at the White House, played matchmaker—a role made easier since Chandler (who had spent time on the Johnson ranch) already knew LBJ.

After preliminary discussions, Chandler, Casey, and Robert Erburu (then a senior vice-president) flew in to see whether a deal could be struck. President Johnson met them in Austin and introduced them to Tom.

Later, Chandler attended a huge reception for the Johnson library and Times Mirror executives. Though the former president was too ill to stand in the receiving line, Lady Bird Johnson and Otis Chandler did. As each guest approached, Tom (who Chandler thought bore a passing resemblance to Clark Kent) would step forward and whisper his or her name along with some bit of personal information. Chandler was amazed that anyone could remember so many people and details about their lives. He inquired about Tom and found out that he was the number-two man at the television station but that he had started in newspapers.

During a break in negotiations, Chandler and Erburu asked LBJ's aide about his career plans. Tom said he was thinking of returning to the newspaper business. Even before the Times Mirror discussions, Johnson had been talking with executives at the *Dallas Morning News,* Knight-Ridder, and Gannett.

Chandler, convinced that the young "Clark Kent" had great potential, asked him to join Times Mirror. Tom would have to prove himself in several demanding positions, said Chandler, but if he passed muster, rewards would follow. He would start as editor of the *Dallas Times Herald.*

Tom had imagined he might be considered for general management, not offered a newsroom to run. Reporters would probably whisper about his LBJ connection; some would resent his parachuting in without paying dues in Dallas. Gaining acceptance could be difficult.

"What do you expect?" he asked.

"Do your very best," Chandler replied. "We would like a newspaper of uncommon excellence in Texas." The effort would have his personal support. Johnson could add staff, recruit nationwide, open new bureaus, take any reasonable measure to attract the most outstanding journalists in the country.

Tom liked Chandler's bold, direct style. As with Moyers, he felt an affinity with Chandler. Though from radically divergent backgrounds, they had a common spirit, a need to measure up to and test themselves against the best.

Times Mirror got the Johnsons' blessings to take Tom with the station; and Chandler duly installed him as editor in Dallas—as two years previously he had installed William Thomas in Los Angeles. Not that Thomas and Johnson had much in common. Thomas was three years older than Chandler; Johnson, fourteen years younger. Thomas had climbed patiently and steadily through the hierarchy; Johnson had come shooting out of Georgia like a bull charging out of a chute—all quick moves and moxie to Thomas's California cool. Yet they shared the one trait that counted: the ability to make Chandler believe that his dream was their dream, that they were, in every sense that mattered, *his* men.

Times Mirror

Otis Chandler

Robert Erburu

David Laventhol

Tom Johnson

Noel Greenwood

Don Wright

Dennis Britton

George Cotliar

Shelby Coffey

William Thomas

CHAPTER 10

CONFLICT AND CONFUSION

The *Times* had been so bad and resistance to change so ingrained that, in the beginning, Chandler's campaign for excellence had seemed a crusade. Excitement had built. Recruits had flocked to the cause. And the newspaper had improved at a dizzying pace.

Yet that very success foreshadowed a time when the momentum would abate. Not only would fewer flaws exist (making the "right" and "wrong" sides harder to distinguish) but the euphoria of battle would inevitably fade.

For the *Washington Post,* that time came just after Watergate, when the big story was finished and the new mission not yet defined. For the *Los Angeles Times,* it came when Bob Donovan flunked his tryout as editor and Bill Thomas was named in his stead. Deep problems remained at the *Times,* but solutions no longer seemed simple.

Thomas, while lamenting the mediocrity among his lower-level editors, knew that replacing them would be a long, complicated process. He endeavored to hire reporters with a flair for language and a taste for innovative, in-depth journalism, yet had to work with many who found a routine story difficult. He set high ethical standards, yet headed a newsroom with numerous journalists who viewed gifts from sources as a privilege of employment. And perhaps most worrisome of all, he found warfare between departments all but impossible to stop.

In some respects, Chandler's reforms had only made matters worse; for as the newspaper improved and editors' staffs increased, areas of potential conflict widened.

The clashes in Los Angeles—among the features, local, and national staffs—were major, but they paled by comparison with the running battle that had developed between the Washington bureau and Los Angeles.

Upon departing as Washington bureau chief, Donovan had successfully lobbied for his deputy, David Kraslow, to succeed him. Some of the editors in Los Angeles had resisted the appointment, thinking Kraslow a bit too pompous, too inexperienced in management, and too much the reporter to administer a bureau of more than a dozen journalists.

Once Kraslow became bureau chief, Donovan, his patron, could no longer shield him. The editors in Los Angeles felt that Kraslow should give up writing to concentrate on administration. They also felt he was fighting their coverage ideas. Relations deteriorated to the point that Dennis Britton, an assistant national editor, was making many of the bureau's assignments from Los Angeles.

Kraslow finally was told he could either resign or be demoted. He resigned and was replaced by John Lawrence, a bespectacled introvert who had built an impressive reputation at the *Times* and the *Wall Street Journal* as a crack editor and administrator. Britton, who had come from the *San Jose Mercury* in 1966 and worked his way up through the editing desks, went as bureau editor and Lawrence's assistant.

After having managed bureaus in half a dozen cities for the *Wall Street Journal* and serving as assistant managing editor in charge of that paper's Pacific Coast edition, Lawrence had been recruited as business editor by the *Times* in 1968. Having moved so much, Lawrence had wanted to settle down and California had seemed a good place to do that. And the *Times* had seemed a paper where he could make a real difference, more so than at the *Journal,* where change took forever and the path to real power was crowded with contenders.

Shortly after Lawrence's arrival, at a lunch with some of the paper's business-side executives, Otis Chandler had motioned toward Lawrence and uttered, "Leave this man alone." Lawrence was grateful for the gesture. Under his guidance, the business staff doubled to more than a dozen reporters, and the section, formerly reserved for writers undesired by other editors, became a showcase for hard-hitting financial analysis.

Though initially unwilling to go to Washington, Lawrence could not help imagining shaking up the bureau as he had the business section. He would free the correspondents from chasing the wire services for spot news and launch them on in-depth, issues-oriented coverage. They would probe the most important subjects of the day—President Nixon's welfare package, educational reform, the revitalization of the economy—and produce insightful journalism worthy of the *Times.*

Unfortunately for Lawrence, he arrived the weekend of the Watergate break-in—June 1972. And the bureau, instead of turning away from spot news, went chasing pell-mell after the hottest spot news story of the decade. Unfortunately for Lawrence also, Britton would directly challenge his authority.

Britton understood *Times* politics better than Lawrence did. And prior to coming to Washington, he had asked managing editor Frank Haven for a job description. His job, Britton was told, was to make all assignments, administer the bureau, and be responsible for correspondents' copy. Britton was perplexed and wondered what that left for Lawrence. At another meeting at which Lawrence and the national editor were present, he again raised the question and received much the same answer. Once in Washington, Britton became a barrier between Lawrence and his bureau; he insisted on making all assignments and even ignored some of Lawrence's suggestions. As the months wore on, he grew increasingly contemptuous of Lawrence, whom he thought too lacking in personality and knowledge of Washington to be an effective leader.

Britton had worked with the bureau from Los Angeles and had occasionally gone to Washington to help out, a contrast to Lawrence, who came in as a virtual stranger. Also, Britton was not held responsible for Kraslow's humiliation. As Kraslow's replacement, Lawrence was seen as the opposition. If reporters were discussing a story and Lawrence approached, the conversation would stop. Finally, Britton called Thomas. "You've got to help us out here," he said, and outlined the situation as an incredulous Thomas listened.

With the Watergate story unfolding in the background and the bureau's reporters scoring one important story after another, they increasingly compared their work to the *Washington*

Post's. The *Post* might get more scoops, they would tell themselves, but the *Post* also made more mistakes. Worse, they perceived a pattern of the *Post* either ignoring *Times* exclusives or lifting their stories from the jointly operated wire service without giving adequate credit.

Resentment came to a head over a story involving Alfred Baldwin, a former FBI agent and a key witness before the grand jury that indicted the Watergate burglars. The *Post*'s Woodward and Bernstein had tried and failed to get a Baldwin interview. *Times* correspondent Jack Nelson succeeded. In October 1972, a detailed account (under Baldwin's by-line) appeared in the *Times* describing both the espionage operation run by the committee to reelect President Nixon and the arrest of the Watergate criminals.

> Across the street in the Democratic National Committee office I could see men with guns and flashlights behind desks and out on the balcony.
>
> It was a weird scene at Washington's Watergate complex. The men were looking for several persons, including my boss—James W. McCord Jr., who was security director for both President Nixon's Reelection Committee and the Republican National Committee.
>
> A short while later McCord and four other men, all in handcuffs, would be led by police to patrol cars and taken to jail.

The story was a major coup, which the *Post* initially declined to use—enraging the bureau, which felt the *Post* was duty-bound to run it and credit the *Times*—despite any embarrassment on being scooped.

The *Washington Star* called Lawrence and asked permission to reprint the story. He agreed, on condition that he clear it with the *Post.* Bradlee exploded. How could the *Times* possibly consider offering the story to the *Post*'s chief competitor? Lawrence responded that since the *Post* was not inclined to print the article, he saw nothing wrong with letting the *Star* have it. Bradlee promised to run the piece in the next edition.

Even after that conversation, *Times* correspondents continued to feel abused by the *Post.* Britton finally began photocopying all Watergate stories as the bureau produced them. He

would send the stories, via messenger, to the networks, the *New York Times,* the *Post,* and other outlets and sources—some nights seventy or eighty packets—to make sure the *Times* got credit.

Lawrence was feeling increasingly isolated, not only because of the bureau's behavior, but because of the vibes from Los Angeles, where national editor Ed Guthman seemed to feel Lawrence and the bureau were bypassing him. When Bill Thomas asked in 1974 whether Lawrence was willing to stay in Washington, he told Thomas he was ready to come home.

Lawrence returned to Los Angeles and was promoted. Years later, he still could not understand Britton's behavior. If Britton had only shown some loyalty, he would say, "the whole thing would have worked a lot better." Lawrence, after all, had quite willingly given Britton all the rope he needed; and Britton had taken that rope and hung it around Lawrence's neck. The experience was a hard lesson for Lawrence in the ugliness of newsroom politics; and for Thomas it was yet another reminder of just how deep divisions ran at the *Times.*

For a brief while the *Times,* constantly in search of respect, flirted with appointing a famous journalist as Lawrence's replacement. Yet as one argument went, the *Times* bureau did not so much need celebrity as it needed cohesive, competent leadership. To parachute in another outsider would be to invite disaster. So the paper advanced Jack Nelson to bureau chief.

Britton came back to Los Angeles as national editor in 1977, to a newspaper as balkanized as ever. His correspondents were forbidden to cover Los Angeles. But periodically—hoping to give national stories a local context—Britton would sneak one or two into town and pray that they not chance upon the metropolitan editor, on whose turf they were treading.

Even as conflict engulfed the *Times* newsroom, a personal and professional crisis enveloped Otis Chandler. In August 1972, a front-page story in the *Wall Street Journal* linked him to the dealings of a longtime friend. Several months later, the Securities and Exchange Commission filed a civil fraud suit naming Chandler and several others as defendants.

The allegations emanated from Chandler's association with Jack P. Burke, a fellow Stanford athlete. Chandler and Burke, a discus thrower, remained friends long after graduating from the university. Burke, an investment specialist, was godfather to

Chandler's eldest daughter and a companion on Chandler's big-game hunts. Eventually, Burke enlisted Chandler's assistance in promoting oil-drilling partnerships. Though Chandler put money into the project, his principal role was to enlist others, which he did spectacularly well. The publisher introduced Burke to some fifty or sixty of his friends—including movie stars, prominent business associates, and local political figures. Chandler also joined the board of GeoTek, Burke's company.

A Securities and Exchange Commission (SEC) investigation indicated that some twenty-two hundred investors lost more than thirty million dollars in the scheme, which seemed designed principally to enrich Burke. Chandler claimed that he had been as much a dupe as anyone else. As the investigation progressed, a secret agreement between Burke and Chandler came to light that absolved Chandler of any financial liability for Burke's dealings. The investigation also revealed that Chandler had received over one hundred thousand dollars in finder's fees and more than three hundred thousand dollars' worth of free shares in Burke's ventures. The SEC held up the agreement and Chandler's financial gains as evidence that Chandler knew of the fraudulent nature of Burke's activities.

Chandler returned the money and consistently denied any knowledge of wrongdoing, but the SEC named him in the subsequent suit. Nearly two years later, the SEC dropped the charges against Chandler, and Burke was sentenced to thirty months in a federal prison. Though Chandler was vindicated, the episode dimmed the aura that had always encircled him. No longer was he a golden-haired demigod gliding along the surf, but a bewildered mortal who had tumbled into the sea.

Indeed, not only Chandler but his company was going through a difficult middle passage.

World Publishing, a book publisher acquired in 1963, was in turmoil a decade later and Times Mirror began selling it off—a public admission that the parent couldn't manage its subsidiary.

Norman Chandler died in October 1973, leaving a legacy of growth and diversification. He had made the company a major player in broadcasting, forest products, and publishing. His obituary in the *New York Times* described his transformation of Times Mirror from a one-newspaper enterprise to a publisher of encyclopedias, paperback books, Bibles, medical books, legal documents, charts, and maps. He was in the "knowledge" business, he had said, but analysts were increasingly beginning to wonder whether the firm really knew what business it was in.

Yet revenues climbed steadily year by year, finally soaring past one billion dollars in 1977—when Times Mirror made nearly one hundred million dollars in profits.

Newsday had launched a Sunday edition in 1972, adding some seventy-five newsroom staffers—amid plans to move the newspaper into a new building. And at the *Dallas Times Herald,* Tom Johnson had advanced from editor to publisher, presiding over a 60 percent expansion in the news staff and working hard to position the paper as something more than an organ for the Chamber of Commerce. By most accounts, he was succeeding; the paper was being touted as one of the most improved in the country, and the dominant *Dallas Morning News'* circulation lead was evaporating.

But in Los Angeles, Otis Chandler's marriage was coming apart and he was questioning his ability to continue pushing himself, to go on juggling the demands of the corporation, the newspaper, and his own athletic pursuits. As vice-chairman of the company and a key member of the office of the chief executive, he was spending perhaps 30 percent of his time on corporate affairs; and he knew he could not avoid becoming chairman of the board much longer. He had taken up surfing, sports car racing, and archery and was competing in an exhausting array of other activities. He was running out of ideas, running down emotionally, feeling drained physically. And for the first time, he began to seriously focus on the question of a successor. Whom could he groom to take his place—or at least to share a major part of the burden?

None of his children was ready for the job, and no one else in the family was remotely qualified. The only person in the company who embodied the qualities he sought was his young protégé in Dallas.

Tom Johnson had shown, to Chandler's satisfaction, that he was a leader, that he had the ability to draw people out individually as well as to work with a crowd. He could give a decent speech and articulate a vision, and he possessed personal integrity. He also had drive enough perhaps to help Chandler realize his vision for the *Times.*

In late 1977, Chandler broached his idea to Johnson, offering him the title of president of the *Times* and a chance to understudy Chandler himself.

Johnson knew that the *Times* had problems, both in the newsroom and on the commercial side. The presses were old and in need of replacement; the paper was not penetrating the market as deeply as it could; the news product was still uneven. He knew that, just as had been the case in Dallas, he would probably encounter suspicion and resentments. *Times* editors might try to freeze him out, seeing him as a bush-league interloper.

He had built a reputation and friendships in Dallas and was comfortable there; and he was giving the *Dallas Morning News* the run of its life. How comfortable would he be in Los Angeles? And having so recently climbed to the top of one mountain, did he have the energy and will to climb to the top of another?

Yet Johnson felt that he could do the job; and he knew he had Chandler's support. Over dinner one night, he told his wife that he had to take the assignment. Otherwise he would always wonder whether he should have.

That August, as he prepared to start his new job, Johnson got a handwritten note (full of underlinings and exclamation marks) that amounted to a call to arms. Therein, Chandler revealed that his decision to move Johnson had been made the previous year, and he continued:

> As you get to know me better, you will find me to be a fighter, an uncompromising advocate of quality . . . and of excellence, and a gambler (not on games but on people and the future) and a fierce competitor.
>
> When I took over the Times . . . I had no interest in the status quo (nor do I now—that's not why you're here!) I set about changing every aspect of the paper in order to make it the best there was. I think we are the best, but we still must get better—that's your challenge (and mine). Together we are going to push the N.Y.T. [*New York Times*] off its perch. Somehow, someday (in spite of the geography, tradition, eastern snobbery and the like) there will be recognized one superior newspaper and it will be located of all unlikely places—way out West in Indian and smog country—L.A!!!
>
> Your charge from me is to study hard, get to know the market, its people, the newspaper and its people, and then

help me move this paper forward, even faster than its present pace.

I never stand still. I take risks (after careful study) but they are risks (in my personal life as well). I think that is the fun and excitement in life. But how many really reach out. How many are truly perfectionists?

So my young friend, you have joined a fast and dedicated team. Some are a bit tired from the pace, others need to be re-directed and revitalized.

I am impatient and absolutely dedicated to excellence, but I need help, some new ideas, some new energy—that's why you're here.

I know you won't let me down.

Johnson was deeply touched by the letter, much as he had been years earlier by LBJ's requesting that Tom be allowed to stay at his side. Once again a mentor was reaching out and binding the younger man's energy and goals to his own. In Johnson, Chandler saw a chance to revive something that was fading, in himself as well as in his paper.

CHAPTER 11

PASSING THE BATON

Friends such as Katharine Graham of the *Washington Post* would ask Chandler how could he think of not being publisher of the *Times*? How could he give up the glamor, the importance, the prestige? Wouldn't he miss the personal meetings with foreign ministers and presidents, the sense of always being on top of the news?

Yet Chandler felt the day approaching when he would have little more to give to his newspaper. Why hang on when his heart was saying let go?

Tom Johnson—bursting with energy, anxious to succeed—appeared to have all the right qualities; he was so bright, so driven, so engaging. But Chandler needed to work with him, side by side, to be absolutely sure. He needed also to know that Johnson would be comfortable in Los Angeles, a community much larger and more complex than Dallas. Chandler sent his executive vice-president into early retirement to open up a position and prayed that Johnson not disappoint him.

At first, Johnson was uneasy. Just finding his way around the labyrinthian *Times* building was a challenge. Los Angeles' endless freeways overwhelmed him. The *Times* dwarfed—in size and reach—any publication he had known. He missed the clean air and open spaces of Texas and felt vaguely out of his element. Yet he knew that he would learn to love his new environment, that he would prove, to his own and Chandler's satisfaction, that he could do whatever the job required. He attacked the assignment as he had attacked everything in life: with the dogged determination of one for whom failure is disgrace.

Johnson poured through marketing data, searching for a key to improve circulation. And he immersed himself in the details of constructing a new plant in the San Fernando Valley and two new presses in the downtown Los Angeles plant. The project would consume five years and $215 million and be touted by Chandler as "the largest single press project in the history of printing." (A short time later, the *Chicago Tribune* would build an even more ambitious facility.)

Given Johnson's status as publisher-in-waiting, comparisons with Chandler were inevitable. And the staff was not inclined to be charitable. With willpower, nerve, and money, Chandler had transformed the *Times.* As managing editor George Cotliar put it, "[We] saw him take this dull newspaper and commit his resources and his name and his backbone to [it]." They didn't know what to expect from Johnson. He supposedly had done wonders in Dallas; but Dallas was not Los Angeles, the *Times Herald* was not the flagship, and—whatever his accomplishments—Johnson was certainly not a Chandler.

During a conversation with Cotliar shortly after arriving, Johnson blanked on the name of the paper's makeup editor. Just as Cotliar chimed in with the name, Johnson pulled a small notebook from his pocket and found it scrawled inside. Cotliar was astonished: "I thought, goddamn it, the president of this paper is writing down the name of a makeup editor." The gesture won Cotliar over, as similar gestures would others.

By April 1980, when Johnson became publisher—adding jurisdiction for the editorial product to his business-side responsibilities—he had gained wide acceptance. He still smarted, however, over the lukewarm welcome editor Bill Thomas had given him, and he wondered whether they could ever click. He also worried about Thomas's distance and aloofness from the newsroom. Still, working largely through Cotliar and a few other senior editors, Thomas had enforced high writing and reporting standards and lifted the quality of the *Times.*

Seeing no reason to fire Thomas, Johnson kept him, though he never came to see Thomas as his lieutenant. And through the years, as they collaborated on several major projects (including the launching of a separate business section and the creation of zoned editions in San Diego and the San Fernando Valley), Johnson thought often of what he would do when his own editor, not Otis Chandler's, was running the newsroom. Until that time, Johnson would devote his primary efforts to the business side of the newspaper (where his first task would be filling the presidency he had just vacated) and give Thomas no cause to be insecure.

As with all of his big personnel decisions, Johnson approached the task of replacing himself methodically. He cast a net throughout the company and after a year-long search came up with Donald Wright, a tall, angular engineer and MBA who was president and chief operating officer of *Newsday.*

Wright had gone to work for the *Minneapolis Star and Tribune* in the late 1950s, just as the industry was embracing management efficiency. Publishers previously had not worried much about high overhead in pressrooms as long as the newspapers came out. Nor had they fretted over delivery schedules or financial projections. When attitudes started changing, Wright's technical training came in handy. Many of the problems—of waste and inefficiency—faced by the *Star and Tribune* resembled those in Wright's old textbooks.

He spent nearly fifteen years with the *Star and Tribune,* in a variety of production and business positions. At one point he even served as executive editor. The idea, revolutionary for its time, was to give Wright an opportunity to broaden his knowledge of the entire newspaper.

Though doing well in Minneapolis, Wright was frustrated. Cowles Media Company, which owned the *Star and Tribune,* was going from one management crisis to another. And while other communications companies were expanding, Cowles was all but standing still. The papers the corporation considered buying would be either in insignificant markets or on the verge of bankruptcy. His future, he decided, required a move; when a headhunter from *Newsday* approached, Wright was receptive, especially since *Newsday* was then owned by Times Mirror, whose potential was unlimited.

He went to *Newsday* as general manager in 1977. A new building was going up, presses had to be moved, and *Newsday*'s management practices needed modernizing.

In many respects, the paper was still managed like the small family business it had once been. Planning was slapdash. Employee practices were inconsistent. Wright expected to spend years setting things straight.

So when he was asked to go to Los Angeles and join Tom Johnson, his first reaction was to refuse. But being a company man, he went, and discovered that the *Times* had challenges of its own.

He had heard the *Times* described as a "velvet coffin"—a comfortable place for an executive to die. Yet when Wright arrived in 1982, with advertising lagging and the nation digging out of a recession, the *Times* was losing its velvet lining. With Johnson's backing, he set out to contain costs and improve productivity.

The paper generated more than six hundred million dollars in revenues that year; but to maintain profit margins, Wright and Johnson played Scrooge, turning down one budget request after another. Chandler, sensing the battle taking its toll, tried in a year-end note to console the man who had become "like a favorite son" and who was responsible for the *Times*—"my favorite object in my life."

"Eighty-five m[illion] p.t. [post tax] ain't all that bad," said Chandler, noting that Johnson had exceeded his expectations. "Don't spend too much time looking at the sidelines for signals," he advised. "You're calling the plays." Such was Chandler's way of telling him his apprenticeship was over; the paper's future—and responsibility for its profits—was in Johnson's hands.

Otis Chandler had always focused on the bottom line, convinced that only with profits could he bring the paper the prestige he craved; but his decisions were reached as much by intuition as by rigorous analysis. Johnson sought quantifiable projections. Casually arrived at hunches were not quite good enough for MBAs such as Don Wright or James Shaffer, whom Wright appointed vice-president for finance.

Shaffer had grown up with a love of math and science and had earned pocket money during his high school years in Bloomington, Indiana, by buying broken television sets and then repairing and reselling them. He later studied engineering and business before family ties led him to the *Star and Tribune* (of which his aunt's husband was publisher).

Like Don Wright, his boss, Shaffer had been appalled at

management's lack of sophistication. He had berated the accounting department for generating useless statistics and pushed it in the direction of long-range planning. He also fought successfully for drastically higher advertising prices (a heretical practice that would drive down linage) by showing how profits would increase.

"As an MBA coming into a company that didn't have a lot of MBAs," he recalled, "I had skills that none of the rest of them had. I could argue these cases with numbers. I could show pro-forma profit projections. I could show how it was in the interest of the shareholders to employ strategy A as opposed to strategy B. And Wright . . . and I found ourselves playing into increasingly higher levels of decision making just because we could relate policy alternatives to profit."

After several years at headquarters, Shaffer left Minneapolis to manage some Cowles-owned weeklies in Maryland. They were sold out from under him just as he thought he was turning them around. The company then sent him to the *Buffalo Courier Express* as associate publisher. Again, just as he thought the paper was recovering, the company lost its nerve. By then, he was weary of Cowles and anxious to join a well-managed company.

Wright hired Shaffer as his right-hand man, indicating Shaffer would be more than the typical chief financial officer. Wright wanted him not only to analyze financial results from last year or last quarter, but to plan for the next, to generate numbers that could be fed into marketing, and to become an integral partner in the shaping of the enterprise.

When Shaffer showed up early in 1983, the national economy was improving, the *Times* was completing construction of its new plant, and management was wrestling with how the *Times* was to grow.

For years, press capacity had limited the paper's expansion; seeking new readers and reaching new advertisers had not been a priority. Instead, executives had been preoccupied with trying to pack advertising into a paper that couldn't accommodate it all. In the recessionary early 1980s, attention had shifted to weathering the economic drought. The new plant (which added press capacity) and the potential of a more robust economy changed the basic assumptions under which the *Times* had operated. Even if Los Angeles did not develop quite as dramatically as in the past, the *Times* should be able to grow—provided Johnson and his team came up with the proper strategy.

After stepping aside as publisher of the *Times,* Otis Chandler had let himself be elected chairman of the Times Mirror board. And as Johnson assumed control of the paper, Chandler puzzled over the corporation.

What kind of company did he want to leave? What should its objectives be?

Times Mirror had grown enormous over the past several years, adding the *Sporting News* in 1977, the *Hartford Courant* in 1979, the *Denver Post* in 1980. The company had interests in forest products, magazines, book publishing, map making, cable and broadcast television, and a wide array of other goods and services. Revenues had reached $2.13 billion in 1981 and were climbing rapidly.

"Do we want to keep adding units . . . so we have more . . . than anybody else? . . . Or is it the quality of the company that's important?" asked Chandler.

The answer, of course, was in the question. Chandler saw no point in trying to "chase Gannett"—a company he believed stood for growth above all else. Times Mirror must stand for quality, and would focus its strengths on publishing and television.

Along with corporate strategy decisions, Chandler (who filed for divorce from his first wife in 1980 and remarried in 1981) faced a personal question. How long would he remain chairman of the board? Certainly not until 1992, when he would reach sixty-five. The job simply could not hold his interest that long. Maybe he would serve for eight years or so and then ride off into the sunset. In the interim, he would have to choose a successor.

When Chandler had become chairman, his confidant, Robert Erburu, also moved up, adding chief executive officer to the title of president, which he had held since 1974. Since Erburu had joined the company in 1961, he and Chandler had hired a number of corporate officers; but most were older than they and would soon be retiring. As Chandler and Erburu talked of succession, it soon became obvious that no one on the corporate staff would be able to replace them; the torch would have to be handed down—to the generation laboring in Times Mirror's properties.

In the early phase of Johnson's tenure as publisher, corporate succession was not a subject much on his mind; mastering the *Times* and its metropolis was.

The population of the area was becoming increasingly dominated by minority groups. In 1980, Los Angeles's population was nearly 27 percent Latino, 17 percent black, and 7 percent Asian. The paper was uncertain how to cover those communities.

One effort was a two-part special report, which ran in July 1981. The first installment, built around a black Chicago family on welfare, analyzed the cycle of poverty in America's inner cities. The second dealt with a subject much more explosive and considerably closer to home: the rape of Los Angeles's suburbs by gangs of inner-city black and Latino "marauders" who wreaked havoc on the lives of peace-loving whites: "In the last 10 years, the ghettos and barrios of the city have increasingly become staging areas for robbers, burglars and thieves who ride the freeways like magic carpets to hit homes and businesses in such areas as Pasadena, Covina, Glendale, Palos Verdes, Long Beach, West Los Angeles and Beverly Hills."

The article, based on a computer analysis, maintained that as crime decreased in the ghettos and barrios, it shot up in the surrounding suburbs, where the pickings were better. ("They was white and they had money," was one thug's commentary on his prey.) Blacks were most likely to be offenders, said the article, but Latinos were more likely to be violent: "Latinos have taken a larger leap into robbery, burglary and illegal possession of weapons," the reporters wrote.

The marauders—under cover of darkness and the influence of cocaine and marijuana—would cruise along suburban streets and shoot victims at random or kick down doors and rape and pillage within, leaving tortured bodies and shattered homes in their wake. Then, apparently incapable of remorse, they would return to their ghettos and to the crap-shooting, dope-drenched welfare households that defined their desperate lives.

The report set off complaints from black politicians and community leaders, who charged that the piece had maligned minorities and whipped up public opinion against them. The National Association of Black Journalists later declared the article one of the worst of the year. And blacks at the *Times* felt the story (prepared and edited by whites) could have been significantly better, as they told editor Bill Thomas.

Thomas thought the reporting was basically sound, but kept hearing an argument he could not convincingly refute. He had never lived in Watts or any other black community; so he and the white reporters he sent in to explain those communities would inevitably emerge with a false view. What would happen, he wondered, if the *Times* did a series using only black reporters and editors?

The resulting articles ran for two and a half weeks. Some were profiles of black corporate executives, athletes, artists, and ordinary people trying to survive. Others were mini-history lessons in the shaping of black Los Angeles. A few were intensely personal—black reporters telling their own stories of discrimination and rejection. One took the news media to task for distorted coverage. And an editorial capped the package, calling for efforts to end racial divisions.

Ron Harris, one of the reporters who worked on the series, thought it "legitimized the black staff." The *Times* realized, he said, that black journalists could do much more than had been asked of them. A few, including Harris, received promotions. And Latinos at the paper—many of whom had simmered since the "marauders" piece—were mobilized. Like the blacks, they felt *Times* coverage of the Latino community had been insultingly superficial—occasional stories on illegal immigrants, Chicano gangs, and Mexican holidays.

Frank del Olmo had brooded over the paper's poor coverage of Latinos ever since joining the *Times* in 1970, following graduation from the University of California (Northridge). That same year Ruben Salazar, a distinguished Latino *Times* man, was accidentally killed by police while covering a Chicano community demonstration against the war in Vietnam. Del Olmo—who had deeply admired Salazar and wanted to carry on in his tradition—had carved out a niche for himself, first as a reporter and then as a columnist, editorial writer, and sometime foreign correspondent; he and other Latinos on staff were so encouraged by the appearance of the black Los Angeles project that "we decided we ought to try to do the same thing," said Del Olmo.

The series ran for three weeks, beginning in July 1983. Much as the package on blacks had done, it traced Latino roots, celebrated diversity, and profiled Latino American doers and dreamers. The effort won a Pulitzer Prize for public service and dramatically improved relations with Southern California's Latino community.

During the 1960s, Ruben Salazar had produced several articles on Los Angeles's Mexican Americans, and the riots had later sparked a similar examination of Watts. But those earlier endeavors did not approach—in time, scope, space, and effort—the productions of the 1980s. Also, the Watts report put together by whites and the Mexican American articles by the paper's lone Latino reporter appeared at a time when blatant newsroom racism was all but condoned. Even in the early 1970s, as blacks and Latinos found their way onto the *Times,* the going was often brutal. They would listen in horror to the night managing editor's racially offensive remarks and try to stay out of his way, lest they become targets. By the 1980s, the days of quietly suffering were over. Minorities were, in effect, telling Tom Johnson and his generation that the *Times* was their paper too—or at least that it could and should be.

Several involved in the Latino undertaking left within a few years of its publication; they felt that despite the Pulitzer, their efforts were not appreciated. But they had made their point: They and their community would no longer meekly accept being taken for granted by the *Times.*

The 1984 Olympics in Los Angeles provided the paper another opportunity to demonstrate its journalistic growth. Some 240 staff members covered the games. Every day the *Times* produced an Olympics color section (in addition to the regular seven sections) of up to forty-four pages and provided the most exhaustive coverage of the contests available anywhere.

Later that year, the Republican National Convention was held in Dallas; and Otis Chandler, Robert Erburu, and other members of the Times Mirror brass came out in force—as was the custom when national political conventions were held in cities with Times Mirror properties.

During the convention, Chandler held meetings with local

dignitaries and with executives of the *Dallas Times Herald.* Criticism spilled forth—from Republicans, Democrats, community leaders, and advertisers, including those who had supported the paper in the past. Delivery, they said, was unreliable and the paper's coverage, inconsistent. Times Mirror executives pored over *Times Herald* statistics on market share, advertising, and penetration and grew increasingly alarmed.

At a reception at the Dallas Museum of Fine Arts, Erburu and senior vice-president Phillip Williams called Johnson over and asked that he return to Dallas following the convention to do a more complete evaluation. Chandler repeated the request in Los Angeles.

Johnson and the Los Angeles–based executives who accompanied him found that the *Times Herald* had steadily lost advertisers and readers to the *Dallas Morning News* (a once sleepy paper that had become a classy competitor) as managers had drifted in and out, leaving bad decisions behind them.

The *Times Herald* had dropped *Parade* magazine; one of the most popular features in the Sunday paper, it was immediately snapped up by the *Morning News.* A program to boost circulation had been so poorly planned that it instead led dealers to turn in orders for phone booths and vacant lots. Key staff members had defected to the opposition.

Johnson was heartsick; before long he was spending two to three days a week in Dallas trying to straighten out the mess, while also running the *Los Angeles Times* and crisscrossing the country trying to recruit an editor and a publisher for the *Times Herald.*

After nearly two dozen interviews, Johnson (who had been made corporate group vice-president) found his publisher in Art Wible, who previously had been president of the *New York Daily News.* Shelby Coffey, formerly of the *Washington Post* and *U.S. News and World Report,* was named editor.

Despite the infusion of new talent, a recession among energy-producing states made the outlook gloomy for the *Times Herald*—as well as for the *Denver Post* (which had also become part of Johnson's domain). Daily circulation in both markets had declined from 1984 (though Sunday circulation had climbed for the *Post*). Advertising linage in both markets had dropped as well, and another drop was predicted for 1986—despite Times Mirror investing some forty-five million dollars in new production facilities in Dallas. Johnson saw a potential loss of some twenty million dollars in advertising for the *Times Herald,* almost all because of the energy recession.

Early in 1986, while in San Francisco for a meeting of the American Newspaper Publishers Association, Johnson attended a *USA Today*–sponsored party to hear Ray Charles perform. By chance, Johnson sat next to Dean Singleton, a young Texas native who had bought his first newspaper only three years earlier and quickly built up a chain of small dailies; in the process, he had gained a reputation for slashing costs and turning marginal newspapers into formidable profit makers. Johnson asked Singleton what his next project would be. Without missing a beat, Singleton replied, "Well, what I'd like to do most is to buy the *Dallas Times Herald* from you guys and show you how to run it."

Johnson had already told Erburu the company should consider selling the newspaper; painful though the proposal had been, he could not justify the drain to Times Mirror shareholders. Nor, given Times Mirror's standards for journalism, could he recommend the draconian cuts that might make the paper profitable. He quickly got Singleton and Erburu together and they began laying the groundwork for a deal—largely financed by Times Mirror—announced that June. Singleton's company purchased the *Times Herald* for $110 million in cash and notes, and after some sharp cuts (and with the help of a cheaper newsprint deal than Times Mirror had), Singleton made the paper profitable.

If, initially, Otis Chandler had thought he might remain chairman for eight years, by 1985, he had had enough. Though he wanted to be useful to the company, he also wanted to get on with the rest of his life. Franklin Murphy, then head of the executive committee of the Times Mirror board, would be retiring at the end of the year; Chandler could take Murphy's position and let Erburu assume the chairmanship. No ready successor, however, was in sight for Erburu, whom Chandler's move would leave with four separate titles: chairman, president, chief executive officer, and chief operating officer. Chandler gave up the chairmanship anyway. But for the first time, he and Erburu talked in earnest about succession.

For months, they played with different scenarios. Using charts and graphs, they assessed a number of Times Mirror executives. Ultimately, they came up with two names: Tom Johnson and Dave Laventhol, then publisher of *Newsday.*

Tom Johnson was by far the better known of the two and the more impressive public presence; but under Laventhol, *Newsday* had flourished—and had recently launched a separate edition to compete head-on against the New York City tabloids. Both were elected senior vice-presidents of the corporation.

The succession talks continued, but Johnson asked that he not be considered. He had been so careful to give Chandler's man—Bill Thomas—space to do his job that Johnson had not yet left his own mark on the *Times.*

To Chandler, the withdrawal made a good deal of sense. Laventhol was eight years older than Johnson. After Erburu retired in five years or so, Laventhol could step up to the chairmanship, allowing Johnson to serve first as president and later as chair.

In order to keep the men's rank roughly parallel, the company made Johnson vice-chair as it named Laventhol president. The announcement was made in May 1986, with the changes to take effect in January 1987.

Laventhol's promotion set off gossip that Johnson's star had fallen, that the Dallas-Denver problems had knocked him out of consideration. "Dave proved that he could make money and Tom didn't," commented one *Times* editor who thought himself in the know. *Newsweek* reported, "Johnson . . . was expected eventually to be Erburu's successor. But Laventhol . . . was recently placed a notch above him on the ladder . . . a move widely commented on in the industry."

Johnson found the publicity painful. Chandler sympathized: "[Johnson] had never had a negative story in his life, and then began to read these stories about . . . losing this contest. Well, Tom was never really in the contest. He wanted to stay as publisher."

Laventhol concurred: "There was no shoot-out. Tom was not penalized for Dallas and Denver. . . . When Tom was in Dallas . . . we did the best in Dallas."

Johnson went to Chandler and asked his advice: "How do I keep from looking like I'm the loser?"

Given the situation, Chandler had no real answer. "Well, you just have to live with that," he said.

Johnson also had to live with the *Los Angeles Times*—whose editor, on turning sixty in 1984, had announced that he would not stay beyond the age of sixty-five. The executive vice-president for marketing was also approaching retirement age.

Appointing their successors would be "the last two personnel decisions that I will confront in the rebuilding of the team from Otis's . . . to [mine]," Johnson would say. But important as the marketing position might be, the editor controlled the paper's voice and ultimately would define what Johnson and the *Times* stood for.

Johnson had overseen a major press expansion and was gearing up for another—an investment in sixteen huge new presses with color capacity that (when completed in 1992) would remove any foreseeable technical restrictions on the *Times* being whatever it wished. The paper would be able to divide itself into an almost infinite variety of separate sections—with room for pullouts on health, science, medicine, or whatever else the editors or advertisers might want. All the more reason to choose an editor with vision.

The new editor, Johnson had already decided, should put his office on the same floor with the news staff, not in the publisher's suite as Thomas had done. Thomas felt he could be more effective where he could better protect his budget, and he liked to hold meetings out from under the newsroom gun; but Johnson wanted *his* editor to be an active part of that newsroom, as Johnson had been in Dallas.

Once Thomas announced his decision to retire, the newsroom grapevine had buzzed with names of possible successors. Even the editorial board meetings had changed, with various aspirants trying to outdo each other with suggestions and questions, showing off their intellects in the manner of beauty contestants showing off their figures.

During the best of times, some of the candidates abhorred each other. With speculation running wild, those tensions were especially near the surface. Whomever Johnson selected, he faced the possibility that some of the others would leave rather than work for him.

Among *Times* editors, Johnson saw four potential choices: managing editor George Cotliar, deputy associate editor Shelby Coffey, and deputy managing editors Noel Greenwood (responsible for metropolitan coverage) and Dennis Britton (in charge of national, foreign, and business news).

Johnson asked each of the four to write a short autobiography and a treatise on his vision of the *Times.* He later shared the editors' writings with Dave Laventhol and Bob Erburu; and he spent hours talking to Thomas and other staffers about the challenges the next editor would face.

He interviewed each aspirant in early 1988—alone and with Laventhol. Then he ranked the four and pondered whether to enlarge the pool. Two hopefuls from outside the paper had come forth on their own; he had consented to see both. A third prospect had been suggested by several sources, and he felt obligated to speak to him as well.

Johnson, who had hoped to keep the selection process quiet, was appalled at the gossip being generated in the industry. Some critics suggested that to make four veteran journalists prance about like so many show horses was humiliating. Yet Johnson felt the job too important to fill casually and concluded he had no choice but to proceed as he was doing—despite any embarrassment suffered by the candidates.

Cotliar, a thirty-year *Times* employee, was the oldest and most senior; but he was seen more as an extension of Thomas than as a presence in his own right. For five years before getting the title of managing editor in 1978, he had served as senior assistant managing editor under Frank Haven, the man he would replace. As Thomas's appointee, he had been the new wave and Haven the old; but for those five years he had tried not to step on Haven's toes. As managing editor, he again had taken the less assertive path.

"I have contented myself with not being in the spotlight," confided Cotliar. "I'm an inside man to a large degree. And that's possibly hurt me. . . . I don't think I have helped myself in some respects by taking a step back and deferring to other people."

Nevertheless, Cotliar thought he had the skills to move the paper where it ought to be. The *Times* had still not learned how to work together; like dancers on a disco floor, each section moved to its own rhythm. Above all, Cotliar thought of himself as a communicator and a coordinator, as one who could get the various editors talking to one another to create a consensus about where the *Times* was going. For it should be one paper, not a collection of sections tossed together.

Britton was also concerned about the paper's drift. "We're at a juncture in which Tom Johnson and his executives have to decide what we are going to be now that we've grown up," he observed.

On the one hand, the *Times* was trying to be a great regional paper, fighting off such competitors as the *Orange Country Register.* On the other, it was functioning as a national newspaper, taking on the *New York Times* and *Wall Street Journal.*

A fifth-generation Californian, Britton had a low-key (at times diffident) manner that hid a driven nature and a deliberative mind. As a child laid up with rheumatic fever, he had covered two years of schoolwork in three months. As a junior reporter determined to learn to take decent notes, he had practiced every evening for several months—repeatedly transcribing tape-recorded conversations until he could get them right. As an editor he would try to make the *Times* preeminent on the prestigious national-international front, where it was already a formidable contender.

For Greenwood, the heart of the paper was local coverage. After all, local readers paid the bills, not pundits in Washington or New York. Instead of always looking to the East for approval, the paper should look closer to home. It could not and *should not* be the *New York Times.* "Let the *New York Times* be the *New York Times,*" he said. The *Los Angeles Times* should be the very best of its kind: a big, regional paper, albeit with national and international interests and operations.

A California native, Greenwood had been a rebel as a youth. He had been fired from a job as radio disk jockey in Santa Barbara because he insisted—against orders—on playing jazz during the dinner hour. And he had been bounced from the University of California (Santa Barbara) because he was unable to develop an interest in any classes other than English. He had worked for a string of small-time newspapers, including one started with a friend in the front office of a laundromat.

When he got to the *Times* in 1967, he was ready for a life and a newspaper with some stability. After becoming metropolitan editor in 1981, he vowed to stop treating the suburban sections as a dumping ground for reporters who couldn't cut it on the regular staff and to upgrade coverage of Los Angeles.

Late in 1987, he finally launched a redesigned and beefed up metro section. The next step, as he saw it, was to "fill in the blanks in our zoning pattern," to start publishing zoned editions for the communities that advertisers had largely abandoned—the central city, the East Side, areas that were poor and largely minority but had news needs just like everyone else.

The fourth candidate, Shelby Coffey, had bailed out of Dallas when the *Times Herald* was sold and come to the *Times* with responsibility for the so-called soft sections of the paper: the magazine, trends, features, book reviews. Before going to Dallas, Coffey had served less than a year as editor of *U.S. News and World Report* and left amid rumors that he and owner Mortimer Zuckerman never really hit it off, that he was reshaping the magazine too slowly to suit Zuckerman.

With his taste for thoughtful, analytical journalism and his skill at being a writers' editor, Coffey seemed tailor-made for the *Times.* But his newness figured against his winning easy acceptance as its editor; and he was plagued at the *Times*—as he had been at the *Washington Post*—by a suspicion that (having made his name in soft news) he could not operate with the big boys on the hard-news side. Of the four prospects, Coffey was the only one whom Tom Johnson had personally recruited into Times Mirror; he alone was, in a sense, Johnson's creation.

For Johnson, the central question was simple: Who could best deliver his vision for the *Times*? Who could make it, over time, the finest newspaper in the United States?

The *Times* certainly had resources enough to aspire to greatness. It pulled in revenues of roughly one billion dollars a year (nearly one third of everything generated by the Times Mirror Company), of which some 20 percent was profit. The paper's weekday circulation, at over 1.1 million, ranked it second among metropolitan newspapers behind the *New York Daily News;* and while *Daily News* circulation had declined during the decade, *Times* circulation was climbing—and could climb further.

On the first weekend in April 1988, Johnson decided that the guessing game had gone on long enough; he would make his choice known that Monday, April 4.

For some time, Johnson had been leaning toward Coffey. He

had called all the places where Coffey had worked in the past and everyone had given glowing recommendations. Johnson had also reviewed his own notes on Coffey. "Superb personal character," Johnson had scribbled, "intelligent, well read . . . a leader, motivator . . . splendid vision of the future, one that we will share . . . commitment to excellence."

In addition, Coffey was a good and willing public speaker—in contrast to Thomas, who had not placed much stock in public appearances. And Johnson felt that *his* editor should get out and show the *Times* flag.

As for the staff's misgivings about Coffey's sparse hard-news background, Johnson thought that, in time, Coffey would win his colleagues over.

Coincidentally, a *Newsweek* item appeared that weekend suggesting that George Cotliar might get the job—all the more reason to get the announcement out of the way and to try to calm the turmoil in the newsroom.

Coffey was promoted immediately to executive editor; he would work alongside Thomas until early 1989 and then move into the top job.

Johnson and then Coffey met separately with each of the other contenders and expressed the hope that they would stay on.

Like Johnson, Coffey regretted that the process had become so public ("You deal with it. . . . You move ahead."), but his eyes were facing toward the future. And as he saw it, the *Times* "will continue to be a road map to the destiny of the West."

For Coffey, that meant that the *Times* would continue to trace the area's development and growth and explore the implications of trade with the Pacific Rim. It would study the massive migration into the area; examine the educational, medical, and infrastructure needs of Southern California; and expand its national and international coverage.

Any changes, said Coffey, "will be part of the natural evolution . . . smart and orderly."

Even before Coffey's appointment, the paper had begun upgrading its standing sections. Ambitious overhauls of the metro and business sections and the Sunday magazine were all part of what *Times* executives called a "core strategy"—an approach that recognized the *Times*' fundamental strength was in its basic product, more so than in its ability (with zoned and special editions) to outdo neighboring community papers' coverage of local news.

Nevertheless, the *Times* intended to push ahead with new regional editions to supplement those it already published for San Diego, Orange County, and the San Fernando Valley. And though a central city section was not on the front burner, eventually, Johnson felt, the *Times* would get around to publishing one, whether or not advertisers embraced it, just as it would probably get around to a science section—prototypes of which already existed—despite the likelihood advertisers would not support it.

Plans were also in the works for a full-scale western edition that would circulate as far away as Mexico, Hawaii, San Francisco, and Las Vegas—extending the reach of the *Times* more magnificently than Otis Chandler could have imagined when he began pushing the *Times* toward glory a generation ago.

In trying to fill Chandler's shoes, Johnson had taken on a daunting responsibility. Chandler had sat in his office acting as "a tremendous shield behind which the news department could operate," mused Johnson. "I don't know whether I can be as strong a shield. . . . Things are different." Yet, as a vice-chairman of the corporation and a member of its board of directors, Johnson was not without corporate clout. He intended to protect the news department's integrity, knowing that he would be remembered for "either having carried the baton handed to me by Otis . . . for the length of the track . . . or not."

Still, certain pressures had intensified since Chandler's day. Advertisers were demanding increasingly sophisticated targeting for their ads and distribution of preprinted supplements that contained no news. A publisher could either give those advertisers what they wanted or watch their business go elsewhere.

Employee problems seemed more complicated—with AIDS, drug addiction, and the sale of illegal drugs on the premises. And the threat of government actions was worrisome—with initiatives surfacing to eliminate the deductibility of advertising expenses and to ban tobacco advertising altogether.

The *Times* was still trying to understand the ramifications of California's changing demographics and the rapid growth of the region's Latino and Asian communities. And it was groping for a coherent response to the growing aspirations of minorities and women, among its staff members and its readership.

In a quarter of a century, the *Times* had matured—like some institutional Eliza Doolittle lifted from journalism's slums. Yet it had not outgrown the need for approval from the powers in the East. In search of such recognition, it had taken out a series of ads in the *Washington Post, Wall Street Journal,* and *New York Times* to show *Los Angeles Times'* journalism to an audience that might not normally see it. And when Ronald Reagan had gone to the White House, the *Times* had put its papers on Washington's news racks and stands, not only to supply the news needs of Californians in Washington but to fly the flag in a territory that mattered.

Johnson knew full well how far the *Times* had come and how awesome was the challenge before him. And he felt both pride and amazement: "For a kid from the wrong side of the tracks from Macon, Georgia, to have an opportunity to be publisher of this newspaper is something akin to . . . the young guy who grew up wanting to be a pilot and ended up becoming the pilot of the lunar lander."

As Johnson looked ahead, Otis Chandler reviewed a job finally done. His goal of simplifying the company was all but accomplished. Most of those units not central to the company's mission or not worth the effort to run had been systematically cast away.

The bulk of Times Mirror's timberlands had been sold, as had been the company's interests in microwave communications, road maps, charts, and atlases. The firm no longer peddled videotex—created to bring computerized banking, shopping, news, and other services to the home—"a technology in search of a market," as described by Chandler.

The troubled *Denver Post* had been sold in 1987 to a company controlled by Dean Singleton, the young entrepreneur to whom Times Mirror earlier had sold the *Times Herald.* The price was ninety-five million dollars, the transaction largely financed by Times Mirror.

While selling off its problems, Times Mirror was acquiring properties that seemed more promising. The Abell company, owner of the *Baltimore Sun* newspapers, was among them. The deal was announced in 1986, almost immediately after the Hearst Corporation announced the folding of the competing and failing *Baltimore News American.*

At Tom Johnson's suggestion, Erburu and Times Mirror vice-chairman Phillip Williams had gone to Baltimore. Erburu had told the owners' representatives that he knew they were not seeking a suitor, but that a lot of family-owned papers not for sale had found themselves on the market. Typically they were sold in the pandemonium of an auction. The *Sun* properties deserved better. He offered six hundred million dollars in cash for the two newspapers and two television stations. The families took the money.

Times Mirror also bought a group of magazines—including *Field & Stream* and *Yachting*—that CBS had recently sold to a company set up by former CBS executives.

The major share of Times Mirror income continued to come from newspapers (which ranged in size from the *Times* to the *Greenwich Time* in Fairfield County, Connecticut, with a daily circulation of thirteen thousand). The company also remained heavily involved in specialized books and journals, and broadcast and cable television.

"I think the chairman's going to have an easier job because of the streamlining of the company," said Chandler. "I think he will be better able to focus on the major operating units and on acquisitions than I was able to. . . . I think succession's in place. . . . We know where we're going."

Wall Street, impressed with the company's new sense of direction, pushed up the price of the stock.

Through the years, the Chandlers' (and other insiders') percentage of outstanding stock had dropped—a consequence largely of issuing stock to make acquisitions. Unlike the New York Times and Washington Post companies, Times Mirror had not originally issued two classes of stock (with most of the voting shares staying in friendly hands) to ensure family control. Theoretically, as inside ownership declined, Times Mirror's vulnerability to a hostile takeover increased. In 1985, with the stock selling relatively cheaply, the company purchased some 7.5 million shares of its own stock—slightly more than 10 percent of the shares outstanding, bringing inside control to over 40 percent. The company also reincorporated in Delaware and adopted measures to discourage a hostile takeover.

"If there were any questions about control, that presumably dispelled those questions," said Erburu.

That there should be concern on the news floor as Chandler moved farther away from day-to-day operations was only natural. "I've shielded them from corporate encroachment, both inside the building and outside the building," he acknowledged. But the tradition was set and the newsroom would be safe—at least for a while. "If you get a different cast of characters, of senior officers, then I think that [corporate interference could become] a problem." But that would not be Chandler's battle.

He looked forward to enlarging his set of big-game trophies, building his antique car collection, climbing mountains, and enjoying his grandchildren: "I think the challenges from here on out will be small ones." He would stay involved in the company, but personal interests would take most of his time.

"I seem to be busier than ever, but I'm not doing important things anymore," he said, in a tone that left no doubt that that was exactly as it should be.

PART THREE

THE CATHEDRAL: THE *NEW YORK TIMES*

CHAPTER 12

LESSONS IN LEADERSHIP

Otis Chandler's selection of the *New York Times* as the standard for his *Times* and Katharine Graham's choice of *New York Times* man James Reston to advise her on the *Washington Post* were natural outgrowths of the paper's unique stature. The *New York Times* ranks as the preeminent newspaper in the United States. It is not the oldest paper in the nation, or in New York, but it has the strongest sense of history and tradition. And—as is the nature of preeminent institutions—it is shrouded by the densest cloud of mystery; a change in its masthead is scrutinized by journalists in a manner usually reserved for leadership change at the Kremlin.

For a quarter of a century, one name—Arthur Ochs Sulzberger—has rested atop the *New York Times* masthead. Sulzberger became publisher during a difficult period for the *Times* and the Times Company, and eventually transformed both. Unlike Chandler in California, Sulzberger was driven not so much by an overarching vision (or a personal need to succeed) as by utter necessity.

In March 1963, after 114 tense days, New York's longest newspaper strike ended. For the *Times*—and for all New York dailies—the disruption was a financial disaster.

Times executives had looked forward to a banner year. Advertising and circulation were at record levels. The shutdown obliterated that progress. The three weeks of the strike that fell in 1962 denied the paper its lucrative Christmas advertising.

That year's revenues barely matched 1961's and profits dropped below half the amount projected. Nineteen sixty-three brought yet more damage. Newspaper revenues (at $101 million) were $17 million below the depressed 1962 level. The *Times* dipped into the red, posting a loss of $527,000. Only through the sale of real estate and dividends from a paper mill in which the Times Company held a substantial interest was the parent corporation able to remain in the black.

At the time, Sulzberger was—by his description—"assistant treasurer in charge of nothing." He had no direct involvement in the conflict, but watched with horror as the *New York Times* stood weakened and bleeding before its unions.

The strike began in the early morning hours of December 8, 1962, when the International Typographers Union and Big Six (its New York local) halted negotiations with New York's newspaper publishers. The printers were demanding higher salaries, a shorter work week, and guarantees against losing jobs or income to automation.

Big Six's strength lay not only in its power to withdraw its own members from work but in its ability to mobilize the nine other newspaper unions. Twelve years earlier, the New York Newspaper Guild had forged a so-called "blood brotherhood" among the unions and successfully struck the *New York World Telegram.* Since then, the brotherhood had grown more confident and powerful. And the publishers had formed an alliance of their own, which included all the New York dailies.

The printers' action was specifically directed against the *Times, News, Journal American,* and *Telegram and Sun.* The other papers were considered too financially unstable to survive a prolonged strike. Nonetheless, to show solidarity, the *Post, Herald Tribune, Daily Mirror,* and *Long Island Star Journal* suspended publication when the printers walked out. And the *Long Island Press* cut off its Queens circulation.

From the beginning, the struggle shaped up as a contest between two self-centered, strong-willed men: Amory Bradford, *Times* general manager and chairman of the Publishers Association, and Bertram Powers, president of Big Six. Educated at Phillips Academy, Yale University, and Yale Law School, Bradford was a handsome, aloof figure given to displays of temper and arrogance. One mediator complained that Bradford's "icy disdain" so chilled the negotiating room that he considered asking the hotel to send up more heat. Powers, a high school dropout and a printer since the age of seventeen, had an ego to match his reputation; associates and antagonists thought the white-haired, nattily dressed Powers one of the best labor negotiators in the country.

Powers opened the talks calling for an increase of $93 a week (on a base wage of $141) while the publishers were offering $8. When the contract expired, the union request was $38—four times management's offer. A few weeks after the walkout, however, an agreement seemed near. At a special session arranged with the help of Mayor Robert Wagner, Powers brought his demand down to $16.42. Bradford haughtily dismissed the concession with, "How do we fit that into a ten-dollar bill?" The moment was lost; the two sides again were at war.

As the conflict dragged on, a number of outsiders got involved. President Kennedy publicly attacked Powers for making demands the president claimed would kill papers and put thousands out of work. Later, *Washington Post* publisher Philip Graham (a close Kennedy friend) held a long private meeting with Powers—during the course of which he called up the president and told him he had been mistaken, that Powers was an eminently reasonable man. Graham offered to help mediate the dispute, but the publishers wanted nothing to do with him. New York's governor and the U.S. labor secretary tried to intercede, also without success.

Only two of the struck newspapers (the *Times* and *News*) had been consistently profitable, and the long campaign was bleeding everyone. In early March, the *Post,* having lost hope for a settlement, resumed publication, placing even greater pressure on the remaining papers. Shortly thereafter, Mayor Wagner injected himself into the negotiations and the two sides pounded out an agreement.

The printers settled for an increase of $12.63 a week—only $2.50 more than the final prestrike offer. They also won a shorter work week, a common expiration date for union contracts, and limitations on the introduction of (and profits from) new technology. The unions had not quite brought management to its knees, but they had come close.

In a long article published after the strike, *Times* labor writer

A. H. Raskin criticized both sides, setting the standard followed more than a decade later by Robert Kaiser, writing in the *Washington Post* after an equally bitter battle at the *Post.*

During the conflict, *Times* managing editor Turner Catledge and Sulzberger met virtually every night in a group that included the circulation director and several others. The dark-haired, unpretentious thirty-seven-year-old heir, with the unlikely nickname of "Punch," looked forward to the meetings, thinking of himself and the rest as something of a club. Catledge, an engaging raconteur originally from Choctaw County, Mississippi, had been a traveling companion and sometime drinking buddy of Sulzberger's father. Twenty-five years Punch's senior, he formed a paternal attachment to the genial young man, who saw Catledge as a mentor.

Sulzberger, viewing events from the perspective of the managing editor's office, concluded that the strike had been unavoidable—springing, to some extent, from a battle among the unions. For years the Guild, whose contract expired several weeks earlier than the rest, had set the precedent for settlement terms. Powers was determined to seize the initiative from the Guild. Members of the Publishers Association were also in conflict and were rarely able to agree on a strategy. Even had the publishers been accommodating, Amory Bradford's icy presence would have destroyed any conceivable harmony.

Watching the paper's earnings evaporate, Sulzberger had lamented the firm's lack of staying power. The Times was a one-product corporation with an affiliated paper mill. When the *Times'* presses stopped, much of the mill's production stopped as well. "It seemed to me that if we were ever going to work our way out of this goddamn union mess . . . we were going to have to have some strength in the company," said Sulzberger.

Following the strike, *Times* publisher Orvil Dryfoos went to Puerto Rico for a rest. During the dispute, Dryfoos had often negotiated late into the night—after spending all day with the skeletal *Times* staff that maintained the news service and the western and international editions. "Certainly these hundred days have been the most awful I have ever lived through," he had written a friend.

Dryfoos's heart began to bother him in Puerto Rico and he checked into a local hospital. When he had applied for military service during World War II, he had discovered that he suffered from rheumatic heart disease. During the labor strife, his doctors had put him on digitalis to regulate his heartbeat. By the time he got to San Jorge Hospital in Puerto Rico, his condition had seriously worsened. He returned to New York and went directly from the airport to the Harkness Pavilion of the Columbia Presbyterian Medical Center, where he died on May 25. Dryfoos, fifty years old, had only been publisher for two years. In a eulogy, *Times* Washington columnist James Reston said that over the period of the strike Dryfoos simply "wore his life away."

Dryfoos's death plunged the paper into another crisis. Arthur Hays Sulzberger, chairman of the Times Company board and former publisher of the newspaper, knew the publisher's position could not stay vacant for long. And he quickly realized that his only son would be the one choice acceptable to all family members. Sulzberger had been impressed with the younger man's maturation during the strike. "You went into it something of a boy and came out of it a man whose judgment was generally respected," he wrote to his son.

Nevertheless, Amory Bradford (who was not only general manager and vice-president but also a board member) apparently thought himself ready for a larger role. Unfortunately for him, Bradford viewed young Sulzberger with less than respect and, in turn, was loathed by Punch. "Orvil, for some inexplicable reason, had a great deal of confidence in Amory. . . . If I had any in the beginning, it evaporated very quickly," said Arthur Ochs Sulzberger.

Some two weeks after Dryfoos's death, Arthur Hays Sulzberger called Bradford to tell him that Punch would be named publisher. Bradford, predictably, did not like the idea. He asked whether all the children were in agreement, and Sulzberger told him that they were. Were any other changes being made? asked Bradford. None at the time, Sulzberger replied. "I'm not sure I want to go along with it," said Bradford. Sulzberger, trying to be both firm and gentle, told him that if he thought things over, he might change his mind.

Arthur Ochs Sulzberger's appointment as president and publisher was announced two weeks later (making him the youngest chief executive in the paper's history); Bradford's resignation was announced the same day. An excerpt from Bradford's statement, published in the *Times,* said he was resigning for "personal reasons" and because "I am not in agreement with the proposed plan of organization."

Punch was profiled by his sister, Ruth Golden, for the *Times* in-house newsletter. The new publisher, she wrote, drank Scotch, loved puns and gadgets, habitually arrived early for planes and trains, and was compulsively neat. "Punch wants his own surroundings orderly and polished, and given a few minutes to spare he will get to work on yours," she wrote. The convivial publisher never remembered names, said Golden, but was "impeccably skillful in either disguising the fact or making Old Nameless feel wanted."

Punch's father had never intended him to be publisher at such a relatively young age. His preparation was far from complete. In a sense, however, he had been training all his life. For to be a Sulzberger, particularly a male heir, was to learn of duty and responsibility almost from the cradle.

At the age of eight, Punch had told his mother that he wanted to be king of the world. Asked what he would do, he had replied that he would stop war, make countries become friends, and "fix up" Germany by making Hitler "into a plain man and make them get a good president." Afterward, he apparently planned to depart for Africa and "kill all the bugs that make people sick."

While in his twenties, Punch and his wife received a long letter from his father, which continued an earlier conversation and defined his concept of "noblesse oblige." To Arthur Hays Sulzberger, the meaning was straightforward: "It seems to me that those of us who are lucky . . . owe more to society than [those] . . . who haven't had the same breaks."

Sulzberger was only nine years old when his grandfather (Adolph Ochs) died: "So I primarily remember him as a grandfather, not as a journalist. . . . If there was any tradition that was passed along, it was passed from my grandfather through my father. . . . Much of anything that we learned about [journalistic responsibility] . . . came rather through osmosis than it did through any stern lectures at the dining room table."

By the time Sulzberger became publisher, the family tradition was firmly enough imbued that no stern lectures were needed. That tradition was due, more than anything else, to the success of his grandfather, who had left Chattanooga, Tennessee, in 1896 in search of a paper to run in New York.

* * *

The *Times* was not the first New York paper to stir Adolph Ochs's interest. He had originally come to look over the *New York Mercury,* which he had heard needed a business manager. After arriving, however, he found he disagreed with the politics of the *Mercury*'s prospective new owners. His own negotiations to buy the paper ended unsuccessfully, but an acquaintance told him that the *New York Times* was in financial distress and might be had cheaply.

Ochs, a somber thirty-eight-year-old, was already a veteran businessman. He had come up through the *Chattanooga Times,* starting as a carrier while eleven years old and subsequently working in every department. At the age of twenty, he had bought the *Times*—with $250 in borrowed cash and an agreement to assume its debts of $1,500. Having made the Chattanooga paper into a grand success, he was seeking to do the same out East.

The owners of the *Times* would have preferred to sell to a local person of substance, but the paper's finances were so precarious that only Ochs was willing to make a serious offer. To help his case, Ochs prevailed upon President Grover Cleveland and other notables to write letters of endorsement.

Ochs negotiated a deal that (for only seventy-five thousand dollars of his own money) would give him majority ownership of the newspaper after three consecutive profitable years. At the time, the publication was roughly three hundred thousand dollars in debt. Virtually everyone but Ochs thought he had about as much chance of turning the paper around as raising its creators from their graves.

The *Times'* founders, Henry Raymond and George Jones, had realized earlier than their peers that a politically centrist, nonsensational newspaper could find a large market in New York.

The two had come together through Horace Greeley's *New York Herald Tribune,* where Raymond worked as an editor and Jones in the business office. They had hoped to buy the *Albany Evening Journal,* but after that effort proved unsuccessful, they started the *New York Daily Times* in September 1851 for a total investment of roughly seventy thousand dollars.

"We shall make it a point to get into a passion as rarely as possible," promised the first edition of the six-column, four-page, one-penny paper. Along with a number of reports from Europe, that issue carried stories about a fire the paper's reporter never managed to find (though a competitor did) and a fight that nearly occurred between rival groups of blacksmiths.

Despite Raymond's intense involvement in politics (at one point, he was a congressman and chairman of the Republican National Committee), he edited a relatively evenhanded, though consistently Republican, newspaper. After one year, circulation was twenty-six thousand. After ten, it had climbed to seventy-five thousand—and the paper (which had dropped *Daily* from its name and was selling for two cents) was solidly profitable.

Raymond died in 1869. Jones, who previously had left editorial direction largely to Raymond, became responsible for the entire newspaper. Under his stewardship, the *Times* courageously led the attack on Boss William Tweed. It also began having financial problems.

When Jones died at the age of eighty in 1891, the paper was no longer piling up profits of more than a hundred thousand dollars annually—as it had several years previously. The paper earned only fifteen thousand dollars in 1890, partly because of construction expenses for a new headquarters. But there had been problems earlier. Jones's 1883 decision to drop the paper's price from four cents to two (to meet the competition of the two-cent *World* and *Sun*) had cost him dearly. The *Times'* refusal to support presidential nominee James Blaine in 1884 had provoked some Republicans to pull their ads. Though many of the advertisers returned, expenses mounted. Jones's heirs, unable to reverse the decline, sold the paper in 1893 to a group headed by editor Charles Miller.

The new ownership was undercapitalized and the Panic of 1893 further undermined the publication's shaky finances. Miller's poor management skills made matters worse. When Ochs arrived, the *Times* was printing nineteen thousand papers daily and selling only nine thousand.

Ochs immediately changed the returns policy, giving dealers a stronger incentive to sell papers. And he introduced several new features, including a book review section and a classy magazine. He also ran a contest for a motto for the paper, which drew twenty thousand entries and generated a lot of hoopla—though Ochs kept his own "All the News That's Fit to Print." His boldest stroke, however, came in October 1898. Because of the Spanish-American War—which had been raucously promoted by William Randolph Hearst's *New York Journal*—the *Times* risked losing much of the ground it had won under Ochs. Not only had it sustained heavy advertising losses during that conflict, but it was thoroughly beaten in war coverage by its better-financed rivals. Ochs, eager to set the *Times* apart, cut the price (then three cents) to a penny.

The *World* and *Journal* were already selling for a cent, but they were considered tawdry, lower-class rags. The *Times* had always tried to position itself as a paper of quality for a select readership. Ochs's new strategy assumed the existence of a price-conscious mass audience ready for an alternative to yellow journalism.

Circulation went from twenty-six to seventy-six thousand between 1898 and 1899. By 1901, more than one hundred thousand copies of the *Times* were being sold daily. Through the years the price crept up, but the readership kept growing. When Ochs died in 1935 at the age of seventy-seven, the *Times* sold more than 450,000 papers daily and was, like Ochs himself, straitlaced, sensible, and insistent on quality. Though uncomfortable with public displays of passion, it had no doubt about where it stood.

Arthur Hays Sulzberger succeeded Ochs as publisher. A stylish sophisticate of forty-four who liked travel, Scotch, and verse, Sulzberger had originally planned a career in his family's textile-import businesses. But after his marriage to Iphigene, Ochs's only child, Ochs insisted that Sulzberger come and work for him. The marriage gave Ochs three granddaughters—Marian, Ruth, and Judith—and, finally, in February 1926, his only grandson, Arthur Ochs. The nickname "Punch" came from a baby book written by his father upon Arthur Ochs Sulzberger's birth. His son, wrote A. H. Sulzberger, would "play the Punch to Judy's endless show."

Though a lovable child, Punch was a lackluster student. "My mother used to move me from school to school about forty-two minutes before they threw me out and I'd end up at another school," he once joked. At St. Bernard's, the very proper Manhattan school he attended for several years after kindergarten, the teachers tried to make him right-handed. Whenever he was caught writing with his left hand, he would be hauled up to the front of the class and beaten with a ruler. "Eventually," said Sulzberger, "you get the point." He switched. As a consequence, he sometimes wrote in reverse—which convinced his mother he was dyslexic. Even as an adult balancing his checkbook, he sometimes would write thirty-seven when he meant seventy-three—a problem he solved in time by getting a calculator that talked.

For as long as he could remember, Punch had wanted to be a marine. To him, the military represented freedom: no more Latin lessons or arbitrary rules or second-guessing of decisions; no more thick books full of meaningless abstractions. Also, a war was going on, and to a patriotic young American the military made a lot more sense than the Loomis School in Windsor, Connecticut.

At the age of seventeen and with his father's permission, Punch left school and joined the marines. Later his mother would tell him that his father had signed the enlistment papers hoping that if he got shot in the head some information might flow in. Whatever the reason, Punch was grateful. For the first time in his life, he was responsible for himself and "the kinds of things I was called upon to do, I could do very, very well."

He enjoyed military service and would later say that he had grown up in the marines. "I found it to be, except when I was scared, a very pleasant kind of life." Punch did not, as he put it, "go charging ashore at Iwo Jima." He worked as a radioman and, for a while, served as a driver in General Douglas MacArthur's headquarters in the Pacific. He also took a U.S. Armed Forces Institute test of general educational development and scored very near the top of the curve, confirming that, despite his hatred of school, he had learned something after all.

Upon discharge from the marines in 1946, he applied to Columbia University; his father, who was a trustee, supported his application. The admissions office, feeling Punch was not quite ready for the regular curriculum, admitted him into the general studies program, where he quickly did well enough to earn normal status. Shortly after graduation in 1951, he was recalled into the marines for the Korean War and served (primarily as a public information officer) for seventeen months. By then he had a wife (the former Barbara Grant), a son (Arthur Ochs, Jr.), and a desire to start a career.

That Punch would one day come to the newspaper had been assured. Under the terms of his grandfather's will, effective ownership of the *Times* had passed directly from Adolph Ochs to Punch and his three sisters—with the controlling shares being held in trust until the death of Ochs's daughter, Iphigene Sulzberger. Given the traditional and dynastic nature of the institution, Punch (the only male heir) could no more reject the *Times* than a crown prince could refuse the throne.

Nevertheless, Arthur Hays Sulzberger had thought Punch should work elsewhere first, and had mentioned that to Washington bureau chief Arthur Krock. While Punch was in the marines, Krock spoke to *Milwaukee Journal* editor J. D. Ferguson about a training program there for Punch. A. H. Sulzberger had followed up by describing to Ferguson what Punch's instruction should cover. He particularly wanted Punch to study the *Journal*'s employee stock ownership program. For Ochs's heirs eventually would have to part with some of their stock; and opening substantial ownership to employees might be one way to ensure the institution's independence.

Punch became a *Journal* reporter in February 1953, returning to New York briefly in 1954 before working as a *Times* foreign correspondent in France (where his first marriage fell apart), Great Britain, and Italy. At times, especially in Paris, he felt like something of a fifth wheel, but his reporting and attitude drew praise from his editors. By 1956, he had begun his progression through a series of nonjobs in New York that seemed designed primarily to keep him occupied. He also began a courtship of Carol Fox Fuhrman and married her in December of that year.

Managing editor Turner Catledge was shocked by the cavalier treatment Punch received and wrote in his memoirs: "Punch's duties were of the most menial sort; he seemed to spend much of his time wandering around the building inspecting things—to what purpose was never clear to me. I several times told [Orvil] Dryfoos that this was a degrading way to treat a future owner of the paper, but Dryfoos would throw up his hands and say he didn't know what to do with Punch."

By then, Dryfoos was the clear successor to A. H. Sulzberger and Punch's turn at the helm seemed far in the future. Six months after marrying Punch's sister Marian in 1941, Dryfoos (at the behest of A. H. Sulzberger) had given up his seat on the New York Stock Exchange and come to the *Times.* He had worked briefly as a reporter and editor and then was assigned to the publisher's office, where he began an apprenticeship not unlike A. H. Sulzberger's. Remembering the frostiness he had sometimes felt from Ochs and Ochs's reluctance to surrender control, Sulzberger had resolved to treat his own successor better—and to resign before dying. He named Dryfoos publisher in April 1961, retaining the title of chairman of the board.

Following Dryfoos's death, Punch assumed the publishership with his sense of humor fully intact. His first day on the job, his sister Judith called and Punch announced, "I've made my first decision."

"What's that?" she asked.

"I've decided not to throw up."

Underlying the easy jest, however, was a determination to change the *Times.* Punch had "the impatience of a man who is underrated and wants to prove himself," concluded Catledge.

Sulzberger had already sized up general manager Amory Bradford and did not want to keep his management system intact. Bradford's method, Sulzberger recalled, was to make sure that circulation, advertising, promotion, production—virtually everything except the newsroom—fed straight into his office. "He didn't want them talking to each other," said Sulzberger. "That was the method he had to try to keep control." Executives from different areas would be lacerated for communicating directly to one another.

Having departments in the same company not talking to each other struck Sulzberger as fundamentally stupid, as did the practice—common at the time—of not preparing successors for important positions. Sulzberger's rejection of that system was, in fact, his first real decision after being made publisher.

In a meeting of senior executives, Sulzberger gave a sense of the type of organization he intended to run. Why, he demanded to know, had the *Times* been forced to go outside the company to find a manager for its international edition? Why had the first manager of the western edition also been recruited from outside the company? What plans had been made for grooming the next treasurer or Sunday editor? He demanded an organizational chart and analysis from each of the executives that honestly assessed the management talent in their departments.

The next year he announced a major reorganization, which he explained in *Times Talk,* the newspaper's internal newsletter:

"I have, on a number of occasions, pointed out that the *Times* reminded me of a tall stand of reeds, each a fine specimen, and each reaching high into the sky. While their roots were in the same soil, when they reached up there was often little to join them together. The 14th floor [where the publisher and general manager are located] . . . at one time had some fifteen separate departments reporting to it."

No more. Under his reorganization, only six departments would report to the fourteenth floor—four commercial departments, plus the editorial page editor and the executive editor.

The new publisher also shut down the western edition. By January 1964, when the last issue was printed, circulation had climbed past eighty-five thousand and was spread over thirteen states. In Sulzberger's eyes, however, it was one big sinkhole for *New York Times* cash. The financial projections seemed weak. Technology for efficiently delivering the paper didn't exist. And the project was diverting the attention of some of his brightest people.

Walter Mattson, then *Times* production manager, had spent a year in Los Angeles working with the edition. He agreed that it was in a sorry state, but thought many of the problems were temporary. It had been launched in a recession and then had been hit with the newspaper strike, meaning much less back-up from the staff in New York. If the company stuck with it over several years, argued Mattson, the western edition would make money. Sulzberger refused to give in.

He thought seriously of closing the money-losing international edition. But with the *Herald Tribune* also publishing an international edition, Sulzberger didn't want to be the first to surrender: "I, frankly, didn't want to haul that flag down."

The pressure for performance was strong and consistent. Secretary-treasurer Francis Cox noted in March 1965 that despite a booming economy, *Times* operations were making a profit of only 1.95 percent. That was not adequate, he pointed out, to provide for the needs of the company or its employees.

By then, senior executives at the *Times* were concluding that, early impressions notwithstanding, young Sulzberger was neither indecisive nor incompetent. Beneath the mild, convivial exterior, lay the heart of a serious executive.

CHAPTER 13

A WHIRLWIND IN THE NEWSROOM

Punch Sulzberger was not alone in 1963 in catapulting to executive status at the *Times.* Abraham Michael Rosenthal was taking a similar leap, albeit on a significantly lower level.

Rosenthal had not sought to become metropolitan editor, but he embraced the assignment with consuming passion; and the former premier foreign correspondent developed into a star editor as well—one whose fire burned so bright that it often scorched those nearby.

Managing editor Turner Catledge had turned to Rosenthal out of frustration. For years, Catledge had been groping for a way to improve the *Times'* lackluster coverage of New York. The problem sprang, in some respects, from the complexities of the city itself. A capital of art, culture, and international finance, New York was also a city of ethnic strife, local politics, and rampant street crime. Only an editor of uncommon talent could coordinate coherent coverage of it all.

Rosenthal (a native of Sault Sainte Marie, Ontario, who had grown up in the Bronx) had originally been a candidate for reassignment to a reporting job in New York. But Catledge had decided that a journalist as gifted and driven as Rosenthal should play a much larger role, though little in Rosenthal's past suggested he was management material.

Rosenthal's early life had been tragic. His father had died in

Rosenthal's youth, laying the foundation for a childhood of poverty. Four of his five sisters died prematurely (three before Rosenthal reached adulthood)—two from cancer, one from pneumonia, and the other within weeks of the birth of her first child. And Rosenthal himself had contracted osteomyelitis, a crippling bone disease that had nearly destroyed his ability to walk.

Instead of being defeated, the bookish intellectual became a fighter, taking on life, rivals, and work with unrestrained zest. Starting with the *Times* as a part-time student correspondent while attending City College of New York, he quickly wrote his way onto the regular staff. He turned a routine story on a day in the life of a United Nations delegate into a resonant feature on the comings and goings of Russia's Andrei Gromyko and was rewarded with assignment to the United Nations. From there, he went to India, Poland (where he had won a Pulitzer and from which he was expelled), and Japan, always performing with distinction.

Rosenthal was so clearly in love with writing and reporting that Catledge feared he might not accept the job of metropolitan editor. Previously, Rosenthal had turned down a Geneva-based job as the *Times'* floating European correspondent in order to go to Japan; and Catledge knew he was in no hurry to leave. Nevertheless, in 1962, when Catledge set off on a round-the-world trip to visit *Times* correspondents, getting Rosenthal to come to New York was foremost on his mind.

Rosenthal was, indeed, quite happy in Japan. He had never seriously thought of editing; and when he had thought of it at all, he had pictured himself foreign editor—"puffing a pipe with the boys on the Council of Foreign Relations or something." Moreover, he had unexpectedly received a letter from editorial page editor John Oakes suggesting that he return to New York and write editorials. That offer held little appeal; but, he told Oakes, if he could get his own column, *that* would be an entirely different matter.

Oakes had not yet responded when Catledge arrived in Japan and offered the metropolitan editorship to Rosenthal. The city staff, said Catledge, should be the heart of the paper instead of a dumping ground for reporters who couldn't make it elsewhere. He thought Rosenthal could bring it to life.

Rosenthal said he was not interested, but Catledge—whom Rosenthal admired deeply—kept pushing the proposal. And as the conversations continued, in Japan and later in India, the editor's charm and determination began to have an effect. At one point, Catledge said the *Times* was calling in its investment. "We want you to be our Nashua."

Rosenthal was stumped. Nashua, after all, was a racehorse—winner of the Preakness and Belmont Stakes in 1955. Only when Catledge explained the reference in a letter, did Rosenthal realize that the managing editor was talking about bringing him in for breeding purposes, that Catledge had this idea that a great reporter like Rosenthal could sire other great reporters and fill the *Times* newsroom with exciting new talent.

The more Rosenthal thought of returning to America, the more sensible the move seemed. His children would probably receive a better education there. And if he performed well for Catledge on the metropolitan desk, Catledge would owe him his pick of assignments. Rosenthal's dream was to report for the *Times* from London or the Middle East; but because Arab countries weren't receptive to Jewish journalists, the Middle East was effectively eliminated. London seemed at least a possibility, since correspondent Anthony Lewis couldn't stay there forever.

Months after the conversations started, and after Rosenthal realized he was not to get a column, the new metropolitan editor arrived in the *Times* city room: a huge, unpartitioned space with something of the feel of a factory. It contained row after row of steel gray desks with Formica tops and manual typewriters set in wells. The most senior and distinguished writers sat in front. Beginners sat in the back. A public address system summoned reporters to the central editing area.

Having never managed anything larger than a part-time secretary and an interpreter, Rosenthal suddenly had the largest staff on the paper. Given his background in running foreign bureaus, he initially assumed New York would not be so different. "I thought that I was going to be like the man at the head of a big bureau, the New York bureau. . . . I'd be one of the boys. . . . We'd all be very collegial."

Rosenthal soon realized that he had too much impact on his colleagues' lives for them to treat him like one of the boys; and the metro desk was simply too massive to run like a bureau. Though he hated to think of himself as an administrator, he recognized that he had to become one.

Still, no one could make him into a run-of-the-mill bureaucrat. "I didn't come here from Tokyo to countersign overtime slips," he told his administrative assistant. "You take care of it all. I'll back you up. If you've got a problem, let me know. If you get into a mess, it's my fault."

His predecessor, Frank Adams, had spent a lot of time working with his administrative assistant at his desk, facing away from the staff. Rosenthal turned his desk toward the staff. It was a small act, but a signal that he intended to be a news executive not a paper pusher.

For Rosenthal, who had spent so much time away, New York was a glorious new world to explore. Yet, the metro staff was not treating it as such: "We weren't covering the city with a sense of discovery. We were covering it by rote. We weren't thinking up our own assignments. What the AP [Associated Press] covered, we covered."

Rosenthal wanted the *Times* to set its own priorities. And he wanted to see writing that sparkled and reporting that astonished. He wished outstanding young journalists to be rewarded with good assignments, even if that meant denying stories to veteran staffers. And his reporters—for they were now *his* reporters—were to get by-lines, just like those writing for the foreign desk.

Not long after arriving, Rosenthal told Catledge that he wanted more money paid certain reporters, such as Gay Talese, who could mean a lot to the paper.

Catledge, not comprehending the significance of Rosenthal's request, replied, "That's great, just recommend them for raises."

"No, Turner," said Rosenthal. "I'm not talking about ten-percent raises, [or] ten-dollar raises. . . . I mean real money, twenty percent, thirty percent." He handed Catledge a piece of paper and added, "Here is the list of people. These are their salaries. That's not enough. I don't want to inch them up. I want them to know a new day is coming and we're going to pay them."

Catledge glanced at the list and said, "I'll think about it."

A few days later, he gave Rosenthal the go-ahead. The increases were to be called "equalization raises"—a new concept meaning writers were to be paid roughly equivalent to their worth. One reporter received a 40 percent raise. Others were lifted from ten to fifteen thousand dollars a year. Subsequently, Catledge held a meeting of senior editors and said, "I want you to look through all the people, and if you think somebody's not getting paid what [he's worth], you tell me. . . . If you've got a real good person, I'll pay them what you think."

Rosenthal sat in the room smugly listening as sports editor James Roach asked in amazement: "Now, let me get this straight, Turner. . . . You're telling us to pay people what we really think they ought to get?"

"Yes, sir," Catledge replied.

Rosenthal's passion for rewarding young talent stemmed partly from dissatisfaction with his own early treatment. In 1964, he confided to rookie reporter Joseph Lelyveld that he had waited a long time for his first foreign posting. As a result, said Rosenthal, he had promised himself that if he ever attained a position of power, young people would get their shots a good deal earlier. He engineered Lelyveld's transfer from the financial staff to the metro staff. And within a few months, Lelyveld was getting regular front-page assignments—covering the then hot story of racial strife in New York City and elsewhere. Within a year, Lelyveld was on the foreign staff and preparing to go overseas—one of the many beneficiaries of Rosenthal's new order.

As Rosenthal got the results he had fought for—broader coverage, better reporting, more insightful writing—he also began to see the consequences. He had started with no idea of the impact his innovations would have on others: "I thought if you suggested change, and it was a good idea, people would welcome it." He hadn't realized that to suggest change was also to imply fault—or at the very least to indicate that the previous way wasn't good enough. To request a fresh approach to city hall coverage, or a different beat system for the municipal agencies, was—however logical—an attack on the old method. To take away good assignments from someone who had been getting them for years and turn them over to a young hotshot reporter was a rejection of the veteran.

Even after Rosenthal realized the effect he was having, his

goals for the *Times* were so important that he continued to shake things up. "I did it, even when I knew after a while that it was causing pain and unhappiness." And one day as Rosenthal looked across the city room, he thought, "My God . . . there are men out there who don't like me." For the first time he truly felt, deep down in his gut, the personal price demanded of an agent for change.

Rosenthal's approach led not only to dissension on the metro desk but to conflict with other editors, particularly Theodore Bernstein—who, ironically, had first suggested to Catledge that Rosenthal be brought back to New York, though Bernstein had been thinking of him as a reporter, not metro editor.

Bernstein was head of night operations, chief of the "bullpen" (where headlines and story play were decided) and author of *Winners & Sinners* (a periodic in-house publication that highlighted the best and the worst at the *Times*). He was also, as described by one admirer, the "patron saint of editing as a craft." His was the final word on language usage at the *Times.* And desk people—copy editors—considered him something of a deity. To Rosenthal, however, who liked reporters who occasionally broke the rules, Bernstein and his dictates were obstructions. They repressed the writing styles of Rosenthal's flashy reporters and blocked those reporters' stories from getting the play they deserved.

Allan Siegal, then a young editor on the foreign desk, recalls Rosenthal's arrival setting off "fairly vigorous and nasty combat" between Rosenthal's and Bernstein's forces: "Abe Rosenthal represented a kind of journalism that had very little use for desk people and very much glorified the individualists among the reporters—stylists, the flamboyant, the stars. . . . There was a star system in the newsroom that Abe instituted. . . . Not only did desk people, in that apparatus, feel disenfranchised, but [so did] the less flamboyant, workaday reporters . . . some of whom felt very much shunted aside by the new Abe Rosenthal ground rules."

However, for the stylists—Rosenthal's favored reporters—the period was a golden era unlike any the *Times* had seen.

Rumors ran rampant about Rosenthal hiring writers for obscene sums of money. And gossip spread outside the *Times,* sometimes printed in the *Village Voice,* that Rosenthal was a tyrant and that great unhappiness existed on his staff. Upon hearing that a senior *Times* employee was checking on morale in the newsroom, Rosenthal confronted Catledge and said, "Look, Turner. When you brought me back, you didn't give me any instructions except to make a better staff. If you're now changing the instructions to make a better staff consistent with what the staff or you or somebody else might think is [high] morale, that's a different ball game. Those are different instructions. . . . So if you want to change the instructions, please tell me and I'll see if I can do it or want to do it."

Catledge took a moment to respond, but told Rosenthal that he should do exactly what he had been doing. Forthwith, the morale auditor was called off—Catledge having decided that, whatever resentment Rosenthal's reforms were creating, the results were worth it.

Local news was not Catledge's only target for reorganization. Catledge had long lamented the newsroom's lack of central control. Various "dukedoms," as he called them, had developed and the dukes were reluctant to concede power. The night-side editors barely communicated with those on the day side. Foreign news was essentially run by a nephew of the publisher from the Paris bureau. And the Sunday paper was put out by a crew of editors operating autonomously from those who put out the daily. For years, Catledge had sought to bring the baronies under his dominion. But when Sulzberger took office, Catledge still had no authority over the Sunday department, which put out the magazine, the book review, "The Week in Review," and other Sunday features.

For some forty years the Sunday department had been the domain of Lester Markel, a brilliant, headstrong editor who reported directly to the publisher—and had ever since the days of Adolph Ochs. Catledge had repeatedly requested an end to the arrangement. The elder Sulzberger had been unwilling; and although Dryfoos was willing, he insisted on waiting until Markel retired.

Less than two weeks after taking charge, Punch Sulzberger had issued a memo announcing that no major reorganization was forthcoming—confirming that the Sunday department would continue operating as an independent entity. The memo had its intended effect—reassuring a management team worried about the unknown intentions of an untried publisher. But when Sulzberger realized that Markel was in fundamental conflict with Catledge, he resolved to do something about it.

When he consolidated many of the business-side functions in September 1964, he also created the title of executive editor for Catledge, adding the Sunday department to his realm. Realizing that Markel would not wish to report to Catledge, Sulzberger gave Markel the title of associate editor and moved him to the fourteenth floor to serve as an adviser to the publisher and head of a newly created department of public affairs. At the same time, he gave the managing editorship (directly under Catledge) to E. Clifton Daniel, a debonair ex-foreign correspondent married to Margaret (daughter of Harry) Truman and whom Catledge hoped to make his successor.

The *Times* was gradually recovering from the 1962–63 strike. Nineteen sixty-four circulation (740,000 daily and nearly twice that on Sunday) and revenues ($137 million) were at record levels. But newspaper profits (roughly 2 percent before taxes) remained razor thin, though they too were edging upward. Profits went up to nearly 3 percent in 1965, despite a twenty-four-day Newspaper Guild strike; and in 1966, they climbed to nearly 5 percent, with daily circulation approaching nine hundred thousand.

New York's other papers were not faring well. Unable to make a go of it individually, three newspapers announced a merger in March 1966—the *Herald Tribune,* the *World Telegram,* and the *Journal American,* forming World Journal Tribune, Inc. The new company was to publish the *Herald Tribune* in the morning and a combined *World Journal* in the afternoon. But before the first paper came out, its workers went on strike. By the unions' reasoning, they had no contracts with the newborn enterprise (which was to lay off nearly half the forty-six hundred employees of its predecessors).

The strike dragged on for several months; and that August, plans were dropped to publish the *Herald Tribune* (a decision its owners, blaming the unions, said would cost another eight hundred jobs). That September—though the unions were guaranteed no new jobs—the *World Journal Tribune* finally emerged, prompting one industry journal to exclaim: "A journalistic phoenix . . . rose from the ashes of three former New York City newspapers on Monday, September 12." The phoenix lived for less than a year, leaving New York with three daily newspapers—and causing *Times* executives to wonder whether they could somehow turn the situation to their advantage.

With the *Herald Tribune*'s death, Sulzberger's main reason for keeping the *Times* international edition alive disappeared. And with the *Post* as New York's only surviving afternoon paper, an opening conceivably existed for an afternoon *Times* effort.

Some months earlier, Sulzberger had asked Lester Markel to chair a special committee to look at the future of the *New York Times.* It was to be one of many such efforts initiated through the years as the *Times* struggled to redefine itself. A more important assignment in many respects, however, was that subsequently given to Abe Rosenthal, whom Sulzberger appointed to head a secret task force to design a prospective afternoon newspaper.

Rosenthal had been given broader newsroom responsibilities (along with the title of assistant managing editor) and was clearly on the rise. For him, the afternoon newspaper project was not only a signal of trust from the publisher but an opportunity to answer the most fundamental questions in the business: What is sports? What is news? What, indeed, is a newspaper?

Rosenthal also saw the task force as a marvelous means of working with the best editors on the paper. "I knew who was good. I picked them all," he said: sports editor James Roach, news editor Larry Hauck, foreign editor Seymour Topping, and nearly a dozen others. The shared experience of trying to create a newspaper would bind the team's members to each other long after the project ended; for in selecting his group for the afternoon newspaper, Rosenthal was essentially selecting those who would march with him up through the *Times.*

James Greenfield was among them. He and Rosenthal had become fast friends while Greenfield was serving as *Time* magazine bureau chief in New Delhi, India, and Rosenthal was covering the region for the *Times.* The amiable Greenfield had worked as a journalist in London and Washington and as State Department spokesman during the Johnson administration. Most recently he had worked for Continental Airlines, before Rosenthal had brought him to the *Times* (at a significant pay cut and initially without a desk of his own) to serve as one of several assistant metro editors. Greenfield loved being back in journalism, particularly at the *Times.* And like the others, he was thrilled to be tapped for the secret project.

Rosenthal's tongue-in-cheek title for the publication was the *Daily No Bullshit,* reflecting his aspiration for a paper that would tolerate no nonsense. He envisioned the paper reporting a press conference with: "Senator Kennedy yesterday . . . made an announcement about a welfare program. There was nothing new in it and he did it because he thought it would be worth a column in the *New York Times.*"

The group intended a paper much more stylish than the *Times*—something closer, perhaps, to the *London Observer,* full of analysis, sleek writing, and also articles to help the reader enjoy New York. The new daily could not detract from or embarrass the *Times*—or compete directly for the same advertisers.

Though the editors had not worked with a design director previously, they accepted Louis Silverstein (promotion art director for the *Times* since 1952) on the team at Sulzberger's insistence.

"He knew nothing about news. I knew less about design. We used to drive each other crazy," said Rosenthal. At times the editors contemplated strangling their designer, recalls Greenfield, as Silverstein insisted on "telling us how long stories could be and how big pictures had to be, and how many stories had to be [in a particular place]." Despite the conflicts, they managed to work together and over the next year came up with a staggering array of proposals, many of them revolutionary at the time.

Silverstein, for instance, proposed placing small pictures atop the sports section with a short description of the story that ran inside. Though considered heretical by the *Times'* conventional editors, the idea eventually found its way into the *Times.*

At one point, the task force played with a concept called the *New York Day:* a six-column format (compared to the *Times'* eight) heavy on entertainment, culture, personal journalism, and graphics, including cartoons.

Later the group unveiled prototypes for the *Evening Times, New York Today,* and the *New York Forum:* all editorially more fashionable and visually more exciting than the staid *Times.*

Sulzberger, however, pulled the plug. Though Rosenthal was never convinced the ideas received a fair hearing, in October 1967, Sulzberger concluded that the new publication would only give current *Times* clients a cheaper place to advertise.

With difficulty, Rosenthal accepted the verdict, and later sat down with Greenfield and several other team members and said, "We've done a lot of interesting things. We're back on the *Times.* How can we bottle it?" The seed was planted. Like Silverstein's photographs, many of the concepts hatched during that period would surface again.

With his work on the task force and in the newsroom, Greenfield made a strong positive impression on his fellow editors, who appreciated his professionalism and agreeable personality.

Like Rosenthal, Greenfield came from modest circumstances. His mother died when he was young and Greenfield was raised in Cleveland, Ohio, by his father—an orphan and onetime boxer who had not finished grade school, was vocally anti-education, and wanted Jim to be an athlete. Young Greenfield, however, fell in love with writing and managed to get into Harvard. Too poor to volunteer his time for the *Crimson,* he worked instead in the Harvard news office and as a stringer (occasional reporter) for the *Boston Globe.*

By 1967, Greenfield had become a sophisticated, graceful journalist—just the sort of person who might head the *Times* Washington bureau.

Ever since James Reston had stepped down as bureau chief in 1964, Catledge had seen the bureau as a huge problem. Reston's successor, Tom Wicker, was widely viewed as a great journalist but a poor administrator. In Greenfield, Catledge thought he had found a solution.

Wicker would keep his column; Greenfield would manage the bureau. And the *Times* would head into the 1968 political season with a strong team in Washington.

The plans were made and the appropriate staff members notified, with Sulzberger himself going to Washington to break the news to Wicker. But shortly before the changeover was to take place, the deal began to unravel. The Washington bureau revolted against an outsider taking over. And though news of Greenfield's appointment had become public, the publisher reversed himself, leaving Catledge feeling betrayed and Greenfield humiliated.

Greenfield resigned but tried to accept the reversal philosophically. (Years later, he would say, "When I was with the *Times,* I loved everything but the last twenty minutes.") He became vice-president for news with the Westinghouse Broadcasting Company.

Rosenthal and Greenfield remained close. But during the next several months, though they talked often, the *Times* was a forbidden subject. Periodically, Greenfield would talk to Sulzberger as well, who one day called and said, "I want you to come back to the *Times.* And I want you to come back as foreign editor."

Greenfield was moved. Long before the torpedoed Washington assignment, Greenfield had told Sulzberger the foreign editorship was the best job on the paper. This time, Sulzberger had not hedged his bet. He had not said, "Why don't you come over as an assistant to the foreign editor, and if things work out, we'll give you the real job."

Greenfield couldn't help worrying about how the foreign staff would respond to his appointment, but he realized, that in his small time there, the *Times* had become his home in a way that Westinghouse never could.

Since taking office, Sulzberger had searched for a way to stanch the hemorrhaging international edition's losses. Early in 1965, when the *Herald Tribune* had appeared willing to explore a combined edition in Europe, he wrote a memo to his senior executives stating, "We still have the albatross of the IE [international edition] hanging around our necks. At last a possibility of removing it with honor is in sight. We had better hurry with care, for some think the bird is starting to rot."

The following year, Sydney Gruson, the immaculately groomed former foreign news chief, was made editor of the international edition. Gruson, a charming bon vivant, had headed *Times* bureaus in several countries and saw the new assignment as a great excuse to get overseas again.

After the *Herald Tribune* folded, Sulzberger instructed Gruson to talk to its president, Walter Thayer, and determine whether they could do business. Gruson found Thayer receptive, as he did Frederick "Fritz" Beebe, who negotiated on behalf of the Washington Post, which shared ownership of the

Herald Tribune international edition. After six months of conversations and analysis, Gruson recommended that the two papers merge. Sulzberger gave the go-ahead, and within two weeks Gruson had an agreement.

In due time, Gruson was to become publisher, an agreement he and Thayer had reached during a recess in ceremonies to launch the new paper. Sitting on the terrace of Gruson's golf club in Saint Germain, France, they had made plans for the publication, which they confidently expected to be profitable.

Later, at a *Newsweek* bureau reception in Paris, Gruson encountered Katharine Graham and arranged to meet her for tea the next day. During tea, Graham turned to him and pronounced it a pity that no place existed for him at the new newspaper. Surprised, he replied, "Kay, I'm going to be the publisher."

"Oh? I would have known about that if that were to be the case."

He realized then that she was serious and surmised that the Post had objected to a *Times* man playing such a prominent role. Disappointed and angry, he returned to New York and was further enraged to discover, as he put it, "the only thing anyone was prepared to offer me was a desk in the general newsroom just to get reacquainted with the American scene on the grounds that I had not been in America very much of my life and it would be good for me."

Fuming, Gruson called Harry Guggenheim, a social friend and owner of *Newsday.* Over dinner, Guggenheim suggested he speak to Bill Moyers, who had recently been named *Newsday*'s publisher. Gruson and Moyers got along well; and a week later Moyers offered him the position of associate publisher.

Sulzberger objected to his leaving, but Gruson said, "I've given Guggenheim my word." Upon arriving at his new job, he discovered that Sulzberger had written a letter to Guggenheim stating that he had failed to get Gruson to change his mind but that at some point he would have Gruson back.

Almost immediately, Gruson began missing the *Times.* "Most of my journalistic friends were at the . . . *Times.* The world I liked to live in was the *New York Times* world."

Also, Guggenheim, who had always been an arch-conservative Republican, was, in his old age, seeing Communists in the newsroom; and he was pressuring Gruson to fire them. After a while, Gruson grew weary of Guggenheim's demands and called up Sulzberger and said, "If you're ready, I'm ready."

He returned nine months after he'd left and moved into an office on the fourteenth floor as assistant to the publisher. (Moyers left *Newsday* shortly thereafter, when the newspaper was acquired by Times Mirror.)

CHAPTER 14

BUILDING A BUSINESS, TAKING A STAND

In 1964, at the first of many Sulzberger-initiated retreats, *Times* executives resolved to modernize the budget process. A year and a half later, Sulzberger wrote, "I feel that we still rely too much on the Lord." The newspaper's first scientifically produced budget and profit forecast, he added, was 100 percent off the mark: "Luckily, it was in the right direction."

Wherever he looked, Sulzberger saw a system in need of revamping. The business departments lacked computers. Top managers lacked ready successors. And the company—which, in those days, was practically synonymous with the paper—had no real program to break the stranglehold of the unions. Repeatedly, Sulzberger pushed his managers to modernize and to plan the company's future. How could the *Times* automate, despite union objections? How could it continue publishing in the all-but-inevitable event of another strike? What standards should the company apply in acquiring other properties?

The self-analysis was unrelenting, driven by Sulzberger's need for tidy planning and by reminders from treasurer Francis Cox and others that the company's survival was at stake.

New attitudes did not come easily. Sulzberger worked hard, for instance, to get editor Turner Catledge to accept the budget, figuring that if Catledge went along, no business department would dare refuse. Catledge not only embraced the planning concept but endeavored to sell it to his business-side colleagues. A few months later, at the first instance of disagreement, Catledge told an incredulous Sulzberger that he was withdrawing the news department from the budget. Sulzberger apprised Catledge that participation was not exactly voluntary.

That Sulzberger could generate any enthusiasm at all was little short of amazing. For in addition to fighting institutional inertia, he was trying to reorient a management team he had not chosen—and whose members were substantially older and more experienced than he.

The Times' lawyers at Lord, Day & Lord, taking note of the situation, offered to try to be helpful. A bright young associate in their employ had been doing mergers and acquisitions, but in 1963, not many such assignments were coming the firm's way. Why not send the young man over to the Times? Assuming things worked out, he would stay, growing up in the company alongside Sulzberger and helping him steer it into the twentieth century.

James Goodale, seven years younger than Sulzberger and a product of Yale and the University of Chicago Law School, came aboard as general attorney for the Times Company. A trim blond with a restless intellect, Goodale had considered a journalism career before deciding a Wall Street law firm offered more opportunity. Still, when he had gone to Lord, Day & Lord in 1959, he had not given up the dream of eventually helping to run an influential newspaper—or perhaps serving in government.

Like Sulzberger, Goodale believed the *Times* was much too vulnerable to its unions and to economic caprice. And as he became more familiar with the corporation, he concluded that part of the problem lay within the culture of the Times. The company had been run for years as the quintessential family concern, neither needing nor really desiring to make a profit, "as long as it got the paper out every day and as long as the company broke even or made a little money" and dividends were paid. Though supportive of Sulzberger's efforts, Goodale believed they were doomed to fail unless accompanied by external pressure.

"I felt that unless the company was public with people looking at its numbers, [it] would never emerge from the family cocoon state that it was in." If the corporation's numbers were scrutinized by outside investors, it would have to become more businesslike and, in the long run, would benefit. A public offering would also generate some much needed cash, both for the *New York Times* and for Adolph Ochs's original paper, the *Chattanooga Times,* which was still in family hands and losing money.

Sulzberger was also concerned about the estate taxes that inevitably would come due. When they did, Adolph Ochs's heirs would either have to break up the company, sell it, or find some way to get money out of it while leaving it intact. Going public would permit them to keep the corporation together and give Times management a convenient way to share ownership with employees and make cash available for acquisitions.

Goodale recalls one strong argument against going public. A great premium was placed on the *Times*' ability to "control its own destiny in editorial matters, not in any sense subject to the demands of Wall Street." Against that objective had to be weighed the ability of the company to move forward as a business.

As Goodale recalls, "We had no cash. We couldn't borrow, because if we borrowed the unions would . . . say, 'Hey, we'll shut you down and we'll bankrupt you.' The only way out of the situation was to diversify and diversify big, and build up a hunk of income that . . . was going to keep you alive if the unions went [out]."

Long before the debate over going public, the company had made some modest efforts at diversification. For years, the Times had owned radio station WQXR. It established a small book division in 1963 and bought a 49 percent interest in a pulp and paper company in Quebec in 1964. It also acquired a controlling interest in a company that developed educational materials for the general market.

Those purchases had already severed a link with the past; for Adolph Ochs, desiring to keep the *Times* pure, had refused to diversify as a matter of principle.

Still, purchasing a few businesses and getting listed on a major stock exchange were fundamentally different propositions. Buying businesses did not require surrendering anything other than money. But going public might mean giving up a great deal more. Like a private castle turned into a showcase for tourists, the Times risked debasing itself for cash.

As discussions went on among the lawyers, managers, and family, the questions and answers weaved themselves together. How could the Times take advantage of the financial markets and still retain the prerogatives of family ownership? The answer, in concept, was absurdly simple: by not selling control along with the stock. Something of a precedent had already been established. Under the advice of Sulzberger family lawyer General Edward Greenbaum and financial adviser George Woods (former head of First Boston Corporation and later of the World Bank), the family had already issued a substantial quantity of nonvoting Class A stock. Some of the voting Class B shares had been issued as well, but the overwhelming majority of those remained in family hands.

Greenbaum had suggested privately selling yet more shares of nonvoting stock. Goodale objected, arguing that instead of offering stock privately, the Times should go public with the nonvoting Class A stock; and it should give that stock enough voting rights to satisfy the American Stock Exchange and to receive favorable treatment from the Internal Revenue Service. (The New York Stock Exchange would not list shares with only limited voting rights.) Meanwhile, the controlling stock would remain right where it was—principally in the trust set up by Adolph Ochs.

The same plan was later used by the Washington Post and a number of other media companies, but Goodale had no model at the time. Still, he was confident that it would succeed in generating cash while also assuring the family it could "control the company with a very small part of the stock but with a very huge vote." It could also, Sulzberger concluded, provide a means to pass the company along "generation after generation . . . without a forced sale."

Sulzberger announced in September 1968 that the Times was considering offering Class A stock on the American Stock Exchange "at an appropriate time." On December 3, the company went ahead with the offering (which was handled by First Boston Corporation) of some 640,000 shares at fifty-three dollars a share. It sold out the first day, reducing the trust's holdings to just over 50 percent of the Class A stock. The trust continued to hold 65 percent of the full voting Class B stock.

That same year, the company acquired Arno Press, a publisher of reprints selling primarily to libraries. It bought *Golf Digest* and Quadrangle Books (later changed to Times Books) and launched its own set of encyclopedias the following year. In

1970, Sulzberger began negotiations for its biggest acquisition to date.

The talks were suggested by a Times executive who thought Cowles Communications—minus its foundering *Look* magazine—might be quite a prize. Sulzberger was intrigued enough to set up a meeting with co-owner Mike Cowles at which he asked, "Would you ever consider selling your company to the New York Times?"

"Yes," Cowles replied, "everything but *Look,*" knowing full well that the Times would never take the problem-plagued publication.

Even without *Look,* Cowles Communications was enormous—containing *Family Circle,* a textbook company, several newspapers in Florida, a CBS-affiliated television station in Memphis, and a group of medical magazines.

The acquisition cost some 2.6 million shares (nearly one fourth of those outstanding) of Class A stock, valued at over fifty million dollars, but it gave the Times a foothold in several new markets and a new vision of itself. "We started to grow from there," says Sulzberger.

Goodale's analysis is decidedly more explicit: "That Cowles deal saved our ass. . . . And we couldn't have done it, if we didn't have the public stock."

Katharine Darrow, a young lawyer who joined Goodale's staff in 1970, was amazed at the company's small size and parochialism. But within months, as work on the Cowles acquisition proceeded, she saw the organization undergoing a fundamental change: "A really very small place, in every sense of the word, was . . . going to become a major publishing conglomerate. Just the size of the deal and the papers connected with it made it obvious to me . . . that this was a watershed . . . for the New York Times Company."

The corporation, she realized, would be forced to manage enterprises of a sort to which it had never given serious thought previously, businesses that—unlike the *New York Times*—had making money as their principal purpose. While the company considered the *Times* "a present which we offer every day to the world community," the same could not be said of those small newspapers in Florida, or *Family Circle.* Decent though those publications might be, they were not hallowed like the *Times.*

The acquisition, Darrow concluded, "made people more open about the New York Times [Company] . . . more able to accept change in the institution. . . . And maybe it made it easier to accept changes in the newspaper itself."

As the Cowles merger was concluding, another major explosion rocked the *Times.* The shock originated in the newsroom, detonated by a report that came to be known as the Pentagon Papers.

Whereas the Papers episode gave the *Washington Post* an opportunity to redefine itself (to prove that it could stand as a virtual equal with the greatest paper in the land), the stakes for the *New York Times* were much higher. The *Times,* after all, broke the story. And while the *Post* was comparing itself with the *Times,* the *Times* was measuring itself against its own image and ideals. "If we hadn't done it," Sulzberger would later conclude, "people would have said the spunk and fight have gone out of the *New York Times.*"

Sulzberger did not anticipate the government's brutal counterattack. He expected, perhaps, a blistering speech from Vice-President Spiro Agnew or an assault on the *Times'* credibility by President Richard Nixon.

Rosenthal and his editors were considerably more apprehensive. To Rosenthal, the continued existence of the *Times* hung in the balance; for if citizens perceived publishing the papers as an unpatriotic act, they might revolt against the *Times.* Allan Siegal, one of the editors who helped prepare the papers for publication, believed it possible that President Nixon "would denounce us for treason, the public would believe it, and the *New York Times* would be destroyed."

Despite all the potential problems, Rosenthal was convinced that refusing to print the papers would be irresponsible. And in early 1971, as the *Times* wrestled with the question, Rosenthal's perspective counted for a great deal.

Far faster than anyone had foreseen, Rosenthal had become king of the newsroom, winning Sulzberger's nod over E. Clifton Daniel, who Turner Catledge had hoped would succeed him. In the abstract, Daniel had seemed the perfect chief editor of the *New York Times.* A very attractive and imposing man, he radiated an aura of omniscience. "He had the most amazing opaque manner," one associate recalled, "so you never knew what was going on in his head." But Daniel was also imperious and abrupt and Sulzberger was never quite comfortable with him.

So after Catledge left the executive editor's job in June 1968, Sulzberger named James Reston to take his place. A two-time Pulitzer Prize winner and former Washington bureau chief, Reston was probably the only journalist on the *Times* with sufficient prestige to move in over Daniel. The following year, Reston returned to Washington, having decided he could not write a decent thrice-weekly column while working as editor of the paper. Reston was given the largely honorary title of vice-president for news, the *Times* announcing the move as "another step . . . to give increasing authority and responsibility to talented younger executives on our staff." At that point, Rosenthal was named managing editor, reporting directly to the publisher. Daniel was named associate editor ("to develop improved methods of news presentation in a wide variety of categories") but no longer had authority over the newsroom, making Rosenthal, in effect, the highest-ranking news executive on the paper.

Once reporter Neil Sheehan acquired the Pentagon Papers, Rosenthal's involvement was assured. And given Rosenthal's sense of journalistic duty, a constitutional confrontation loomed.

Sheehan, a Harvard graduate and former Vietnam War correspondent, had been outraged by the growing U.S. involvement in Vietnam and the governmental conspiracy to cover it up. After returning to the United States, Sheehan was assigned to the *Times* Washington bureau, where he encountered Daniel Ellsberg—also a Harvard graduate who had spent time in Vietnam and had been sickened by the behavior of the men behind the war.

Ellsberg had helped produce an official (though classified) history of the Vietnam conflict for Defense Secretary Robert McNamara. He had tried, without success, to interest the Senate Foreign Relations Committee in releasing the study publicly. Finally, in desperation, he had gone to Sheehan—who, early in 1971, spent several days (and fifteen hundred dollars) in Cambridge, Massachusetts, with his wife copying Ellsberg's mammoth report.

Rosenthal's great fear was that the papers were fake, that some kids at Harvard—or worse, at Students for a Democratic

Society—had conjured up the documents in order to embarrass the *New York Times.* He imagined such a group sitting around a desk and plotting: "Okay, you be the CIA and I'll be the Joint Chiefs, and we'll [fake these papers and] dump them on the . . . *Times.*" He relied heavily on Greenfield, with his years of government experience, to verify the authenticity of the documents.

Greenfield quickly concluded the papers were legitimate, and, indeed, discovered, among the volumes, cables that he himself had signed off on. But worried lest the *Times* inadvertently reveal some crucial secrets, he had *Times* editors cross-check information in the papers against scores of books and articles written by former government officials. The process revealed that despite the material's "top secret" classification, the information had been aired to a fare-thee-well by former agents of the government. "We weren't starting something," said Greenfield, "[those officeholders] in their books had gabbed beyond belief about their conversations within the government."

As Sheehan and what grew to be a team of twenty others toiled in secret, James Goodale was consulted. He agreed the papers should be published. But his former colleagues at the Times' law firm were adamantly opposed—so much so they declared that if the *Times* insisted on publishing top-secret papers, it would do so without the representation of Lord, Day & Lord.

The Washington Post's lawyers had also been opposed, but they had stayed on until after the papers were published and the legal battles fought, not leaving while the company was in the midst of deciding how to proceed. Goodale, however, could not sway Lord, Day & Lord and—at the eleventh hour—recruited the firm of Cahill Gordon to assist in the *Times'* defense.

As Goodale worked through the legal mine fields, Sheehan and a legion of editors whipped the mass of material into shape. The original articles consisted largely of analyses and paraphrases from the documents, but *Times* editors rejected those pieces. By then Rosenthal and his colleagues had decided that the *Times* had to print the actual text. "Maybe they will argue with our analysis of the Pentagon Papers," reasoned Rosenthal. "Let them argue with the text." Stories summarizing the papers were meticulously annotated by Allan Siegal and others, but the heart of the *Times* report would consist of the documents themselves.

The *Times* men, working in secret at the New York Hilton, feared news of the project would leak out and they would be arrested. For Rosenthal, in particular, the pressure was agonizing. The *Times,* he knew, was breaking totally new ground—for itself and for the American press. In declassifying government documents, the newspaper was saying, in effect, that the government's right to secrecy was superseded by the public's right to know. The papers were much more than a great news story; they were a historical treasure, showing how one presidential administration after another had secretly laid the groundwork that had pulled the country into Vietnam. Once those papers were published, no one could write a history of Vietnam without them, and no one could look upon the government in quite the same way as before.

On Sunday, June 13, 1971, the *Times* published its first excerpts, along with stories by Neil Sheehan and Hedrick Smith describing the study and its origins. Sheehan's dry, matter-of-fact prose summed up the documents with little elaboration, giving no insight into the turmoil the papers had set off at the *Times:* "A massive study of how the United States went to war in Indochina, conducted by the Pentagon three years ago, demonstrates that four administrations progressively developed a sense of commitment to a non-Communist Vietnam, a readiness to fight the North to protect the South, and an ultimate frustration with this effort—to a much greater extent than their public statements acknowledged at the time."

That Monday morning, Sulzberger (who had made a point of carrying on with business as usual) left for London for a previously scheduled trip concerning the company's magazines. He was awakened in his hotel room later that evening by a call from the *Times* informing him that Attorney General John Mitchell had sent a telegram requesting that the *Times* halt further publication of the documents. After listening to the arguments, Sulzberger gave the order to continue.

Washington bureau chief Max Frankel had been summoned to New York, lest he be served with papers in Washington for a case the Times was preparing to defend on its home turf. While there, Frankel typed out an affidavit that described in detail how various government sources routinely leaked classified documents when it suited their purposes. That affidavit was to play a key role in convincing the courts that the Times' position had merit.

That Tuesday, the government won a temporary restraining order blocking further publication, which was overturned by the Supreme Court later in the month.

The encounter, Rosenthal later concluded, forever extended the boundaries of news: "If something is going to affect the public, then that is news." Though the papers had been stolen, the information they contained belonged to the public all along. While the case did not license newspapers to print troop movements or other information that could get people killed, he believed it did license them to look the executive branch squarely in the eye and reject its rules when they made no sense.

For Goodale, the case was a fitting climax to an exceptional year. Not only had he worked on the Cowles acquisition, but on a case involving *Times* reporter Earl Caldwell, from whom the Justice Department was seeking his sources for stories on the Black Panthers. Then the Pentagon Papers had come along.

If the *Times* had not published them, said Goodale, "it would have been the complete turning point in the history of journalism."

Greenfield saw the events in less sweeping terms. They helped change the view that the press was an arm of government. And the months of clandestine labor proved the *Times* could keep a secret. But "did anyone learn anything from the Pentagon Papers? I doubt it. Look at Iran."

Sulzberger also thought the impact of the papers was limited. The adventure had served as a great tonic: "It revitalized the staff to a great extent."

One revitalized staffer was Allan Siegal, a leader of the Pentagon Papers editing team. A native of the Bronx, where his father had owned and operated a truck that delivered seltzer and soda water, Siegal had intended to become a high school English teacher. But at New York University he discovered the journalism department with its teachers, largely former journalists, from a world he thought glamorous and wanted to join.

He was hired as a copyboy at the *Times*—where he would carry finished copy from the editing desk to a pneumatic tube that took it to the composing room. Often, he would read the copy as he walked, and sometimes he would return to the editor to point out a mistake. His knack for catching oversights led to his being given a crack at editing and to his assignment to the prestigious foreign desk. When the Newspaper Guild went out on strike, Siegal waived his strike benefits and refused to walk the picket line; though he belonged to the Guild, picketing the *Times* was an act of sacrilege.

He had considered working on the Pentagon Papers a privilege, a judgment validated when the *Times* won a Pulitzer for its efforts. Sulzberger had a replica made for each member of the team. Some sixteen years after the papers were published, Siegal stared at his framed replica, touched it, and said softly, "Editors don't win Pulitzer Prizes. . . . It's a nice thing for an editor to have on his wall."

New York Times

Arthur Ochs Sulzberger

A. M. Rosenthal

Allan Siegal

Max Frankel

Arthur Ochs Sulzberger, Jr.

Katharine Darrow

Walter Mattson

Jack Rosenthal

CHAPTER 15

REMAKING THE *TIMES*

Like a ship being pulled by a tugboat, the *Times* was responding, with magisterial slowness, to Sulzberger's insistent nudging. But though the *Times* was changing, the market was changing as well—and, in many respects, more quickly and more profoundly than the paper.

For a while, financial success had seemed assured. Lance Primis, a retail advertising salesman in 1969, recalls that so many advertisers were trying to get in the paper that year, he had to tell some, "We can't run your ad. No room." By the time the paper had adapted to accommodate the ads, the first of the 1970s recessions had hit.

Even as revenues—boosted by acquisitions—increased, profit margins remained low. The corporation earned $9.5 million on revenues of $291 million in 1971. Four years later, it was earning $12.8 million on revenues of $390 million—an abysmal performance for a major newspaper company. And with New York City itself on the verge of bankruptcy, only the most drastic steps promised to turn the *Times* around.

Sulzberger was prepared to take such steps; and he had a strong ally in Walter Mattson.

Six years younger than Sulzberger, Mattson was a tall, no-nonsense executive with an encyclopedic knowledge of newspaper production. A native of Erie, Pennsylvania, he had grown up working in the printing office of his uncle's weekly. Through much of high school and college, he had earned extra money as a printer, always assuming accounting would be his profession. Finance fascinated him and he was good at it. But by the time he got out of the marines, his career plans were a muddle. For some inexplicable reason, he didn't like accounting anymore. So after finishing his degree in business, he became advertising manager for his uncle's two weeklies near Pittsburgh.

His wife hated Pittsburgh. And Mattson disliked working for his uncle. "You never know if you're doing okay because you're working for your uncle, or you're doing okay because you're doing okay." Mattson, still in his twenties, left for Boston. His wife's family lived nearby and Boston was big enough to offer plenty of opportunity.

Mattson found a production position with the Boston *Herald-Traveler* and later worked in commercial printing and as a consultant in graphic arts—picking up an associate's degree in electrical engineering at Northeastern University in his free time.

The constant travel involved in consulting left little time for his family, and he accepted a job in production with the *Wall Street Journal* that offered more opportunity for a home life. But after he and his wife spent a night in crowded, dirty New York, they decided they could not live there. That Monday morning, he called to turn down the position.

When the *New York Times* made an offer, Mattson refused, citing dislike of the city. Over the next several months, he realized he hated living out of a suitcase even more. The *Times* called again, offering more money and a better assignment, and he said yes. In February 1960, at the age of twenty-seven, he started as assistant production manager.

Mattson quickly gained a reputation as a hands-on manager who could move into a department and whip it into shape, and who even knew how to repair the machines on which his men worked. He went to Los Angeles to help with the *Times*' western edition and returned to New York to shape up the composing room and engraving department.

He was made a vice-president in 1970, senior vice-president two years later, and in 1974 became general manager of the *Times.* Like Sulzberger, he felt surrounded by risks. New York was going broke. Readers were leaving the city. Circulation was fragile. Advertising was weak. Suburban competition was increasing. "It was pretty clear that we had to put our house in order."

The first step was negotiating labor peace. And in May 1974, he worked out an agreement with printers union leader Bertram Powers.

The next step was cleaning house. Sitting in the den in the publisher's suite that September, he told Sulzberger that the department managers were too weak for the *Times* of the future; he asked for a year to bring in a totally fresh team—a new advertising director, circulation director, production chief—top-notch executives to turn the place around. Sulzberger consented. The last replacement arrived just two days short of a year.

One recruit was Donald Nizen, a blunt iconoclast with a working-class Brooklyn voice who had been circulation director for the *Times*' west coast edition before going to the *Miami Herald.* He enjoyed working at the *Herald,* where—unlike in New York—new ideas could be implemented without approval from a thousand different unions; and he wasn't sure he wanted to leave. What, he asked Sulzberger, was the newspaper's "marketing position"? Sulzberger shrugged and replied that he did not know, that perhaps Nizen could help them figure it out.

Later, at the Algonquin Hotel, he met Rosenthal, who, bubbling with enthusiasm over the latest edition, gushed, "Isn't this the most exciting, dramatic front page of any newspaper you've ever seen in your life?"

"No. I think it's kind of boring and cluttered," Nizen shot back. Fully aware that Rosenthal was growing angry, Nizen pushed on, asserting that the paper would look better with a six-column format instead of eight, and that it should have more pictures and fewer stories that jumped inside. Also, the *Times* was totally missing the boat with entertainment and cultural coverage by running such stories on Sunday instead of Friday. Anybody planning for the weekend was out of luck. Why not produce a Friday package for the weekend?

Rosenthal lashed out at the inability of the idiots in marketing and circulation to sell such a great paper as the *Times.* And Nizen left convinced that he had alienated Rosenthal. He was shocked when Rosenthal called that weekend and asked him to join the newspaper. The call convinced Nizen to accept the job;

and the argument with Rosenthal grew into a series of discussions.

Rosenthal pressed Nizen for ideas on the special weekend package. Adding "Weekend," Nizen speculated, would mean printing a four-section paper instead of the current two—since the press was not equipped to produce a paper in three sections.

"You can have 'Weekend' in ninety days," Rosenthal announced at one point. And in April 1976, true to his word, Rosenthal unveiled it—a potpourri of features on Broadway, opera, art galleries, jazz, and sundry activities in New York and environs. The first of the *Times'* so-called C (or third) sections, it was unlike anything that had appeared in the weekday paper before. It was agreeably stylish and made liberal use of graphics and photographs. And in an unusual departure for the typically serious *Times,* "Weekend" suggested frivolous activities for readers.

The section immediately increased Friday circulation by thirty-five thousand. Nizen, like a proud parent, glowed with satisfaction. Yet many of the ideas that went into "Weekend" had been kicking around well before Nizen and Rosenthal sat down at the Algonquin Hotel. Some originated with the afternoon newspaper project. Others came from previously held meetings and study groups focusing on the *Times'* future.

A series of such meetings had recently taken place in Tarrytown, New York. Walter Mattson, among others, had lectured on the need for increased profits. At the same time, *Times* executives were absorbing the findings from a huge market study that found readers weren't getting as much out of the newspaper as they wished. More chillingly, it showed that even faithful supporters read the *Times* significantly less than they themselves thought.

The *Times* was already experimenting with modest change. The paper had grown so large that it was difficult to print in two sections. And editors had worked with the production department on a method of publishing the paper in four. Also, weeks before launching "Weekend," the *Times* had gone to a six-column format—which was becoming the standard for newspapers across the country. The *Times* had switched very carefully, lest the readers become alarmed at the transformation.

"We kept playing with the type and playing with the pictures until we couldn't tell the difference between the eight-column *Times* . . . and the six-column *Times,*" recalls James Greenfield.

The talk of sickly *Times* profits had made the editors very nervous. Rosenthal and Seymour Topping (Rosenthal's deputy) decided they had to develop a more exciting paper that would attract more readers and revenue. Otherwise, they feared, the publisher would one day tell them, "Your news budget is going to be cut."

Previously, the news department would come up with ideas only to be shot down by the more cautious business departments. But with Mattson's new team in place, said Topping, the business side "was ready to engage with us. They were willing to take risks . . . that the previous business establishment had not been willing to take." They were, in fact, demanding that the *Times* shake itself out of the doldrums.

With "Weekend" such a phenomenal success, Rosenthal and Mattson decided to launch other C sections.

Arthur Gelb, a former drama critic who had become metropolitan editor, was given responsibility for coordinating their creation. But much as the editors wanted commercial success and the additional readers the new sections might bring, they were terrified of creating a monster that would alter the basic nature of the *Times.*

Early on they decided that regardless of the areas covered by the C sections—from home design to food preparation—the articles would reflect *Times* standards. They would not be mere listings of recipes and events. "Abe [Rosenthal] and I would sit there and argue whether this picture of a fish was better than that picture of a fish . . . with the same vehemence we argued on Washington stories," recalled Greenfield.

Uncertain of reader response, Rosenthal proposed putting entertainment, television, and culture in every C section—not just Friday's. "I had a terror of them saying, I'm not interested in 'Living,' or whatever, and throwing it away. But if you put entertainment and culture in the back, they can't throw the damn thing away."

The *Times* launched "The Living Section" in November 1976, with tips on painting, cooking, and "planning a pool for your apartment."

"For the very first time," said Mattson, "we were willing to acknowledge that people who read the *New York Times* ate." "Home" came out in March 1977, with articles on furniture, home design, and reducing heating costs with solar heat. In January 1978, "SportsMonday" debuted, and in May of that year, "Business Day" appeared—a self-contained daily presentation of business news and analysis, the fourth section of the four-section paper.

As executives rejoiced—and the new publications pulled in readers and advertisers—many journalists were horrified. The new "soft" sections appeared, in the words of one, "a corruption of everything we stood for." Even those who generally supported the changes saw disturbing aspects.

Joseph Lelyveld, one of Rosenthal's young stars, was among them. After serving tours in South Africa and India, Lelyveld had voluntarily left the foreign desk to rediscover the United States, which had seen the arrival of a sexual revolution, an antiwar movement, and hippies while he was away. Upon returning, he had been entrusted with some of the hottest stories of the day (Chappaquiddick, Woodstock, New York's education crisis) and was later given an American scenes column in the magazine.

Initially, he had been encouraged by the C sections and the accompanying format changes, which signaled a breaking down of rigid barriers and perhaps a greater freedom for writers. Instead, he found the editing more heavy-handed and sensed an attitude that said: If the *Times* is going to have all of that soft stuff—those long articles on guacamole and gazpacho—then the hard news "had better be very hard," meaning a loss of flexibility for those reporters who wrote it. In addition, the newsroom was becoming more bureaucratic, adding layers of deputy and assistant editors. "Though the paper was developing in a very positive way, internally something was going a little wrong, at least for people like me."

The internal dynamics of the paper was not the only thing going awry. Rosenthal wasn't enthusiastic about Lelyveld's column, and the necessity of "popping up somewhere in America every week" to write it was disrupting Lelyveld's family life. Lelyveld told Greenfield he might like a change; Greenfield suggested he become deputy foreign editor.

Until then, Lelyveld had never really thought of editing, had never even understood why a good reporter would want to be an editor, but at that juncture, editing offered a noble escape. And he resolved to use his new post to fight for the writers, like himself, who were being crushed by the weight of the changing *New York Times.*

As *Times* executives debated the character of the fifth and final C section in mid-1978, another strike intruded on the New York newspaper world. Following a walkout by *New York Daily News* editorial and commercial workers, management published without them. Rocks and bottles were thrown at the delivery trucks, whose drivers had crossed picket lines. The third day, the Newspaper Deliverers Union stopped carrying the paper, citing violence and danger. The strike ended after five days, having established, beyond a doubt, that a newspaper could be printed (even if not distributed) during a strike.

The pressmen (with the other unions' support) struck the three New York newspapers that August, taking issue with management's plans to reduce, through attrition, the number of pressmen on a press. The publishers stood firm, convinced that the war over staffing levels and automation had to be fought. Late in September, the *Post* reached a separate agreement, placing pressure on the *Times* and *News* to settle. In mid-October, the *Times* reached a tentative settlement of some of the issues—job guarantees and reduced manning through attrition. The paper began publishing again in November.

The agreement ushered in a new era of labor relations, forming—as the more brutal *Washington Post* conflict had done—a foundation for modernizing production of the newspaper.

Against the background of the printers strike, a much quieter battle had raged inside the paper. The news and business departments were at odds over the final C section. Advertising was pushing for a fashion spread. But Rosenthal felt the paper was at a tipping point. The readers had accepted all the soft sections so far, but now was time for a serious section, one that would cause readers to say, "By God, that's the *New York Times.*" He thought of his good friend Theodore White, author of the *Making of the President* books. "Teddy had kept faith, even when he saw the asparagus stories." But Teddy rated something more substantial. Rosenthal did not want the *Times* to lose money, but it could not sacrifice its integrity.

The interruption in publication was an additional reason to

come back with a really hard section that would make readers take notice. A science package, he thought, would do that nicely.

During the strike, some management employees painted the presses and locker room, attempting to create a pleasant atmosphere for the workers' eventual return. Rosenthal's team made improvements in the metropolitan report, but their real priority was the science section. Despite the business departments' objections, Rosenthal continued to work on it, figuring out schemes to succeed despite business-side opposition: "I knew that once 'Science Times' came out, there was no turning back."

Donald Nizen, who controlled the promotion budget, listened one day as Rosenthal explained his concept. " 'Science Times'?" asked Nizen. Who in the world would read it? Who would buy advertising in it? Test tube and beaker manufacturers weren't exactly big *Times* spenders.

Nizen had gotten the two sections he wanted—"SportsMonday" and "Weekend." Advertising had gotten its sections with "Home" and "Living." Maybe the editorial guys deserved a shot. But he didn't like the idea of money walking out the door. And he had a weapon to use. He threatened not to promote the section.

Mattson kept the peace, pointing out that Rosenthal, indeed, was owed a section. And how, at any rate, could Nizen promote four days and not the fifth?

"Science Times" came out after the strike, and at first, advertising executives couldn't figure out how to sell it. Later on, they suggested a computer columnist, as a bridge into the growing personal computer market. They also discovered the section attracted readers willing to study detailed advertising copy—making it a perfect place for a company such as Mercedes Benz to explain a new disk brake system. Before long the section was generating enough revenue to satisfy the advertising department.

As the new format and special sections took shape, Sulzberger tackled another piece of unfinished business. Years earlier, he had promoted managing editor Turner Catledge to executive editor in hopes of unifying the Sunday and daily departments. Instead, as Sulzberger saw it, Catledge had been seduced. "What he did . . . was fall in love with the Sunday department."

Catledge had left the department largely untouched; and in April 1976, with change already exploding all about, Sulzberger announced the joining of the news and Sunday departments under Rosenthal.

"Like all institutions, the *Times* has been shaped by many forces, some perceived, some accidental," said Sulzberger, explaining the change to readers. "As a result, we were blessed by a vigorous and creative Sunday department that came to produce 5 of the 10 sections that now make up the Sunday paper: the *Magazine, The Book Review, Arts and Leisure, Travel* and *The Week in Review*. . . .

"We have reached the moment when there is no longer any conceptual division between the works of the two departments. . . . This merger will enable us to pool the talents of our staff so as to enhance all sections, prepare for new journalistic ventures, and better exploit the new technology which we are introducing."

At the time, the Sunday department was headed by former Washington bureau chief Max Frankel, a caring intellectual whom colleagues sometimes found emotionally elusive. "You feel you have this invitation to intimacy and then you bounce up against this velvet wall," observed one.

Following the uproar over the aborted James Greenfield appointment, Tom Wicker had stepped down as Washington bureau chief. Frankel, who replaced him, was determined to play peacemaker. Washington's revolt against New York had embarrassed the *Times* before the world. The bureau still felt pushed around and abused. Frankel had an unquestioned commitment to the *Times* but also the confidence of those in the bureau; and he thought that he could bridge the gap between Washington and New York.

Like Rosenthal, Frankel had grown up at the *Times.* And he had decided on journalism early—within a few years after emigrating to the United States. Born in Gera, Germany, Frankel had come to America at the age of ten, following a long and difficult journey, via Poland, from Adolph Hitler's Germany. His family had settled in Washington Heights, a working-class uptown Manhattan neighborhood largely made up of immigrants. A high school English teacher had introduced him to journalism as a way of stimulating his interest in the readings for her class. Makeup, pictures, writing, interviewing opened up a great new world. He became editor of the student newspaper at Columbia University, and more important, he became the Columbia correspondent for the *Times.*

Within a few years of starting as a full-time reporter, Frankel was dispatched to Austria to report on the Polish and Hungarian rebellions, and in 1957, while still in his twenties, he became the paper's Moscow correspondent. Russia exerted a profound influence on him, forcing Frankel to digest and interpret for his audience some basic questions of politics and freedom. Why were the Soviets so patriotic despite their abuse by Stalin? How did a nation change from one system to another? Were the Russians really becoming more like Americans, or would they forever be in another world? "You can't come back to your own society and look at it in the calm way or the unexamining way that you did before," he later observed.

By 1961, Frankel was in Washington, having covered the Caribbean and the United Nations. He liked the feeling of reporting on events from the center of the world. And a vigorous young president and the spirit of the New Frontier made Washington even more exciting.

He quickly established himself as a bureau standout. His name even came up as a possible replacement when James Reston stepped down as bureau chief. Instead, Tom Wicker was selected. The Friday after the appointment, Frankel wrote a letter of resignation. After reflection, he decided he could not leave the *Times* and withdrew his resignation the following Monday.

The notion got around that Frankel had resigned in anger over Wicker's appointment. Frankel would later say that his reason wasn't so simple. The *Reporter* magazine had made him a very substantial offer, an opportunity, as he read it, to inherit the publication from its editor, Max Ascoli. The discussion of his becoming Ascoli's successor had gone on for months and merely happened to coincide with Wicker's appointment. "It looked terrible, as if I were running away in protest against what was happening at the time," he said. "I wasn't happy about what happened at the *Times,* but that was relatively minor."

The idea of heading the bureau had definite appeal—but primarily because the job came with a column. "I saw that Reston became bureau chief and got a column. Tom Wicker became bureau chief and got a column. And that seemed to be the way to do it." As Washington boss, Frankel channeled his taste for column writing into analytical news pieces—for which he won a Pulitzer Prize for international reporting after traveling with President Nixon to China.

When asked to come to New York and run the Sunday department, Frankel was surprised; but he prepared to return to New York by the end of 1972, just as Watergate was exploding in Washington.

Frankel arrived with little knowledge of the Sunday operation and no experience in running a department; but the more he learned, the more convinced he became that the Sunday department shouldn't exist—that having so many important publications divorced from what was happening at the daily paper was, at best, illogical.

He also, much to his dismay, became ensnared in office politics. Though Reston was no longer executive editor, Rosenthal had not been given the title. Reports became rampant that Rosenthal and Frankel were locked in combat for the position. At some point, Frankel had indeed been told one reason for his New York assignment was to develop his management ability. Still, the rumors were dispiriting and more than a bit ridiculous. For if he was fighting a battle with Rosenthal, the odds were most uneven.

"I had no troops. . . . All the troops were in the news department putting out the daily paper. And once the idea spread, somehow . . . that I was put there to compete with [Rosenthal, the situation] became even more strained, because he wasn't about to let the Sunday department benefit from the talent that was in his army. He made a point of telling people he didn't want to read anything in 'The Week in Review' that he hadn't read in the daily first, and [he was] not making writers available for the magazine. We were begging and borrowing. . . . He could assign . . . three reporters to take three months to look at a situation and write a big blockbuster in the daily, and I could afford to pay somebody two thousand dollars for a magazine piece that would take just as long."

Frankel was not a natural warrior. Faced with battle, he sometimes judged it wiser to walk away. In junior high school, for instance, a gang of thugs had repeatedly stolen his pens. At first Frankel had lied to his mother about the loss, but he finally turned the gang in to the teacher—so enraging the toughs that they started beating Frankel every afternoon. He insisted on being transferred, having concluded he could neither win the fights nor go to school shaking every day.

As the news department prepared for "Weekend's" debut, Frankel knew the time had come to retreat. He told Sulzberger and Mattson that "Weekend" was, in essence, another version of Sunday's "Arts and Leisure"; he and Rosenthal inevitably would be competing for the same critics and reviewers. Frankel traces the dismantling of the Sunday department to that discussion.

Intense as the politics were around the Sunday department, those swirling around Frankel's next assignment were even more so. After several months of travel, domestically and abroad, Frankel was to become chief of the editorial page, replacing John Oakes—Sulzberger's cousin—who had edited the page for fifteen years.

Sulzberger had grown uneasy with the editorials. They were too predictable and too antibusiness. The change he decided to make, however, was to exert an awful emotional price and would take on the appearance of a bloodbath.

After deciding to consolidate the Sunday and daily staffs, Sulzberger had persuaded Oakes to step aside to make room for Frankel and to come upstairs as a senior vice-president and adviser to the publisher. Oakes, a Rhodes scholar who had been valedictorian at Princeton University and a highly decorated World War II veteran, was roughly a year away from mandatory retirement.

Oakes had assembled a spirited editorial page staff. Among its members was Roger Wilkins, who had resigned from the *Washington Post* over what he considered editorial page editor Phil Geyelin's rude and racist behavior. When Wilkins had gone to the *Post* in 1972, Rosenthal (who Wilkins knew socially and who had no authority over the *Times*' editorial page) had asked him why had he not come to work for the *Times.* Wilkins, a bit surprised by the question, had responded, "Two reasons, Abe. They asked me and you didn't."

During his years at the *Post, Times* executives had approached Wilkins repeatedly for suggestions for a black editorial writer. He offered some names, but no black was hired—until Wilkins himself became available in 1974.

Wilkins was fond of Oakes, whom he thought of as a passionately decent man, despite being "handicapped by the narrowness of his [privileged] background." And he had watched with consternation what he took to be the humiliation of Oakes, who was not permitted to stay until normal retirement age.

He became enraged after the paper's endorsement in September 1976 of Daniel Patrick Moynihan for senator in the Democratic primary. Sulzberger had ordered the endorsement over strong objections from Oakes, who (along with most of the other editorial writers) favored former congresswoman Bella Abzug. Moreover, Sulzberger put the endorsement in the paper when Oakes was on vacation.

Oakes had insisted on his right to dissent, and Sulzberger had allowed him to run a short letter of disagreement. Several blacks on the paper had also taken exception to the editorial and approached Oakes and asked permission to voice their protest on his page. Oakes refused, saying that the paper's policies prohibited it. But he agreed to permit Wilkins, who favored former attorney general Ramsey Clark in the race, to write a personal column opposing Moynihan. Oakes showed the piece to Sulzberger. Another confrontation ensued, and the article's publication was delayed until after the primary—which Moynihan won with 36 percent of the vote to Abzug's 35 percent.

That episode, combined with Oakes being kicked upstairs, left the editorial page staff dispirited.

Frankel had barely read the page before being told he was to run it. Though he craved to be a columnist, he had never dreamed of writing anonymous editorials. Nor was he convinced he could easily attract other good journalists to write them. He was less concerned about his ability to create a tone Sulzberger would find congenial. "I told him from the beginning, 'I don't know how to work this thing. But all I can do is go and try to put out a page and write in a tone of voice that's natural to me. And if you don't like it in a year or so, you tell me and you give me a column and I'll go away.' "

Frankel told Sulzberger that he could not single-handedly transform the page. The editorial board, he pointed out, had only a dozen writers, each an expert in his or her field. "How am I supposed to change what they're doing?" he asked. "I can't take their pencils in my hands and write." Rosenthal would have to be persuaded to take some of those writers off his hands and perhaps make them distinguished correspondents somewhere. Then Frankel could bring in four or five of his own people, preferably from the *Times* news staff, "but if Abe won't give them up, from outside."

Sulzberger agreed. But some of those Frankel wanted to reassign took his suggestion as an insult and quit. Others, whom he wanted to stay, left in anger over the treatment of their colleagues and Oakes or because they were not chosen to be Frankel's deputy. "Before we knew it," said Frankel, "two thirds of the people were out. . . . Close to half were literally gone before I even arrived formally to take the job. It was chaos. . . . The idea was right. The execution left something to be desired."

Roger Starr, a former New York City housing commissioner and author who had published in the *New Yorker,* was among those Frankel brought onto his staff. Starr recalls feeling isolated. "I had a feeling in those first six or eight months that I was here that people wouldn't speak to me in the elevator because I was one of the new guys who had forced everybody out."

Peter Passell, a Ph.D. economist from Yale and another of Frankel's recruits, said, "At some point, fairly early on, I got the impression the world thought this was a conservative revolution and that John Oakes had left because of disagreements on ideology. . . . And while the people [who remained from] the old board . . . seemed to have a kind of edginess and resentment, and they sometimes cast it in ideological terms, I never quite believed it." After all, Frankel seemed liberal and deputy editorial page editor Jack Rosenthal—no relation to Abe—was certainly liberal.

For his part, Jack Rosenthal came to the job with very mixed feelings. He realized that "there was blood all over the floor." And he wasn't convinced that writing editorials was what he really wanted to do. He accepted the position because, as he read the personalities and politics of the time, he had little choice.

Like Frankel, Jack Rosenthal was an immigrant whose family had suffered under Nazism. His father, a judge in Berlin, had one day climbed the steps to the front door of the courthouse and found two storm troopers with crossed rifles barring his entry. Just as they started to push him down the stairs, the chief judge arrived and interceded. The elder Rosenthal left Germany within two weeks, settling first in Palestine (where Jack was born) and then moving to Portland, Oregon, a few years later.

Rosenthal felt "quite foreign" in Portland—largely because his mother forced him to wear short pants as a child—but he never experienced discrimination as a Jew. And when he got to Harvard on scholarship in 1952, he was surprised that such a big deal was made of racial and ethnic distinctions.

From childhood, Rosenthal had dreamed of being a journalist and chose Harvard largely because of the opportunity to be on the *Crimson*—which he eventually edited. After graduation and a stint in the army, he returned home to a job as a reporter on the Portland *Oregonian,* where he had once worked as a copyboy.

In November 1959, the *Oregonian*'s stereotypers went out on strike, protesting the installation of a machine that would eliminate most of their jobs. The labor conflict dragged on for more than five years. In the interim, Rosenthal helped launched an alternative newspaper, the *Portland Reporter* and was offered an opportunity, in early 1961, to become a press assistant to Attorney General Robert Kennedy.

To Rosenthal (who, as *Crimson* editor, was intensely proud of having opposed Senator Joseph McCarthy), Robert Kennedy represented the best of liberal America: "I would have offered my testicles to work in the New Frontier."

Indeed, during those years, Washington was a magnet for young Harvard men who took seriously John Kennedy's exhortation to get the country moving again. At one point, Rosenthal counted some thirty-five ex-*Crimson* writers who, like him, had come to Camelot to save the world.

John Kennedy's death shattered some of the magic. Two days before his assassination, Rosenthal had taken his wife to a White House reception. "He's beautiful," she had murmured, after meeting the president.

Despite the pall after Kennedy's assassination and despite Rosenthal's discomfort with Lyndon Johnson's "kick shit" style, he stayed on. After Nicholas Katzenbach was named attorney general, Rosenthal became his principal assistant and later worked with him in the State Department.

By then, Rosenthal was eager to return to journalism and thought to make the transition via Harvard; but while a fellow at Harvard's Institute of Politics, he was tapped by old friends in Washington to help write the 1968 Kerner Commission report on riots and race relations in America.

Rosenthal wanted terribly to get the point across to America that the riots were not the plot of a bunch of Communists but sprang from deeply felt grievances that demanded attention. He was very proud of a line in that report that he wrote and that summed up much of the problem: "Our Nation is moving toward two societies, one black, one white—separate and unequal."

His time with the commission and at Harvard made him want to write more about urban America; but when he approached Abe Rosenthal and tried to explain his idea, the *Times* man told him the paper already had a writer covering urban architecture and another covering housing: "You're a bright fellow, obviously. Why don't you come back to us sometime when you have a better idea of what you'd like to do."

Furious, Rosenthal took a job with *Life* as an urban affairs correspondent. Shortly thereafter, Frankel—who had been Washington bureau chief for roughly a year—offered him an urban affairs beat with the *Times.*

Rosenthal worked closely with the cluster of other reporters writing about urban America and helped organize a series of tours for *Times* reporters through America's inner-city ghettos; he felt he was making an important contribution to understanding those communities' woes.

When Frankel became Sunday editor, Rosenthal went as his deputy. And in November 1975, Frankel gave him responsibility for the magazine. A few months, later, however, Frankel was no longer in control.

"Here I was, finally with my own ship, my own flag to fly, and then . . . bam, the skipper is knocked out of the box and suddenly I report to Abe [Rosenthal]."

Jack and Abe had always been polite to each other, but the relationship had never been comfortable. And Jack didn't much care for what he had heard about Abe's management style. "Well, all of a sudden, here I was, his boy, except I wasn't *his* boy. I was probably suspect because I was Frankel's boy. And so, the only thing was to go to him and say, 'I know I don't have any constitutional right to this job. In a perfect world, I would like to keep it indefinitely, but you have the right to appoint anybody you like. . . . Here's my resignation and you can accept it whenever you want to.' "

Abe was effusive. The last thing in the world he wanted was for Jack to leave. Jack stayed; but as the months wore on, he felt Abe was torpedoing him at every opportunity. Jack was working around the clock trying to put out the best magazine that he could, but his budget was being cut, permission to replace staff withheld, and his judgment called into question.

"It wasn't even personal," he said later. "I think it was that in some deep way he needed to put his stamp on [the magazine]."

Sulzberger came down to Jack Rosenthal's office that November and asked him to become deputy editorial page editor. The position came with a big raise and, in the *Times* hierarchy, it was a substantial promotion. Still, he found himself wishing that Sulzberger would say, "You be editor of the magazine instead of Abe." He knew that was not in the cards, so he accepted, thinking deputy editorial page editor wasn't such a bad booby prize.

A month later, Abe Rosenthal was given the title of executive editor (confirming the status he had already acquired, with the editorial page remaining outside his domain). At the same time, Sulzberger announced Jack Rosenthal's promotion and several other staff changes. The past year, he said, had been a period of major growth and change—with the creation of special sections, the expansion of the business report, the development of two regional weeklies, and the beginning of automation of news operations. In 1977, he said, the paper would continue to grow. Other new sections would be launched. Business and financial news would be further expanded. "The new organization of the top news management group is designed to handle all this and perhaps more."

Katharine Darrow was also promoted in December 1976, to assistant general attorney of the New York Times Company, in recognition of the increasingly important role she was playing in the affairs of the company and the newspaper.

Compared to the news department, the legal staff was tiny and virtually invisible; but sooner or later the paper's most troublesome problems landed on the lawyers' desks; and in the late 1970s, as Darrow sorted through discrimination suits filed by women and minorities, she hoped the *Times* family was not tearing itself apart.

Darrow's work was made more complicated because she was sympathetic to the complaints, having spent much of her life struggling against discrimination.

A Chicago native and the daughter of immigrants from Nazi Germany, Darrow had initially planned to be a mathematician; but after the family moved to a Philadelphia suburb during her teens and Darrow became involved with nearby Quaker organizations, she decided she liked working for the poor. She nevertheless entered the University of Chicago as a math major, but soon changed to history and philosophy of science while trying to determine what she really wanted to do. Following graduation, she enrolled in the university's law school (despite having resolved not to model herself after her parents, both of whom were lawyers), joined a law student civil rights research group, and went to work part-time for a firm active in civil rights.

That summer—1965—Martin Luther King, Jr., marched in Chicago. Darrow's firm defended many of the demonstrators and she came away depressed. King's methods, she decided, couldn't work in Chicago: "It was . . . too big and much too complicated and much too political." And the war was too bitter, not only between blacks and whites, but among different groups of blacks.

That realization made her question her choice of a profession and made her see her hometown and the civil rights struggle in a different light. She no longer knew "whether being a lawyer was going to enable us to do something for people." Also, her marriage was collapsing. Distraught, she dropped out of law school and came to New York.

After working briefly for the Legal Aid Society, Darrow enrolled at Columbia University Law School, which she found passionless after Chicago.

Searching for a summer job that first year was disheartening. Despite her superior grades, no law firm wanted her. One interviewer, noting her law school transfer and civil rights work, accused her of instability. Another was initially enthusiastic, but turned chilly after realizing the firm had hired one woman that summer and apparently saw no reason to hire another.

She had nearly given up hope when James Goodale called

and offered a job (for which she had interviewed weeks earlier) at the Times. She accepted immediately and was thrust into an exciting new world of First Amendment and labor law.

The *Times* had a most unusual cast of characters, which she realized while sitting in a meeting of senior editors discussing a possibly libelous column written by C. L. Sulzberger—European correspondent and Arthur Hays Sulzberger's nephew. Darrow meekly suggested that a minor change be made in the column, and the assemblage grumbled its concurrence and continued to talk about what to do.

"It soon became clear to me that the whole issue here was not the legality, or whether I was right, or whether the change ought to be made. The whole issue here was that no one wanted to call [C. L. Sulzberger]; no one wanted to incur his wrath." After much shuffling around by important *Times* editors, she was instructed to call Sulzberger herself, which she did, yanking him out of an opera in Paris, which infuriated him much more than the change she was suggesting—and to which he agreed.

Shortly after graduation in 1969, Darrow joined the Times legal department, but left in the spring of 1971 to accompany her second husband to London. Her job was still open when she returned two and a half years later. Though she wanted to wait until the New Year to start work, the Times insisted that she come immediately to deal with the class-action suit filed by women employees against the *Times.*

The advertising department, she knew, had systematically discriminated against women for years. The news department would be much easier to defend. The *Times,* she concluded, could almost certainly win the case. Yet she was disturbed, "because I knew perfectly well that the company had discriminated in various ways for years like all companies had and it made me unhappy to be in a position where I seemed to be denying that which clearly had taken place."

As the case wore on and bitterness grew on both sides, Darrow and senior management realized that the *Times* could not afford to go through the agony of litigating the lawsuit. As she prepared Sulzberger and Walter Mattson and other senior executives for the trial process, everyone saw that the defense would have to consist of publicly tearing the women down, of attacking their abilities at every opportunity. Working together harmoniously once the battle was over would be virtually impossible. "The trial would have been so disruptive, we would never have recovered."

The company settled before trial in 1978, as it did in 1980 with a similar action filed by minorities in 1974. In both cases, the Times put the best corporate face forward.

"We regard today's announcement as total vindication of the New York Times and as full refutation of the charges against us," said James Goodale in a statement issued when the women's case was resolved. After the minorities suit was settled, the corporate public relations office issued a press release noting, "The agreement . . . specifically states that the *New York Times* has not been found guilty of any discriminatory hiring practices."

Darrow thought the minorities' and women's suits fundamentally different. "I always felt in the women's case that it was like a divorce or a custody proceeding. It was really a family being rent asunder with all the hideous bitterness and personal animosity that that can [engender]. . . . There wasn't any of that in the minorities case. And, I suppose, it's for a very simple reason. There were so few minorities, so few longstanding preexisting relationships, you didn't have the sense of a family being rent asunder. The gap was too wide. You were talking about people at much lower levels, people who had been here for shorter periods of time."

Another difference was that the *Times* was generally proud of its accomplishments with women: "We had nothing to hide and nothing to be ashamed of. . . . In the minorities case, we didn't have those feelings. We knew damn well that we weren't any better than anybody else."

Roger Wilkins had left the *Times* editorial page shortly after Frankel's arrival. Frankel had asked him to stay, but Wilkins had been unenthusiastic—particularly after discovering that Jack Rosenthal, whom he had worked with (and developed an intense dislike for) in the Justice Department, would become Frankel's deputy. Wilkins suggested the paper make him an op-ed page columnist. Several months later, he was given an urban affairs column—though in the news section instead of on the op-ed page.

As a former assistant U.S. attorney general, Wilkins was deeply knowledgeable about legal strategy and anticipated the

Times' defense of the racial discrimination suit. As a preemptive strike, he submitted a long, blistering affidavit accusing Abe Rosenthal and Sulzberger of encouraging racist practices at the paper.

"I figured they'd settle." If the case had gone to trial, *Times* lawyers and executives "were going to tear people apart. . . . They would have gone at the innards of each and every one of us. . . . A lot hinged on me. . . . They had offered me the editorship of news in 'The Week in Review' and I turned it down. . . . Had I been promoted to that job. . . . it would have been a terrific defense for that lawsuit. . . . I was going to destroy that aspect of their defense for good. . . . What I hoped would happen would be that we would . . . force them into a settlement that would change the system, improve the life chances of minorities at that paper, and improve the paper."

Wilkins resigned in 1979.

In many ways, the 1970s ranked as the *Times'* most extraordinary decade ever. With its C sections and new format, the paper had transformed itself, while broadening the very definition of news. It had won a wrenching constitutional clash with the federal government, forced its unions to accept automation, and backed down from potentially disastrous battles with its women and minorities. Meanwhile, the parent company had grown from a large family business into a hungry conglomerate. Revenues had nearly tripled from $283 million in 1970 to $731 million in 1980. Earnings had gone from $14 million to $41 million.

At the center of it all sat Sulzberger, who was not only publisher of the *Times* but chairman of the company, and who was to close out the decade with another major decision—making Walter Mattson president of the company. Though the move had been in the offing for some time, it stunned some who had expected James Goodale to be named.

Both Mattson and Goodale were executive vice-presidents of the company. Sydney Gruson, who had returned as Sulzberger's assistant after his short stint as associate publisher of *Newsday,* was also an executive vice-president (serving as chief adviser to Sulzberger). Along with Sulzberger, the three made up the company's executive committee (deciding implementation of company policy)—and had since 1974.

As the years passed, however, a rivalry developed between

Goodale (who oversaw the legal department and was heavily involved in acquisitions) and Mattson (who ran the business side of the newspaper) that made the arrangement no longer workable—and that subjected their respective underlings, as one described it, to "frequent bouts of jealousy and mild insanity . . . [as the two men] kind of jockeyed around."

Periodically, Sulzberger had commissioned management studies of the paper. In the late 1970s he asked McKinsey & Company to tell him how to restructure top management.

The final report, delivered in April 1979, was titled *Building the Management Team in the New York Times Company.* It recommended that Sulzberger appoint a president who would serve as chief operating officer and a vice-chairman to lead a major and sharply focused acquisitions and diversification effort.

Sulzberger had all but decided on that course of action before calling in McKinsey to recommend it. "I knew very well that the structure that I had and the way I liked to operate . . . a three-headed monster . . . was not going to work in the long run." But calling in the consultants gave him a certain comfort and helped him to think through basic strategy for the company.

The choice of a president boiled down to decisions about three human beings, all of whom Sulzberger respected and cared about deeply. Gruson was already in his sixties in 1979. "I just don't think there are enough years left," Sulzberger told him during an emotional conversation that left both men distraught.

A combination of personal chemistry and practical considerations led Sulzberger to Mattson—who had already proved himself as a manager, tamed the labor unions, and systematically built up the paper's business departments. Goodale was more of a visionary but less of an administrator.

"Walter Mattson's operating style, his abilities, [the] work he had done before, his general managership of the newspaper, his restoration of the strength of the newspaper, all lent themselves to a very early decision in Sulzberger's mind that it would be Mattson. . . . Mattson's determinedness, his stick-to-itness, his disciplined approach to things impressed Sulzberger," said Gruson.

Another executive who had worked closely with both men observed, "If Goodale had some of Walter's qualities—namely, the ability to be quiet, the patience for negotiation, and a little less ego and less susceptibility to the blandishments of people who work for him—he could have been president. In some respects, he would have been a better president. But Walter was, of the two, the [better] choice. . . . Gruson would have been [chosen] if he had been five years younger. But neither [Goodale nor Gruson] could have run a newspaper company as well as Walter."

Gruson became vice-chairman and premier corporate deal maker after Mattson was named president in late 1979.

Goodale professes to be mystified by talk of a power struggle. "I didn't have any desire to be the chief operating executive of a company. . . . My plan had always been to [work for] the *Times* until I was forty-four or forty-six and then either go back to a law firm or go into government. . . . I didn't want to spend the rest of my years in a family company. . . . If it was my ambition to be chief operating officer, I would have gone around and kissed everybody's ass. . . . I grew up in an academic family. . . . When you grow up in that kind of atmosphere, to be the head of the business side of the paper draws sneers."

When Mattson was made president, Goodale, like Gruson, was made a vice-chairman of the company, without any substantial duties he could discern. The role of editorial adviser and confidant to Sulzberger, which Goodale might have found interesting, was already occupied by Gruson. Perhaps if Sulzberger had decided to make him publisher or chairman of the editorial board, or given him another position where he could really affect public policy, then he would have stayed. But that was clearly not in the cards. "I was surprised at the way the thing was organized, but I had other things I wanted to do anyway."

Shortly after the reorganization, Goodale left to become a partner in the law firm of Debevoise & Plimpton.

CHAPTER 16

SULZBERGER'S LEGACY

Almost since the day he had taken over, Punch Sulzberger had been preparing the *Times* for the day he no longer would be in charge. Coming into office untrained and at a time of crisis had forced him to think deeply about corporate stability and management transitions—and to realize that neither could be taken for granted. From the beginning, future-oriented committees and planning exercises had received his enthusiastic support; and before long, assorted consultants with computerized crystal balls were brought in to assist. All the planning efforts essentially had the same goal: to protect and enrich the legacy with which Sulzberger had been entrusted.

By the end of the 1980s, Sulzberger would be nearly sixty-five. The family business was no longer what Arthur Hays Sulzberger had built but what his son had made it. And much of the 1980s would be devoted to preparing to pass it on.

Sulzberger's earliest goal—a company strong enough to weather a prolonged *Times* strike—had been achieved. Ironically, the *Times* was significantly less likely to face a strike. Negotiations had resolved many contentious issues of the past, and technology had given the paper the ability to publish in defiance of its unions.

Technology also had given the *Times* the means to publish a national newspaper. For the western edition of the 1960s, the copy sent from New York had to be typeset, made up, and printed in California. (It had also been hindered by a poor advertising strategy, a recession, and a wrenching strike.) By the 1980s, a page could be beamed, via satellite and virtually ready to print, anywhere in the world.

The *Times* had long distributed papers nationally, but it had not produced a specific national edition. The effort had consisted of flying newspapers to a few major cities. National circulation was roughly twenty thousand daily and eighty thousand on Sunday—largely in the Chicago area. And the paper was full of advertising for local stores and businesses whose proprietors had no interest in Chicago. When the energy crisis and airline deregulation hit, many flights used by the *Times* were cut from schedules. The paper faced a choice—either find some other way to distribute nationally, or give up trying to develop a national market.

As executives researched the technical feasibility of transmitting the *Times* to distant printing sites, they also studied market acceptance for a paper stripped of many New York features and advertisements—developing a prototype for a two-section national edition in 1979. Lance Primis, then director of advertising, recalls that one research project consisted of piling as many of the papers as would fit into the publisher's plane and flying them to Detroit, Chicago, and Cleveland and determining whether people would buy them.

Those first readers, the *Times* discovered, were largely ex–New Yorkers. Allan Siegal, then head of the news desk, described them as people who "were using us, in a highly emotional way, to cling to their identification [with New York]." They didn't want New York news and advertisements left out. And once the edition was launched, the *Times* received hundreds of vituperative, complaining letters. Market research had predicted the reaction. Even so, Siegal and others were jolted by it.

As time passed, the *Times* discovered another base—readers who had never lived in New York but enjoyed the *Times'* coverage of arts, culture, international news, and finance. Unlike the failed western edition, the national edition was aimed at businesspeople and firms that wanted to reach them—particularly financial advertisers who knew serious investors were likely to be readers of the *Times.* By 1985, having started with one plant in Chicago, the national edition was being printed at six sites and more were planned—even as major expansion and restructuring of the company itself were taking place.

The McKinsey & Company study of 1979 had criticized the unfocused nature of Times diversification. Acquisitions should neatly fit into a larger strategy, said McKinsey, in recommending the company create a "corporate development" staff to identify and investigate potential acquisition candidates. The *Times* took the recommendation. And over the next several years, Sulzberger, Mattson, and vice-chairman Sydney Gruson unloaded several subsidiaries.

Us, a personalities and gossip magazine launched in 1977, was among those properties the company ditched. It had never made money for the Times. But more important, "It just wasn't a fit for the New York Times Company," said Mattson. "None of us had an interest in that kind of report. And in order to make it with a popular book, you had to do things we were even less happy about." The company also sold its computer operations and microfilming businesses and its book division—which had generated considerable tension by requiring *Times* writers to give Times Books first crack at manuscripts growing out of their work at the paper.

As Times Mirror had earlier, the Times rejected McKinsey's suggestion of diversifying into areas far afield of its expertise. The Times chose to stay in businesses "we know something about and where we can bring something to the party," said Mattson. As a result, the Times invested in small, nonunion papers in growing markets, and to a lesser extent in magazines, broadcast television stations, and cable television. The company also became increasingly profitable.

Profits increased two and a half times, from $41 million to $100 million, from 1980 to 1984—at a time when gross revenue growth was strong but unspectacular (going from $731 million to $1.2 billion).

Even as the financial picture brightened, Sulzberger could ill afford to relax. In 1987, Abe Rosenthal would turn sixty-five, the customary retirement age for officers of the company; and Sulzberger would have a final opportunity, before he himself turned sixty-five, to appoint an editor charged with steering the paper into the 1990s and beyond.

* * *

For a brief period, Craig Whitney thought he might be that someone. And like a few other *Times* men similarly encouraged to dream, the former Moscow correspondent with thinning hair and a patrician face eventually came crashing to earth.

In September 1983, Abe Rosenthal took Whitney to lunch and asked, "How would you like to be an assistant managing editor?" (a rank, at the *Times,* just below managing editor with areas of responsibility defined by the executive editor). Whitney, appointed foreign editor only the year before, was overwhelmed. Yes, he said, the idea appealed to him quite a lot. Rosenthal explained that he would appoint other assistant managing editors over the next two years, with varying duties; none of them would appear on the masthead. But as Whitney understood the conversation, the chosen few would be candidates for Rosenthal's job—or, perhaps, for managing editor. That Whitney was being chosen first meant nothing in itself, except that he was one of the field.

If a prototype existed for a ranking *Times* news executive, Whitney came extremely close. Virtually his entire adult life had been spent at the *Times.* And his ticket had been punched in all the right places.

Growing up in a small, rural town near Boston, Massachusetts, Whitney had originally thought he might be a teacher like his grandfather. His father, a postal worker, went off to World War II before Craig was born and returned when he was two. His maternal grandfather, a French teacher in a private school, had become the father figure, imbuing Whitney with a love of languages, literature, and learning.

That Whitney get a good education was very important to his parents, neither of whom had gone to college. Scholarships took him to Phillips Academy at Andover and to Harvard University. Following his sophomore year, a friend got him a job as a summer replacement reporter on the *Worcester Telegram*—whose real news struck him as much more interesting than the "pretend" journalism practiced on the *Crimson,* which he had no desire to join.

Whitney quickly became a committed newspaperman and planned to pursue graduate studies in journalism at Columbia University, but dropped those plans upon being selected as clerk to James Reston, the *Times* Washington columnist—another choice for the real world as opposed to the pretend.

During his year with Reston, Whitney received his draft notice, which prompted him to volunteer for the navy. Reston's neighbor—naval secretary Paul Nitze—had Ensign Whitney detailed to the Pentagon, working as his speechwriter. The job was unremittingly boring and after two years of it, Whitney got himself transferred to a public relations post in Saigon—right after the Tet offensive of 1968. He was discharged in mid-1969.

Not until Whitney returned to Vietnam as a *Times* correspondent in 1971 (having worked, in the interim, on the paper's metropolitan staff) was he to understand how flawed the war effort had been. As a reporter, he traveled much more extensively than as a naval officer—when the Vietnamese people had been dismissed as "gooks or prostitutes." Finally, he saw full human beings; he also saw that the war wasn't working.

Following Vietnam, Whitney had gone to Bonn and then Moscow, before returning to New York in 1980 to become deputy foreign editor. He liked shaping other writers' stories and getting them into the paper. He even enjoyed the daily page-one meetings—sessions dubbed "the Abe Rosenthal terrorism course"—during which each editor pitched stories for the day. Whitney found the ever-present possibility of being hit by one of Rosenthal's unpredictable attacks "stimulating," like participating in a high-stakes poker game. He also thought the *Times* he had come home to, with its C sections and expanded coverage, was a much stronger paper than the one he had left. His promotion to foreign editor in 1982 was a natural progression; and his being tapped for the assistant managing editor's job seemed a confirmation of his steady ascent.

But once in his new job, Whitney discovered that senior management could be intensely frustrating at the *Times.* Despite the higher title, he exercised less authority than as foreign editor, where he had supervised correspondents. He was placed over the paper's "Living" and "Home" sections—which meant the editors in charge were to consult with him, though they really reported to Rosenthal. "I was somewhat frustrated by the feeling that either I wasn't taking full advantage of the opportunity that he [Rosenthal] had offered me or that I wasn't being allowed to," said Whitney. "I know that both things were at work. . . . I know that Abe tried to delegate authority the best way he knew how and that it just wasn't in him."

Warren Hoge, who followed Whitney as foreign editor and

who was also considered a potential Rosenthal heir, experienced fewer frustrations than Whitney, largely because Hoge's expectations were lower. Unlike some of his contemporaries, who hoped for the executive editor or managing editor title, Hoge wanted only to be a member of the new management team. More important, as a close friend and admirer of Rosenthal, he had a more realistic view of how the process would likely end up. He knew that "Abe loved the job so much, inhabited it so totally, that it would be difficult for him to focus on an individual who could replace him."

Hoge, a former metropolitan editor of the *New York Post,* had known Rosenthal socially before coming to the *Times* in 1976. Periodically, during his years at the *Post,* Hoge would have an evening cocktail in Rosenthal's office. Speaking editor to editor, Rosenthal would pump Hoge for opinions of writers of the *Times.*

They did not discuss jobs in those days, recalls Hoge, "but I think I had the sense that if I got into trouble at the *Post* . . . I might have a card to play [at the *Times*]."

He was happy, however, at the *Post,* where he had done well—becoming a senior editor well before the age of forty.

His father was a prominent New York trademark lawyer. His older brother became publisher of the *Chicago Sun-Times* and later of the *New York Daily News.* Warren, slim and rakishly handsome, was a singer and adventurer.

He was kicked out of Exeter preparatory school for running a gambling operation, but was later admitted to both Harvard and Yale. He chose Yale, not only because big brother Jim had gone there but because it had a better singing program. Though singing was his passion, he knew that he would one day turn to journalism. As a teenager, he had spent summers working in the kitchens of ships and would write long letters to his parents about his experiences. "I had the sense that I hadn't seen something, that I hadn't really experienced it until I put it on a piece of paper."

In 1963, his last year at Yale, the *Washington Star* selected Hoge as one of two trainees and later promoted him to reporter. He became the *New York Post*'s Washington correspondent three years later and worked out of the home office during the summer of 1970 filling in for editorial writers on vacation.

Gay Talese, the writer, was away for the summer, and Hoge rented his town house apartment on East Sixty-first Street. The first morning in New York, as he walked out of the building and strolled to the subway, he fell in love with his hometown and said to himself, "I'm never going back."

Even though it meant giving up writing, Hoge stayed and quickly rose to become metro desk chief. The excitement of directing a talented staff on a hungry tabloid thrilled him; but, after a few years, the strain of pumping up a barely surviving paper with no real mission wore him down. Moreover, he was tired of running other people's lives and too young to condemn himself to the closed-in life of a manager.

Having concluded that he could not comfortably write on the *Post,* whose local staff he had headed, Hoge joined the *Times* as a metropolitan reporter. As his first day approached, Hoge was terrified. He called up an old colleague who had also defected from the *Post* and asked, "Will you have breakfast with me and welcome me to the company?" The friend agreed. Another friend arranged a luncheon at Sardi's. He spent much of the first morning humming an inspirational tune from a Frank Loesser musical. "I Believe in You" still danced through his head as he screwed up his courage, walked into the *Times,* and sat in the back of the enormous city room.

His stage fright vanished almost immediately, and for the next five weeks Hoge was blissfully happy writing. But then Rosenthal approached him with an offer to become regional editor—overseeing the suburban editions.

"It's a great priority of ours," said Rosenthal. "The publisher himself has great interest in this." The offer came with a generous budget and a substantial staff. And it was the last thing that Hoge wanted to hear. For a year, he had searched his soul, sorting out what he really wanted to do. Finally, he had convinced himself of the advantages of getting off the fast track and returning to reporting. And now, five weeks into the job, Rosenthal was trying to change his mind. Hoge refused the job and, as he recalls, came "that close"—fingers nearly touching—"to being fired as a result."

The next day two editors revealed that they had been told not to talk to him; one arranged to meet him for breakfast and the other called him at home. Rosenthal, they told Hoge, was deeply offended. "This guy's not for us," Rosenthal reportedly had said. "He's not *Times* material. Who is he to say he's going to turn down this job?"

Hoge decided he had best take the job. Rosenthal acted as if Hoge did not deserve it.

"You will never know that I didn't want this job," Hoge told Rosenthal. "I will give it the best shot I've got." Rosenthal approved the promotion and Hoge went on to inaugurate weekly sections in Westchester County (New York) and Connecticut, and shepherded those already existing in Long Island and New Jersey. At every opportunity he would tell Rosenthal that he longed to be a writer, especially a foreign correspondent; and Rosenthal would always respond that it would never happen.

Hoge groused about his misfortune to his friends, including Sally Quinn, whom he had dated before she began seeing Ben Bradlee. Fed up with his whining, Quinn told him that if he wanted to write, then write. So what if editing tied up his day, he still had his evenings and weekends and vacations. Hoge began using his evenings to write pieces on the theater and his vacations to write about Hollywood. And he would shove them at Rosenthal as if to say, "See. I can write."

"Okay, I've got the message," Rosenthal said one day, and the two worked out an accommodation. Hoge was made deputy to the metropolitan editor with the promise of a writing assignment to follow. Early in 1979, he became chief of the *Times* bureau in Rio de Janeiro, Brazil.

He loved the travel, the writing, and being back on the street, but before long, like some latter-day Faustus forced to surrender his soul, Hoge was asked to give up his pen.

Rosenthal came to Brazil in 1983 and offered him the foreign editorship. He did not have to take it, Rosenthal emphasized, and could still remain one of the paper's two or three star foreign correspondents. "But you'll be sending us a message you don't want to be thought of as part of the new generation of people."

The thought stopped Hoge cold. For, if he had to be an editor, the foreign editorship was the best job on the paper. And though his heart told him to continue as a foreign correspondent, he had responsibilities that hadn't previously existed. He was newly married with two stepchildren and another child on the way, and had a growing desire not to be left out of the new team of leaders at the *Times.* He returned to New York in time for 1984's New Year fireworks, which the children watched from the apartment window—crying because they weren't in Brazil.

The newsroom he came back to was in convulsions, swept by rumors about who would succeed Rosenthal, how and when the succession would take place, and what it would all mean for the paper. Over the next two years, Rosenthal appointed a host of new assistant managing editors with varying responsibilities. Journalists inside and outside watched in bemusement. In addition to Hoge and Whitney, a number of others seemed in contention, including Washington bureau chief Bill Kovach, editorial page editor Max Frankel (who alone of those in contention did not report to Rosenthal), and John Lee, who had previously overseen economic, business, and financial news before being appointed assistant to Rosenthal.

In October 1986, Sulzberger decided the time had come to calm things down and announced that Max Frankel, fifty-six, would become executive editor effective November 1. Rosenthal was to be an associate editor and columnist, reporting directly to Sulzberger. Deputy managing editor Arthur Gelb was to replace managing editor Seymour Topping, who was retiring from the *Times* to help upgrade the company's smaller newspapers.

Roughly a year before the announcement, Sulzberger and Frankel had lunched in a private executive dining room. Frankel, aware he was a contender, wanted to be sure Sulzberger understood his feelings. He asked Sulzberger not to say anything, but to listen. If Sulzberger wanted him to do the job, he was available—and eager. Others might argue he was not qualified; those arguments were without merit. On the other hand, if he did not fit into Sulzberger's plans for executive editor, he could accept that with no complaint. But he would have been editorial page editor for ten years and wanted Sulzberger to be creative and find something else for him. And though Frankel did not mention it explicitly, he hoped Sulzberger would ask him to write a column.

Sulzberger replied that he had always thought well of Frankel; and that, of course, Frankel was on his mind for Rosenthal's job.

For the next several months, the men said nothing about the executive editorship. Periodically, vice-chairman Sydney Gruson would talk to Frankel about activities in the newsroom and

Sulzberger's thoughts on succession. Frankel never knew whether Gruson was sounding him out for Sulzberger or simply sharing observations with a friend. He never asked.

Frankel and Sulzberger had another lunch that July 15. Toward the end, after discussing everything but the looming appointment, Sulzberger said, "I've decided."

"I always had Max in my hip pocket, at least in my judgment," Sulzberger would say later. And when the process of sifting through the younger talent was over, he still felt more comfortable with Frankel. "I knew his temperament, knew what kind of journalist he was. . . . I'd taken my risks. I didn't feel I had to take another great big one."

In a sense, Sulzberger was doing with Max Frankel what he had done nearly two decades earlier with James Reston: bringing in a trusted hand after a period of deep turmoil to calm the waters. For Rosenthal's way had been to stir things up. "And, Jesus, the next thing you know the whole place went wild," said Sulzberger. "And then he'd calm it down, and then something else would come along. . . . And that's all right for a while. And it is kind of fun. . . . But there's fallout . . . every once in a while from running things like that."

Reston's caretaker approach, however, was not to be Frankel's. The new executive editor expected to be an agent of change.

Once the appointment was made, many journalists speculated that the fix had been in for Frankel all along. Yet, in the beginning, Sulzberger had thought a successor might be found in the newsroom; and he had asked Rosenthal to give editors real responsibility in order to test their potential.

Meanwhile Frankel, as editorial page editor, had been completely out of the news operation, "and the whole spotlight was on the news department," points out Sydney Gruson. Frankel became the obvious choice, Gruson adds, only when "Abe's efforts to initiate a process by which a successor would naturally emerge were clearly not [working]."

When he gave Rosenthal responsibility for the news department, Sulzberger had asked him to be a hands-on editor, to bring warring departments under control. "He didn't sit with me at five o'clock in the afternoon and have a cocktail and chat about the world," said Sulzberger. "He was in there, making up page one. Practically all major decisions were taken over by

Abe." Having assumed such power, Rosenthal clearly had great difficulty giving it up.

Rosenthal seems genuinely puzzled as to why the newsroom contenders felt they never got a fair shot. As assistant managing editors, they certainly had responsibilities, he believes, and they clearly had opportunities to show what they could do. Frankel's star simply glowed brighter than the rest.

In the years preceding Rosenthal's retirement—with potential successors fighting to prove themselves, with Rosenthal resisting retirement, with constant speculation inside and outside the *Times* on who was up and who was out—the newsroom had whipped itself into a frenzy. Frankel's first priority was to ease the tension.

William Connolly, then deputy editor of "The Week in Review," was stunned when Frankel came into the "Review" office the Saturday after his appointment just to chat. "I thought the staff was going to faint," said Connolly. Workers in the telephone recording room (where dictation from correspondents is transcribed) were likewise shocked to find Frankel shaking hands with clerks.

"The whole atmosphere in the room is lighter," observed Gerald Fraser, a *Times* writer for twenty years.

Not all the turmoil ended with Frankel's appointment. Washington bureau chief Bill Kovach, disappointed at being passed over, left in December 1986 to become editor of the *Atlanta Journal* and *Atlanta Constitution.*

John Vinocur, a former Paris bureau chief who was made metropolitan editor in early 1986 (and who was also viewed as a possible contender for one of the two top jobs), became executive editor of the *International Herald Tribune.*

Those who stayed behind comforted themselves with assurances that their time would come, delighting in Frankel's management style after the chaos of the past few years.

Craig Whitney, whom Rosenthal had approached in 1983 with the offer of an assistant managing editorship, became Washington bureau chief after Kovach's departure—with considerably more autonomy, Whitney believed, than he would have had under Rosenthal.

"Abe was chaotic . . . in a good sense as well as a bad sense," says Whitney. "[He was] impetuous, arrogant, imperious, dictatorial, inspiring, and inspirational. . . . He inspired fear . . . respect . . . toadyism. . . . The good side . . . is that he inspired people . . . to do the best job they could."

Indeed, many of the *Times* editors—forceful, dynamic, even brilliant individuals—responded to Rosenthal like frightened children, cowering before his whims. "I've been in meetings with Abe," said one editor, "where Abe has made some stupid proposals and he would say, 'Do you all agree with that?' And we'd all sit there sheepishly and say nothing because nobody was going to be daring enough to put his neck out there." As Frankel pushed decision making down the line, some editors initially had difficulty believing that they were actually expected to make decisions on their own.

Well before the newsroom chaos began, Joseph Lelyveld had left the deputy foreign editorship to return to South Africa as a correspondent. He subsequently took time off to write a book on the experience (*Move Your Shadow,* which won a Pulitzer Prize) and was again in New York near the end of 1984. Rosenthal had talked vaguely about a senior editing job for Lelyveld, but it never materialized. After working briefly on the magazine staff "as a stopgap until somebody could figure out where I belonged," Lelyveld concluded that Rosenthal didn't want him around and left to report from London.

He came back as foreign editor in December 1986, thankful he had missed the stress, confusion, and unhappiness of the transitional year, and grateful to be a senior editor under Frankel.

"Abe . . . just brooded over the *New York Times* all the time. And . . . he loved to give people opportunities, but *he* gave them." While Rosenthal would always embrace a great journalistic idea, his executives largely executed Rosenthal's wishes. Frankel was more inclined to leave his managers alone. "The number of people licensed to second-guess each department has been drastically reduced."

Early in Lelyveld's tenure as foreign editor, the *Times* correspondent in South Africa was expelled and his designated successor denied a visa. In the pre-Frankel days, conjectured Lelyveld, crisis meetings would have been held in the executive editor's office. As it was, Lelyveld took about a week to present a recommendation to Frankel. Afterward, he thanked Frankel for giving him time to solve the problem. "It gave me the sense I really was the foreign editor. The decision waited for me to make it."

Allan Siegal, who had been head of the news desk, was made an assistant managing editor (responsible for presentation and production of the news product) shortly after Frankel's appointment. When Siegal had come to the *Times* as a copyboy more than a quarter of a century earlier, he had fantasized about one day having such a job, but eventually had concluded he never would: "Rosenthal, who had had a very tough time as metropolitan editor, swimming upstream against Ted Bernstein, did not ever again want the editing side of the paper represented at so high a level."

Several desk editors took Siegal's promotion as a sign that Frankel would not treat career editors as second-class citizens, that they too could aspire to be part of the leadership of the newspaper.

Like others, Siegal was struck by Frankel's willingness to delegate.

"Abe sometimes impressed me as believing that the news department organization chart consisted of him in the middle and a thousand lines leading into that box. . . . Everybody in the newsroom reported directly to Abe. . . . If you got a raise, you got it from Abe. You got a bonus, you got it from Abe. You got a new assignment, you got it from Abe. If you had a problem, you wanted a decision, you went to Abe. . . . Max is changing that. . . . One person in the news department reports directly to Max, and that's [managing editor] Arthur Gelb. Four people [the assistant managing editors] report to Arthur Gelb, probably a group of thirty to forty people report to the four of us."

Shortly after taking over, Frankel handed out copies of their budgets to department heads. Many had never before seen them and were stunned to find the information being shared. Frankel also told them that, henceforth, they would be responsible for handing out merit raises.

By giving them the budget, Frankel was also making them responsible for keeping the news department—which had overspent the previous year—within allocation.

"It's astonishingly different," said Siegal, who as news editor had supervised several management-level subordinates whose salaries were unknown to him. "But I was told to give them their new numbers, and told that next year I would decide their new numbers. This is a radically different way of managing. It's the way the rest of the building is managed . . . but it wasn't Abe's way. And it was very hard to feel responsible for the product when he was calling all the shots."

Frankel traces the development of his management style to his experience as Sunday department chief. How, he had wondered, could one person run five sections? "Now, suddenly, I had those five sections and fifteen more." The only sensible course was to give each department head more responsibility. Nevertheless, the *Times*—if no longer a tyranny—is "still a monarchy. People still look to see whom I talk to, whom I smile at, and whom I'm allegedly down on, up on. . . . They want to take their cues from me."

Under Frankel, a certified public accountant began working full time with the news staff on the budget, signaling a further dissolving of the barriers between the business and news sides. Unlike a woman from the business side who had come in briefly under Rosenthal and quickly been labeled a "spy," the new accountant was winning acceptance. "If we can co-opt [the CPA] and persuade him, he can help us sell our story to the business side," said Dave Jones, editor of national editions.

Even with goodwill freely flowing, Frankel's early months saw some glitches. In mid-1987, for instance, Whitney was publicly and embarrassingly overruled by Frankel.

Whitney had sent a letter to all major presidential candidates requesting access to personal information for in-depth profiles. He wanted to view birth certificates, school transcripts, net worth statements, medical records, income tax returns, military records, and school transcripts—plus waivers of privacy rights for FBI and law enforcement agency files. The request arose, said Whitney, because of the importance of personal character as a presidential issue.

The candidates saw the *Times* letter as the equivalent of a subpoena.

"We're all running for the presidency, not for saint," wrote Senator Paul Simon in reply. That June, Frankel (in a memo to staff) stated that the request had gone too far.

Under Frankel, the *Times* also ran the most prominently displayed correction in its history—a two-column headline on the front page of July 13, 1987: "A CORRECTION: TIMES WAS IN ERROR ON NORTH'S SECRET FUND TESTIMONY." The story confessed that a previous *Times* report on Oliver North "went beyond Colonel North's actual words and stated incorrectly that he had testified that neither the President nor the Congress were to be informed about the secret fund."

The headline stunned *Times* watchers, who had never seen such a conspicuous acknowledgment of the *Times'* fallibility. But Frankel believed the retraction should be as prominent as the original story.

Frankel adopted a similarly direct approach in the *Times'* relationship with its black journalists.

When the changing-of-the-guard process began, minorities had wondered how they would fare. No minority member was ever in contention to be executive editor or managing editor. Paul Delaney, deputy national editor and a black, was the only ranking minority editor on the paper. For many minorities on staff, Delaney was a role model, confidant, and godfather—the only senior manager many thought truly understood them. They had assumed that, once the transitional dust settled, Delaney would be at least one rung closer to the top.

Like the rest of the staff, minorities had welcomed Frankel's appointment. "We were encouraged by the fact that Max had sought out minorities on the editorial board and a number of us had been told that Max was largely responsible for hiring minority copy aids when he was in charge of the Washington bureau," recalls Tom Morgan, a *Times* staff writer and former assistant metropolitan editor.

Morgan and a number of his fellow blacks grew concerned when, instead of rising in management, Delaney was made bureau chief in Madrid. They became more troubled when a white reporter, after a luncheon meeting with managing editor Arthur Gelb, claimed Gelb had said the paper's "affirmative action" hires did not meet *Times* standards.

Gelb heard the alleged remark was making the rounds of the newsroom and sought out several black reporters to deny the rumor; and on Christmas Eve of 1986, a number of those reporters met with Gelb and Frankel in an executive lunchroom to talk about their concerns.

They wanted no special treatment, said the black reporters, only to know that they were part of the *Times* family and that the opportunities for them were as bright as for anyone else. Through the years, they had seen a number of whites come onto the paper and receive assignments and opportunities to grow that minorities had not had.

Frankel promised that minorities would not be left out of the new order. All he asked was a chance to prove himself. He had a lot on his plate, but was not hostile to them or unsympathetic to their concerns. If they had problems with the paper or with him, they should talk directly to him; he had no intention of sweeping their difficulties under the rug.

Shortly after the meeting, Frankel named a black editor on the metropolitan desk. By and large, minorities saw the appointment as a positive sign, but hoped it was not the *Times'* way of washing its hands of the issue.

Paul Delaney, whose reassignment had raised eyebrows, acknowledged his situation had not worked out as he had hoped. Though management strongly denied he had been demoted, Delaney was unsure exactly what the transfer meant.

Delaney was fifty-two when Frankel was appointed executive editor. A native of Montgomery, Alabama, and the son of a carpenter, Delaney—like many black journalists of his generation—had great difficulty entering mainstream journalism.

Following army service, he had enrolled in Ohio State University's journalism school and, after graduating in 1958, applied to some seventy-five dailies across the country. A few invited him for interviews—which always ended abruptly once the editors discovered he was black. The only job he could find was writing for the *Baltimore Afro-American.*

The work consisted largely of making up letters to the editor, and Delaney soon quit and returned to Cleveland. He worked as a taxi driver, but continued to write scores of letters and was finally hired by a black paper in Atlanta. He quickly found himself at odds with his employer because the paper—fearful of losing its ads—refused to report on civil rights demonstrations.

In the early 1960s, daily newspapers began to recruit blacks and Delaney got a job in Ohio with the *Dayton Daily News.* He joined the *Washington Star* in 1967. Two years later, he received an invitation from Max Frankel to join the *Times* Washington bureau as a member of the "urban cluster" that included Jack Rosenthal.

Delaney accepted enthusiastically and carved out a niche covering civil rights, black politics, and black business. As the only black member of the Washington staff, he felt responsible for giving *Times* readers a window into the black community and for giving black newsmakers access to the pages of the *Times.* But lest he be pigeonholed as a reporter who could only write about blacks, Delaney insisted on covering nonblack subjects as well.

In 1974, Delaney was transferred to the Chicago bureau. And in late 1976, when the bureau chief's job came open, he assumed it would go to him. Instead, his editors moved someone else in. Delaney—normally a team player—was shattered and protested loudly. His editor explained that the new bureau chief had been ordered out of his previous job—and they felt compelled to find the man a position of equal rank. "Yeah, but you didn't have to find him *my* place," grumbled Delaney.

Several months later, Delaney was asked to be assistant national editor and subsequently became deputy national editor. He was pleased to move into management and soon became a magnet for minorities seeking advice: "It was a natural thing that happened to me and I accepted it." When coming up, Delaney had never had "anybody's shoulder to lean on, anybody's ear I could bend." And he had promised himself that if he was ever in a position to help those who came after him, he would do what he could.

He worried, however, that his own career might be stalled. To climb much higher at the *Times* normally required overseas experience. Years ago, he had tried to get that experience and the paper had refused him; he had done everything other than go abroad to qualify for the next step. Now, when he was no longer asking, the paper was volunteering to send him away.

When Frankel took over, Delaney had made it known he no longer wished to stay on the national desk. After nine years there and dealing with national news his entire career, Delaney wanted to do something else. Heading the Washington bureau or the metropolitan desk were reasonable options, but neither was offered. Madrid was a chance to buy time. In two years or so, he would return—hopefully to something higher than what he had left.

Before Delaney departed, two New York parties were held in

his honor. One was hosted by colleagues on the national desk, the other by a black friend and former *Times* reporter. Very few black *Times* staffers came to the one and very few whites to the other—a sign of how wide was the chasm that Frankel was trying to bridge.

During his first senior staff meeting, Frankel had told his editors that if they were looking for carnage, to look elsewhere. The editorial page bloodbath would not be replayed in the newsroom. He had come as a peacemaker.

In reaching out to career editors, to minorities, to women (from whose ranks he named the national editor and Sunday business editor), and in giving department heads more control over their domains, Frankel was trying to keep that pledge. But like any editor, Frankel knew that he would ultimately be judged not so much by how he treated his staff as by how he molded the publication. By sheer determination and brilliance, Rosenthal had made the *Times* his own; he had been shaped by it and then had shaped it, to dazzling effect. Now Frankel had a mandate from the publisher and an editorial budget of over ninety million dollars a year to show what he could do.

He would have roughly nine years to put his stamp on the paper—not as long as Rosenthal, but a healthy chunk of time for a man of action and ideas. And shortly after Frankel took over, the *Times,* ever so slightly, began to change.

Shorter stories ran on page one—sometimes alongside snazzy new graphics. A Sunday television supplement appeared. A consumer page emerged, as did columns on fitness, law, child rearing, and participatory sports. The paper became more tightly organized, even as the editing loosened up and allowed the writing to breath.

No executive editor of the *Times,* said Frankel, would dream of "wanting to tear it all up." Yet every decade or so, "major things have happened to the product. And you hope that they're not all just technologically or commercially driven, that some of them reflect deliberate journalistic policies and intentions."

Some of Frankel's decisions were relatively easy. The science section had been a smashing journalistic hit and its staff had won two Pulitzer Prizes in a row. The natural next step was to create a health staff and give them a segment of the paper—and to do the same with education. Many *Times* writers, particularly women, were upset by the "Style" page. Though it treated sophisticated subjects, it also showcased fashion and seemed too much like the old women's pages to be a part of the changing *Times.* Frankel did away with it.

Many of the decisions—and even framing the right questions—were difficult. How, asked Frankel, was the paper to cover the New York metropolitan region properly for New York readers while also catering to the needs of readers in Stamford and Hempstead and Newark? What is the function of a major newspaper that "sort of glides above the city and only penetrates at best into 20 percent of the homes around here and that is national in its impact and international in its aspiration? . . . What can it do that's constructive and intelligent without letting every tabloid horse us around?"

Frankel's tenure will answer those questions. But already the general direction is clear. The new *Times* will have more short articles, more people pieces, and more service and coping features than the old.

James Greenfield (one of four assistant managing editors), who oversees many of the "soft" sections, forecasts that the magazine will be more on top of the news and have much to say about current social trends. He also sees more specialized sections aimed at specific groups and more aids (lists and directories) to help the reader through an increasingly complicated paper. Other editors forecast a less rigid page one, more graphics, and the use of color in the news pages. "We'd be crazy if we didn't think about turning to color in one shape or form," says Sulzberger.

The new *Times* will also have a significantly greater national presence than the old, as printing sites open and the paper becomes more widely available. In 1987, national edition circulation hovered near two hundred thousand. Dave Jones, editor of that edition, thinks it can go considerably higher.

Circulation vice-president Russell Lewis believes much of the *Times'* future growth will come along the Northeast corridor—with the target remaining the high-income, well-educated readers *Times* advertisers like to reach.

Greenfield argues that Rosenthal's attempts to groom a successor may not have been a failure after all. Both Greenfield and managing editor Arthur Gelb would soon be retiring and the managers likely to replace them had surfaced through Rosenthal's efforts. Warren Hoge was made assistant managing editor for administration (handling personnel and related matters). John Lee, the former head of business news, was made assistant managing editor for news (serving essentially as deputy to the managing editor). Other senior *Times* editors also had been named. All of which will make it easier in time for Greenfield to "phase myself out."

Similar thoughts were on the mind of president Walter Mattson. "Punch and I have worked together for a long, long time . . . since 1970, when I was a made a vice-president. . . . That's one of the longest-running Broadway shows in history. We feel that things have gone well. We have an obligation to leave things in good order. And that means to bring along people to build the organization. We've been talking about that for a couple of years. . . . People are getting a chance to be tested, to show us what they can do in a controlled way."

By any standard, the Arthur Ochs Sulzberger era is one of staggering accomplishment. Company earnings have increased more than a hundredfold since Sulzberger took over. Corporate profits—$160 million in 1987—vastly exceed total company revenues in 1963. And gross revenues, at $1.7 billion, have been multiplied nearly seventeen times. Total employees (10,500 in 1987) have roughly doubled as the Times has gone from essentially a one-newspaper firm (with a radio station and interests in a couple of newsprint companies) to a corporate colossus with more than two dozen dailies; numerous weeklies, magazines, and broadcast outlets; a cable system; and substantial interests in three Canadian newsprint companies. And the *Times,* which Sydney Gruson calls the "great diamond in the tiara," boasts a news budget whose size approaches total corporate revenues of a quarter of a century ago. Throughout, the Sulzberger family has stayed firmly in charge.

To ensure that family control continues, stockholders approved a plan in 1986 that would allow family members to sell much of their stock without giving up the reins of the company. Since going public, the family had already increased its share of Class B stock (which elects 70 percent of the board of directors) to 80 percent of the total. Under the 1986 provisions, Class B stock could not be sold to outsiders unless offered first to the family and, second, to the company at the prevailing price for

Class A stock. If neither the family nor the company wished to purchase the shares, they would have to be converted into Class A stock (which elects only 30 percent of the directors), share for share, before being sold to outsiders. The scheme virtually guarantees that the potential desire of some family members to cash in their stock would not lead to a forced sale of the paper—as has happened with several third- and fourth-generation newspapers in the United States.

That such effort goes into keeping the Times a family company seems almost quaint in an age where corporations casually change hands. Yet precisely because corporations are so fickle and corporate values so fragile, the Times' transformation (and its success in moving one leg solidly into the world of commerce and keeping the other anchored in Sulzberger family values) is remarkable. Former vice-chairman James Goodale maintains it is also an argument for the value of the Times stock structure. "I think the best policy argument for having this kind of stock is what happened at the Times," said Goodale, "because if we hadn't had this stock, the Times wouldn't be the institution that it is today." The institution is, of course, largely what Adolph Ochs and the Sulzbergers have willed it to be. And with the naming in January 1987 of Arthur Ochs Sulzberger, Jr., thirty-five, as assistant publisher of the *Times,* the family essentially served notice that, for another generation at least, the Sulzberger legacy would be tended by one of its own.

With his dark, curly hair and attractive (almost delicate) bespectacled face, Sulzberger looks more like an artist than a business tycoon—or future press lord. But beneath the angelic appearance and easy, wisecracking manner, lies a tough intellect and a formidable will. One Times executive and admirer of Punch Sulzberger called the appointment "a watershed." Sulzberger, Jr., he said, "will be even better than his father. . . . He's not worried about controversy. He's . . . willing to make mistakes."

Young Sulzberger's elevation occasioned little fanfare. And his modest eleventh-floor office—on a different level and out of view of both the newsroom and the publisher's suite—is not prominently placed. Yet, unlike his father, who at a similar age was relegated to the newspaper's fringes, Sulzberger, Jr., was designated head of a committee grappling with the central question facing the *Times:* What will the paper be in the future?

Former Sunday editor Lester Markel had chaired a similar committee some two decades earlier, but Sulzberger's was the first such exercise run by the person who eventually will control the paper. It was not merely an intellectual exercise, but stemmed from the *Times'* decision to build a new four-hundred-million-dollar printing plant.

The plant (scheduled to be operational by 1990) should eliminate a persistent problem—the inability of the daily *Times* to expand to accommodate advertising or news. The presses will also permit the printing of full color in many sections and will significantly increase the number of sections the paper can turn out in any day—presenting the editorial department with a dazzling array of possibilities, the reader with a dizzying assortment of choices, and the circulation department with a heavier paper and a potentially major headache.

Determining what sort of newspaper would come off of those new presses was a matter of great concern to young Sulzberger. How was the *Times* to balance its allegiance to tradition with society's demand for change? How was the paper to grow into more sections offering more options to readers without overwhelming them—and without alienating those who had traditionally taken the *Times*? And how was it to respond to the challenge of increasing specialization?

Times coverage of international affairs is read both by the general public and by professional diplomats. Its stories on advertising are read by general consumers as well as by "fundamentally, every advertising executive that matters," notes Sulzberger. How, he wonders, as society increasingly fragments into narrow, specialized groups, can the *Times* best continue to serve the generalist and the expert?

Like his father, Sulzberger the younger attended the Browning School in New York and received his basic journalism training away from the *Times.* But his experiences have been quite different from his father's; he is as much his own man as his father's son. Instead of attending Columbia University as Punch did, Sulzberger chose Tufts University in Medford, Massachusetts, largely because his half sister was already there.

In high school and college, much to his father's chagrin,

Sulzberger vocally opposed the Vietnam War. That he was too young to cover "the best story of my generation"—the war and its effects on the United States—remains a source of regret.

Though he never considered anything other than journalism as a career, he wonders whether his unquestioning acceptance of a role in the family enterprise says something unflattering about himself, about a possible self-satisfied approach to life or an unwillingness to explore beyond what he already knew.

After completing his degree in political science, Sulzberger became a reporter on the thirty-four-thousand-circulation *Raleigh Times.* ("You don't learn journalism at the [*New York*] *Times* if your name is Sulzberger.")

Sulzberger next joined the Associated Press in London. He chose England largely because he wanted to work abroad and didn't speak a foreign language; he also figured that his wife—whom he had met at Tufts—would be able to find work there.

Sulzberger returned to the United States in 1978 as a correspondent in the *Times'* Washington bureau. The paper was on strike, but Sulzberger went to work anyway, and was surprised at his colleagues' uncritical reaction: "There seemed to be an . . . acceptance that there were some lines I couldn't cross, and a picket line was one I was going to cross."

He spent much of 1981 covering Mayor Edward Koch in New York and later spent time editing. As Sulzberger switched from assignment to assignment, he tackled each one energetically and was unavoidably aware that his treatment was not the norm for a young *Times* reporter: "I was spared a lot of the agony that some of my brethren down there went through. . . . I was able to ride above all that."

By 1982, Sulzberger was an advertising salesman. Having spent so much time as a journalist, he found the transition difficult. He had a vague notion that advertising simply poured into the *Times.* As he perceived parallels between reporting and advertising (the daily pressure was identical, as was the sense of feeding copy to the paper), his enthusiasm grew. Sulzberger personalized each sale. Instead of merely selling space in the paper, he was generating money so the Washington bureau could add another reporter, or so a *Times* correspondent could make another trip.

The contacts from his reporting days came in handy. For several of the officials he had covered in the Carter administration had gone to work for the Wall Street firms whose accounts Sulzberger handled.

Other assignments took him to production and corporate planning, and even to Harvard Business School for three months of intense study. The next stop, he assumed, would be circulation. Instead, he was told that the time had come for his name to go on the masthead. The position of assistant publisher had not previously existed, which Sulzberger took to be a great advantage: "No one's ever had it before, so no one . . . can tell you you're doing it wrong."

One of the assistant publisher's first tasks was to host some of the publisher's luncheons formerly run by his father. At those luncheons, held in a private dining room of the *Times,* heads of state and other renowned newsmakers break bread with senior *Times* editors in hopes that the accompanying exchange will translate into sympathetic coverage. One of Sulzberger's first sessions was with President Amin Gemayel of Lebanon. As he reached out to shake the president's hand and felt seven security guards watching his every move, Sulzberger's imagination took over. "They think I can't be the assistant publisher," he said to himself, as he envisioned being cut down in a hail of bullets.

Of course, no bullets came. But at times Sulzberger himself has difficulty believing that he is heir to the *Times.*

While in Washington, Sulzberger got to know Donald Graham of the *Washington Post.* "There have been occasions when I've called and said, 'Jesus, Don, I need your advice. . . . Talk to me.' He's been around the track; he knows all this stuff. He may not know all the players, he may not know the whole situation . . . but he's got a good sense of the possible."

Helpful as Graham has been, Sulzberger has not patterned himself after Graham. "What he did was no worse and perhaps better than what . . . I am doing. . . . But there are different pressures. The *Times* . . . has its own vision, different from the *Washington Post* vision. And there's a different family structure here than Don has. . . . There has been no model. And, quite frankly, it isn't as if I have been laying out this course myself."

Even Sulzberger's father cannot serve as an exemplar; for the paper that his father inherited no more resembles the one the son was destined to run than a biplane resembles the Skylab.

During most of the Punch Sulzberger era, Walter Mattson held responsibility for the business operations of the newspaper and Sulzberger for the editorial side. "It works fine for the two of us," said Punch Sulzberger. "I would suspect the next publisher would want to bring his business department and his newspaper back together under one roof."

Though the paper is more complex, it also is infinitely more sound. And the "diamond in the tiara" is staffed with a new generation of talent. "The thing I'm proudest of is . . . generally speaking, I've chosen the right people," says Sulzberger, Sr.

The team that Sulzberger, Sr., and Walter Mattson put in place—Frankel in the newsroom, Jack Rosenthal on the editorial page, and Lance Primis as *Times* executive vice-president and general manager—was a source of continuing comfort to Sulzberger, Jr. All arrived in their jobs, like young Sulzberger, with a highly developed sense of mission.

Not surprisingly for a man with roots in the New Frontier, Jack Rosenthal wants to see more causes and more crusades on his page: "I know that works and I know you can make a difference." If one of his editorialists feels strongly about the homeless, for example, Rosenthal intends to encourage the writer to focus on it and "get something accomplished about it."

Primis, a former University of Wisconsin athlete who chose sales over a professional baseball career, became *Times* general manager in 1986 and brought with him a reputation for motivating those who work for him and a determination not to take the market for granted. His energy and enthusiasm match Sulzberger's, and his irreverent style meshes with that of the witty, sharp-tongued heir. Sulzberger represents "a contemporary view," says Primis, who believes Sulzberger will inevitably spark a debate between change and tradition.

Nearly a year after his promotion to assistant publisher, Sulzberger, Jr., said he was happy not to have his father's job. He could host publisher's luncheons, putter around the newsroom, run projects such as the committee on the future, and avoid decisions he was not ready to make.

"When push comes to shove, I can defer if I have to, or if I want to. . . . I don't have to be the son of a bitch. I can go around and be involved in all these things, and help people arrive at decisions; and bring the business side and the news side closer together; and start that process of intermingling. . . . And then when they say, 'Yes, but is it coming out of my space or is it coming out of his space,' I can say, 'Well, gee, maybe the publisher ought to answer that one.' And I won't piss off anybody. So it's easy for me right now. I've got tremendous freedom. So the fact that . . . the day may occur where, in fact, I can't defer the questions somehow . . . is scary.

"On the other hand," he said, pointing in the direction of Lance Primis's office, "I've got, across that hall, the brightest newspaper businessman in the country, bar none. And on the third floor, I've got the finest newspaper editor in the country, bar none. They're too smart to let me fuck it up. . . . They're just too good. . . . And that's a nice reserve chute to have when you jump out of the airplane. . . . This is a good place to be right now. . . . I can get to know [Frankel, Rosenthal, and Primis], and they can get to know me. I don't report to them; they don't report to me. I can learn. I've gone from being a low-level manager to being a senior executive in one step. There's a lot here that I don't know. And this is the chance to learn."

Arthur Ochs Sulzberger announced the promotion of his son to deputy publisher in April 1988. At the same time, Primis was named president of the *Times.* The promotion gave young Sulzberger responsibility for the news and business departments (and made him Frankel's and Lance Primis's boss). The editorial page continued to report directly to the publisher. Clearly, in the opinion of one whose opinion mattered, Arthur Ochs Sulzberger, Jr., was learning his lessons just fine.

PART FOUR

THE CHAINS: GANNETT AND KNIGHT-RIDDER

CHAPTER 17

EXPANDING HORIZONS

To admirers, Allen Neuharth is a businessman-cum-prophet who has shown fellow publishers a golden path to the future. To critics, he is a scourge of biblical proportions who has lowered journalistic standards, homogenized newspapers, and led an entire industry down the road of superficiality. Whatever their feeling about the Gannett Company chairman, newspaper people view him as a legend who has lifted himself out of poverty, his company out of obscurity, and divided time into two distinct eras: pre- and post-Neuharth.

In another age, Al Neuharth might have been a pirate, taking by cunning that which was not his by birth. But as a child of the twentieth century, he became a corporate prince, sneering at convention while racking up an unparalleled record of business expansion and earnings growth—building Gannett into the largest and one of the most profitable newspaper chains in the country.

No newspaper executive better represents the industry's shift from family domination. And no one has enjoyed the benefits of that transition more conspicuously or unapologetically.

Ferried about in limousines and personalized jets, enveloped in Gatsby-like glitter, Neuharth glides comfortably through the world of privilege, a conquering potentate enjoying the spoils of war. With his wavy, silver hair, glittering smile, and elegant gray, black, and white wardrobe, the diminutive press lord looks more the pampered, aging playboy than the ruler of a corporate empire.

Beneath the nouveau-riche gloss, however, lie the memories of a disadvantaged small-town boy who saw other kids playing with toys he could not have and his widowed mother enduring snubs he could not abide. If, in some respects, Neuharth remains the kid on the wrong side of the tracks, he has edged ever closer to the dividing line (or perhaps simply brought the dividing line closer to him).

Many who consider the *New York Times* a cathedral call *USA Today*—Gannett's flagship and Al Neuharth's biggest triumph—a journalistic junk-food palace. Such sniping notwithstanding, *USA Today* has significantly altered the character of newspapers in the United States, even as Gannett has redefined the newspaper business. And Neuharth himself—with an annual cash compensation of $1.5 million plus stock options (which netted $3.5 million in 1987)—has become an icon to those who cherish the spirit of Horatio Alger.

The second of two sons, Neuharth was born in 1924 in Eureka, South Dakota, two years before his father died from injuries suffered during a farm accident. His mother found work wherever she could, waiting tables, taking in laundry, always struggling to make ends meet. For Neuharth, his mother's example was both inspirational and depressing. He still rankles when recalling the discrimination she faced as a single mother trying to make it alone: "I saw how much harder she had to work and how much less she got in rewards for it than the men who were making a living in that town."

As a youngster, Neuharth realized he was a have-not and that many of the haves in Alpena, South Dakota (the town of four hundred where he was raised), looked down on him. He hated that, but his mother taught him the only way to overcome it was "to work a hell of a lot harder" while surviving by "scratching or clawing" or doing whatever else was necessary. "My mother proved that she could survive, despite being discriminated against."

While she never made very much money, she vigorously competed in her own arena and made Neuharth realize he would have to do the same—"because nobody's going to give you anything if you don't go after it."

Neuharth coveted the new bicycle owned by the children

across the street, but had to settle for one that was secondhand. "I felt, from those days on, that if you are able to earn material things, go ahead and enjoy them."

He worked first as a newspaper carrier (thereby earning the five dollars for his used bicycle) and later in the composing room of the weekly in Alpena. When a dislocated knee barred him from high school basketball competition for several weeks, Neuharth became active on the school paper. In his junior year, he became the paper's editor.

For Neuharth, as for other young American men coming of age in the early 1940s, a war loomed. Pearl Harbor was attacked his senior year in high school. Within months, he had joined the army and subsequently served four years as an infantryman in Europe and the Pacific.

Neuharth came home with a Bronze Star and a hatred of war—even though he felt World War II a necessary conflict: "In politics today, I believe . . . most hawks didn't carry guns, or fire bullets, or weren't fired at."

The war years developed Neuharth's political consciousness and introduced him to a much larger world of possibilities: "There is no other way I could have broken out of that small arena and, in . . . forty-three months, developed a global perspective. I trained in many places in this country, from Texas to California to New Jersey. And I served in both the European and Pacific theaters. So all of a sudden, this eighteen-year-old country kid . . . comes back nearly twenty-two years old [and] has had the whole world opened up to him."

In that world, he would become so wealthy and so famous, so much more than anyone from Eureka, South Dakota, had ever been before, that no one would ever look down on him again.

While completing his journalism degree (under the GI Bill) at the University of South Dakota, Neuharth talked to a friend about starting a weekly tabloid that would cover every spectator sport in the state—and that could serve as the flagship for similar publications across the country. The friend, Bill Porter, went on to earn his law degree and Neuharth became a reporter for the Associated Press, but they clung to their entrepreneurial dream.

After two years with the Associated Press, Neuharth quit to become editor of the proposed publication. Porter became business manager. With fifty thousand dollars raised from selling stock, the two would-be somebodies founded *SoDak Sports.* The ten-cent tabloid was an immediate hit with readers, but never caught on with advertisers. Two years later, their money ran out, and *SoDak Sports* closed its doors.

The failure was a deep disappointment and a source of considerable shame. But later Neuharth would say, "In the thirty-plus years since [the publication's failure], there have been many, many occasions when I have just multiplied what I did in *SoDak Sports* that worked, multiplied it many, many times and done it again; or . . . stopped short of doing . . . on a big scale what I screwed up on a small scale."

Following the failure of *SoDak Sports,* Neuharth became a reporter with the *Miami Herald,* one of Knight Newspapers' leading publications: "I was just grateful to have a reporter's job at ninety-five dollars a week, because I was bloodied and I was broke." And he prayed he could perform up to *Herald* standards.

Neuharth's fears were quickly laid to rest: "I was astonished that the journalistic standards necessary to star in the *Miami Herald* newsroom were not all that much different than what they had been with the Associated Press in South Dakota or with *SoDak Sports.*" Neuharth was promoted to assistant city editor and discovered competition for management jobs was not very tough either. At that point, Neuharth decided to concentrate on being in charge.

In rapid succession, Neuharth became executive city editor and then assistant managing editor, gaining a reputation for ruthlessness along the way. Six years after joining Knight Newspapers, Neuharth was appointed assistant executive editor (the number-two editorial position) of the organization's *Detroit Free Press.*

Neuharth's prospects in the Knight organization were bright. His boss, Lee Hills, was a fast-rising star, serving not only as publisher of the *Free Press* but as a key executive for the entire Knight Newspapers chain. Jack and James Knight, the two brothers who controlled the company, were Neuharth supporters. Still, when Neuharth received a feeler from the smaller Gannett organization in early 1963, he felt compelled to explore it: "I did a coldly calculating analysis of whether Neuharth, then age thirty-eight, would be better off in ten or twenty years in an organization like Knight or Gannett."

He enlisted the help of J. Montgomery Curtis, executive

director of the American Press Institute (API) and the person who had recommended Neuharth to Paul Miller, Gannett's president. After tabulating the advantages and disadvantages of each news organization on a chart, the men concluded that Gannett offered Neuharth a better shot at one day being boss.

No Gannett family members worked in the company. And Miller, then fifty-six, was looking for an understudy to be his successor. Miller claimed that no insider had emerged, which translated to Neuharth as, "The [CEO] job is yours if you come in and earn it because nobody's tagged for it."

Knight was a significantly larger and more prestigious organization, but Neuharth felt that, with the right managers and a firm commitment to expansion, Gannett could move itself into Knight's league.

Neuharth signed on as general manager of Gannett's morning and evening newspapers in Rochester, New York. He received no guarantees concerning the top job, but he had considerable faith in his own abilities. Also, if within five years a path was not cleared to the top, he would be young enough to join a company that might make him its chief. (Ironically, four years after Neuharth came to Gannett, Montgomery Curtis left the API to become vice-president, development for Knight Newspapers, the very company he had convinced Neuharth to leave.)

At the time, Gannett was a small-town, regional company with a string of undistinguished dailies, the largest of which were the flagship *Rochester Democrat and Chronicle* (133,000 circulation) and *Times Union* (131,000 circulation). But Paul Miller dreamed of expansion.

As a board member of the Associated Press (to which he was elected in 1950 and of which he became president in 1963), Miller had met many newspaper owners. With Neuharth to help run the company, the tall, handsome Miller could spend more time on the golf course and over dinner tables charming those who might sell to Gannett.

In characterizing the contributions of the three foremost architects of the company, journalism scholar Ben Bagdikian wrote, "Frank Gannett had a limited vision, Miller broadened it, and Neuharth built it into a modern conglomerate empire."

Frank Gannett was not so much a man of limited vision, as one whose vision was limited by his time. When he began building his company shortly after the turn of the century, the age of big business was only beginning (most people still worked on farms or in small businesses) and the age of conglomerates was decades away.

Frank Gannett was born in 1876. His father was a failed farmer who later became a marginally successful hotel manager. Gannett's family had no money for his education, but he attended Cornell University on scholarship. His writings for the student newspaper led to a warm and mutually admiring relationship with university president Jacob Gould Schurman. When President William McKinley appointed Schurman to head a commission of inquiry to the Philippines in 1899, Schurman took his protégé along as his private secretary. Though Gannett could have remained in government service, he chose newspapering—which seemed a more stable profession—but maintained a lifelong interest in government and foreign policy. In 1900, Gannett was named managing editor of the *Ithaca Daily News,* then owned by a member of Cornell's faculty.

Six years later, Gannett was ready to strike out on his own; and, after a few false starts, he came upon the *Elmira Gazette,* in which he and some associates bought a half interest. Gannett's share was three thousand dollars in cash, five thousand dollars borrowed from a bank and a two-thousand-dollar note from friends. By the early 1920s, Gannett (having effectively bought out his primary partner) owned papers in Elmira, Ithaca, Utica, and Rochester, New York (where he set up company headquarters in 1918 and merged Rochester's *Union and Advertiser* and *Evening Times* into the *Times Union*).

A teetotaler, Gannett refused liquor advertising well before Prohibition was passed. "A newspaper, to suit me, must be clean, one that I would be willing to have my mother, my own sister, or my daughter read," Gannett told the Hartford, Connecticut, Chamber of Commerce. He opposed gambling and "rotten movies" and believed in local editorial autonomy for his newspapers.

Originally a Democrat, Gannett thought the New Deal (and the corporate taxes and deficit spending it represented) a disaster and viewed Franklin Roosevelt's attempt to pack the Supreme Court as an outrage. His frustration with national policy led him to offer himself for the 1940 Republican presidential nomination. Only at the convention—when he received a mere thirty-three delegate votes on the first ballot and Wendell Willkie got the nomination—did Gannett realize how outrageously flawed his political calculations had been. He subsequently served as vice-chairman of the Republican National Committee.

All the while, Gannett's newspapers prospered. Generally acquired for modest prices, they tended to be located in noncompetitive markets, making profitability easy to achieve. Gannett also was not above collusion with the competition—working out an agreement with William Randolph Hearst in 1937 to kill two Gannett papers in Albany, New York, in exchange for Hearst killing two papers in Rochester—ensuring a monopoly market for each publisher.

Gannett fractured his spine in a fall in 1955 and never totally recovered. He arranged in April 1957 for Paul Miller to succeed him as president. A former Washington bureau chief for the Associated Press, Miller had joined the company in 1947 as Frank Gannett's executive assistant. Gannett, eighty-one, died the December following Miller's promotion, having amassed twenty-two daily newspapers, four radio stations, and two television stations. He was survived by his widow, a daughter, an adopted son, and a foundation that bore his name.

The Frank E. Gannett Newspaper Foundation, controlled by company officials, held majority ownership of Gannett's newspapers. It had been created in 1935, according to Gannett's widow, to ensure that the newspapers "would not pass into the hands of interests who might change their character and cause them to have an unwholesome influence on their communities."

In short order, Miller sold off six newspapers he considered marginal—five going to local managements and one to the Hearst Corporation. He also disposed of UHF television stations in Elmira and Binghamton, New York—in preparation, he said, for growth.

By the time Neuharth arrived, Miller's ambitions had soared. "Paul had a vision of breaking out of the regional mode and trying to develop a national company, and I certainly did," said Neuharth. "The only question was how quickly we could do it."

In 1964, Miller made his first major acquisition: the nine New York City–area Westchester-Rockland Group dailies, with a combined circulation of nearly two hundred thousand.

The next year, Neuharth got Miller's backing for a new daily newspaper to replace the tiny, lackluster *Cocoa Tribune* in Florida. The idea had stemmed from Neuharth's days with Knight in Florida; he had become convinced that the Cape Canaveral area could support an aggressive daily. With considerable nervousness, the board went along with the Miller-Neuharth plan to buy the *Tribune* and use it as the stepping-stone for a new newspaper.

Phil Currie, then a young reporter for the *Rochester Times Union,* recalls a change in the atmosphere in Rochester as the Cocoa project progressed and as "a lot of people kept disappearing . . . to Florida." Employees felt that the company was on the move, that it "wasn't afraid to try things."

Even as the action heated up in Florida, in Rochester—where Neuharth was general manager—a number of new people began appearing in the building. They would form the nucleus of the Neuharth team.

John Quinn was among the first. Though outwardly relaxed—even laid-back—he was nearly as driven as Neuharth; but having weathered a heart attack in his early thirties, he had learned how to pace himself. In time, Neuharth would refer to Quinn as the conscience of Gannett—a strong voice battling to protect editorial integrity.

A year and a half younger than Neuharth, Quinn had been day managing editor at the *Providence Journal Bulletin.* Starting as a copyboy while still in college, Quinn had been with the paper for twenty-three years. But Quinn's immediate superior was a relatively young man who had no intention of stepping aside for Quinn. The position Neuharth offered—as ranking editor of the two Rochester papers—was a step up from Quinn's old job. But he was not so much taking a job as buying into Neuharth's dream. Neuharth clearly wanted nothing less than to run the company and promised a great adventure to those who would join him. Quinn's title, director of news, was uncommon. But Neuharth was to make a practice of giving titles so unusual that the responsibilities could encompass whatever he wished.

Ron Martin, destined to become executive editor of *USA Today,* was also drawn to Neuharth's vision. A native of Joplin, Missouri, Martin had met Neuharth while working as an assistant city editor at the *Detroit Free Press.* Before going to Gannett, Neuharth had said to Martin, "I'm not suggesting you should ever leave the *Free Press,* but if you ever do, you ought to keep us in mind in Rochester. There'll be interesting things going on there."

The comment stayed with Martin, who had come to Detroit in 1959 straight out of the University of Missouri Journalism School. Martin, in his late twenties, was beginning to worry (in the way of young, ambitious men) that his career was stagnating. During five years in Detroit, he had advanced through a lot of different jobs, put behind him his small-town awe, and was ready to move up. If that meant taking a chance on something new, fine. He had been responsible for making his own way ever since his widower father had died when Martin was eighteen; so far he had always landed on his feet.

Martin arrived at Gannett in 1964 with no set job. He floated through a variety of assignments—editing on the city desk, creating a Sunday television magazine—and headed to Cocoa in early 1966 to help with the new paper.

Cocoa was abuzz with activity—as Neuharth presided over a plant expansion, market studies, and the production of prototypes; and in late January, he announced that on March 21, Brevard County, Florida, would have a new paper named *Today.*

The ten-cent tabloid called itself "Florida's Space Age Newspaper." The lead story for its first edition was a report ruling out radio sabotage in the failure of the Gemini 8 spacecraft. Inside, an editorial crowed, "Today for the first time Brevard County has a county-wide newspaper of its own," and went on to rave about Brevard as "the birthplace of the Space Age—an area alive with the promise of discovery and the adventure and mystery of the unknown."

After a few weeks, circulation had reached thirty thousand copies daily and by August 1968, the paper was in the black. Neuharth's reputation as publishing's Midas was born.

Martin saw *Today* as a turning point for the company. Even as papers failed all over the country, Gannett was standing up and shouting, "We can start a newspaper."

Back in Rochester, Neuharth was playing corporate hardball with Miller. In the midst of trying to make *Today* succeed, Neuharth had been offered the executive vice-presidency of the *New York Daily News*—with a clear shot at becoming publisher shortly thereafter. The job would place Neuharth in position to control the biggest metro daily in the country—in a city no one could take for granted. He told Miller he found the offer attractive but that running the Gannett organization could be even more so. Miller named Neuharth executive vice-president of Gannett and promised to make him president within five years.

Before turning over the reins of the company, Miller hungered to make Gannett into a large, powerful publishing entity. Miller, Neuharth, and their financial advisers pondered how to make that happen. Issuing public stock seemed, by far, the easiest way to obtain the financial muscle and flexibility that would permit Gannett to pursue an aggressive acquisitions program—particularly since many board members didn't want the company to borrow large sums of money.

In 1966, Gannett's revenues cleared the hundred-million-dollar mark for the first time. Profits before taxes were slightly over fourteen million dollars and net income was just over seven million—a respectable financial performance, but hardly spectacular enough to finance a major expansion program out of corporate earnings. Miller already had passed up some attractive deals because money was not readily available.

Financing acquisitions was not the only reason for going public. Issuing public stock would give the company an easy way to share ownership with executives and, ultimately, with other employees. Going public would also permit the company's foundation—through the sale of its stock—to diversify its holdings and avoid conflict with proposed prohibitions against foundations holding majority ownership in corporations.

Miller and other board members worried, however, that issuing stock might mean giving up control. What if shareholders demanded a voice in editing the newspapers? Or objected to editorial positions?

Such arguments struck Quinn as comic. If anything, shareholders were likely to be considerably more responsible than "a publisher who owns the whole damn thing telling you how to edit your newspaper."

In October 1967, Gannett offered some five hundred thousand shares in the over-the-counter market. Nearly seven years later Miller wrote: "Our stock offering did not receive any particular ovation in Wall Street. On the contrary, we quickly learned that too few in the financial community knew much about newspapers—beyond the disasters that had befallen some in New York—and fewer still knew or cared much about Gannett. . . . Our stock came out at $29 . . . and shortly dropped to $20 and less. It moved upward later, but haltingly."

Alarmed, Miller decided a full-scale promotional campaign was necessary. Wall Street's analysts and players would have to be told that even though papers were failing in New York City, they were thriving in small markets across the country—and big money could be made by those clever enough to buy. "Paul Miller and I did a lot of preaching," said Neuharth.

Although Gannett's low-profile news staff "tried to be community oriented and local," recalls Quinn, the high-profile Miller-Neuharth campaign triggered "cheap shots" from critics, who assumed Gannett cared only about money.

Though the news staff agonized over the response to the chain's growing reputation, the promotional efforts were having their intended effect. Wall Street was taking notice. Newspaper owners were flirting. And Miller and Neuharth were more eager than ever to dance.

Gannett

Al Neuharth

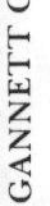

Tom Curley

Cathleen Black

John Quinn

John Curley

Gerald Garcia

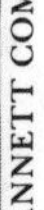

Nancy Woodhull

CHAPTER 18

BUYING INTO THE BIG TIME

Only winning a bank full of cash might have equaled the impact on Gannett of suddenly having thousands of shares of publicly traded stock. The effect was as if a huge supermarket were opened, the shelves stocked with newspaper companies, and Miller and Neuharth invited to race up and down the aisles and toss selections into their basket. They went on a shopping spree unlike anything previously seen in the newspaper world—and changed the sleepy, regional firm into a rah-rah corporation that rewarded entrepreneurial skills and the ability to manage rapid change.

Several months after going public, Gannett agreed to buy Times Mirror's San Bernardino newspapers. "We thought that was pretty hot stuff," recalled Neuharth. "Here . . . is this . . . company headquartered in Rochester and all of a sudden we're in both Florida [with *Today*] and California. . . . From that point on, the determination to make it a national media company was stronger and stronger."

Paul Miller was constantly on the prowl for acquisitions. After receiving a routine letter from Federated Publications president Louis Weil in 1969, he noticed that the stationery identified the seven Federated newspapers (in Michigan, Indiana, Idaho, and Washington state). Miller dashed off a note: "I looked at the map on your stationery. Gannett and Federated don't seem to compete or conflict anyplace. We ought to talk about a merger."

After two years of wrangling, Federated was acquired for sixty-seven million dollars in Gannett common stock. In the interim, Miller and Neuharth were busily shopping elsewhere, picking up papers in Honolulu, Guam, West Virginia, Vermont, and wherever else prospects were right. Gannett was not interested in big newspaper problems or highly competitive markets, but focused on dominant small and medium-sized newspapers in growing areas. The deals very often were for stock, and of a magnitude Gannett would have found difficult to finance as a private company.

With merger and acquisition activity heating up, Neuharth decided to hire a savvy Wall Streeter to specialize in deal making. He settled on Douglas McCorkindale, a graduate of Columbia College and Law School who was a partner at the firm of Thacher, Proffitt & Wood.

When approached by a headhunter on Neuharth's behalf, McCorkindale was practicing securities and corporate law and expecting to continue to do so for a long time; but he was intrigued enough to meet Neuharth for drinks in New York's Waldorf-Astoria. Later, he met Miller and other Gannett people. Though he liked them, he was reluctant to leave his prestigious law firm.

Gannett continued to woo him and McCorkindale (then living in Saddle River, New Jersey) increasingly wondered whether he wanted to spend the next several years catching the 8:42 train every morning and the 5:47 every night. One Tuesday he went into the law firm's regularly scheduled meeting and told his colleagues he intended to take the job in Rochester. They laughed in disbelief but after he convinced them he was serious, they voted to keep his partnership agreement alive for two years—should he come to his senses.

No grand acquisitions strategy existed when McCorkindale arrived in 1971, but he soon realized none was required. Many newspaper owners were getting on in years; they faced successor problems or estate tax problems and were looking for help. Part of his job—following Miller's and Neuharth's lead—was to persuade them that selling to Gannett was the most desirable solution.

Though McCorkindale initially found Rochester an insular, cold town, he soon learned that Gannett's name opened doors. He also discovered that deal-making opportunities abounded.

During his first nineteen months with the company, nineteen newspapers were acquired.

Absorbing the new properties was a major challenge. But the process was no easier for those acquired—most of which were previously owned by families or small corporations.

Brian Donnelly was a rising executive with the Westchester-Rockland newspaper organization when Gannett took it over in 1964. By 1971, he had become assistant general manager of the group but was still not accustomed to Gannett's style. The previous owners had been reserved businessmen who wouldn't dream of raising their voices to advertisers or making speeches that might offend their peers. Suddenly the mercurial Neuharth was railing against "cockeyed" advertisers and a fossilized newspaper industry. "We would just sit back in horror," recalled Donnelly.

Equally unsettling were Gannett's management requirements. The first corporate publisher sent to Westchester-Rockland by Gannett was much more budget-oriented than the family member who had run the papers previously. When Federated joined the company and brought in a sophisticated budgeting system of its own, Gannett became even more rigorous. "All of a sudden we went through a budgeting revolution," said Donnelly, "and we found that the financial people we had at Westchester were inadequate and . . . couldn't provide us with what [Gannett] needed."

By the end of 1971, Gannett owned fifty-three daily newspapers. The next year the company bought papers in Tennessee and Texas. Charles Overby, then editorial page editor at the *Nashville Banner,* recalls Neuharth dropping by after a morning run to look over the new property. "He was like some guy from another planet . . . all sweaty . . . just kind of looking around. In this *white* running suit."

To many, Gannett itself was looking like a predator from another planet with an appetite that grew stronger with every newspaper consumed. "There are 34 states in which we are not now doing business," Miller told *Finance* magazine in 1973, leaving little doubt that—if Miller got his way—that situation would soon change.

In those early days, many owners came to Gannett almost solely because of Miller, who had converted his leadership of the Associated Press into a hunting ground for the company. But

Neuharth, who had received the titles of president and chief operating officer in 1970, believed Gannett could grow faster than it had: "It was no secret to my associates that I was chomping at the bit to get the CEO's hat on my head. And when that happened in '73 . . . I was pretty aggressive and ambitious—some thought too much so—but I didn't waste too much time [before] trying to move things in the direction I had been wanting to go: bigger markets, bigger acquisitions, bigger dreams, and more entrepreneurship."

Since the early growth had come more easily than he had expected, the potential, he reasoned, was greater than he had assumed. Also, he remembered his mother's exhortations not to rest on his laurels, to push himself harder after reaching each goal. As Neuharth pushed, Gannett grew and operating executives raced to keep up.

Along with his other jobs, Quinn was responsible for the Gannett News Service (GNS), whose main operation was in Washington, D.C. GNS reports were transmitted from Washington to Rochester and sent from there to Gannett papers elsewhere. In the beginning—with Gannett papers clustered in New York, New Jersey, and Connecticut—the mechanics were simple.

The stories were delivered, via wire, to most papers in those states and sent, by mail, to Gannett's sole distant paper—the *Commercial News* in Danville, Illinois. Leasing a wire simply to send reports to Danville (or even for some of the smaller nearby properties) struck Gannett as prohibitively expensive. (GNS reports to the paper in Ithaca, for instance, were sent by bus from the paper in Elmira.) As the corporation expanded, adding properties throughout the country, the question of how to serve them inevitably came up.

"That was the time to make the hard decision," said Quinn. "When we said we provided the Gannett News Service so all newspapers would have firsthand coverage out of Washington and the state capitals, did we mean it? Or did we mean it only if you could get there by bus? . . . We went through some very expensive and difficult technical years trying to figure out how realistically we could justify carrying a wire all the way to California for . . . the *San Bernardino Sun.*"

Gannett concluded that if the company was going to grow,

the news service had to grow with it. The company invested in the wire, and the age of the bus-delivered news service ended.

As growth had accelerated, Neuharth had delegated more of his news responsibilities to Quinn, making him vice-president for news and a member of the Gannett operating group in July 1971. Quinn, in turn, was cultivating new managers under him, many of whom would rise to key positions in the company. None would advance more spectacularly or with less apparent effort than John Curley and his younger brother, Tom—destined to become, respectively, Neuharth's successor and president of his most precious publication.

Raised in Easton, Pennsylvania (population: roughly thirty thousand), where Middle American values reigned and sports lay at the core of the culture, the tall and athletic Curley brothers could have walked straight out of a postcard from America.

John, nearly ten years older than Tom, played a big part in raising his younger brother, taking him for pick-up basketball games, teaching him to catch a baseball, providing a solid set of footsteps for Tom to follow.

Both parents started out as teachers, the father later becoming a school principal and superintendent of schools. He worked two jobs until he was well into his sixties, without ever having much money. The boys, though instilled with their father's sense of public responsibility, decided early on not to share his fate.

As teenagers, they worked on the hometown paper. Tom decided on a newspaper career early. John thought of becoming a lawyer and running for political office, not entirely giving up those dreams until the age of thirty—after spending summer and fall of 1969 as press secretary to William Cahill in his successful race to become governor of New Jersey. In the rough and tumble of the campaign, John found he hated politics; he left Cahill after the election.

The editor of the *Perth Amboy* (New Jersey) *Evening News,* where John had once worked as night editor, contacted Quinn on John Curley's behalf and mentioned that Curley was job hunting. "And boy, if you've got any sense, you'll grab him."

Curley was already an experienced journalist, having worked nights for the Associated Press while earning a master's degree in journalism at Columbia University. Upon graduating, he had gone to the AP operation in New Jersey before joining the Perth Amboy paper. Quinn was sufficiently taken with him to create a position as suburban editor of the Rochester *Times Union.*

With his low-key, affable style, Curley impressed Quinn as a gifted, hardworking editor who could spot talent and manage it well. When the editorship became open at the *Courier-News* in Bridgewater, New Jersey, several months later, Quinn did not hesitate to recommend him. Within a year of Curley's arrival in Bridgewater, the publisher became terminally ill. Curley took up the slack, juggling the jobs of editor and publisher, leaning on the business manager for assistance with budget matters and turning to the plant supervisor for help overseeing installation of new presses. Quinn would visit and walk away amazed at Curley's energy and dedication. "Curley was down there banging a sledgehammer on the press . . . [then] back upstairs writing headlines," recalled Quinn in disbelief.

In August 1971, little more than a year after his arrival, Gannett promoted Curley to publisher and president of the *Bridgewater Courier-News.*

Around the same time, the editor who had alerted Quinn to John Curley told Quinn over drinks, "If you like John Curley, you should see the younger one. He's better."

While earning his political science degree at La Salle College in Philadelphia, Tom had worked at the *Woodbridge News Tribune* (previously the *Perth Amboy Evening News*) as an intern reporter and later as a copy editor. Quinn (who by then was responsible for news at all Gannett papers) proposed Tom start as a reporter at the *Press & Sun-Bulletin* in Binghamton, New York. Tom held out for an editorship, which was offered the following year—in Rochester, where he stepped into his brother's old job as night suburban editor.

John Curley left Bridgewater to become head of the Washington bureau in 1974, adding the title of general manager of the Gannett News Service the following year. The news service had always been run by reporter types, but Quinn felt it had grown to the point that "it couldn't be run by a bureau chief who wanted to spend all his time covering politics and letting the clerk pay the bills." The company also wanted a more substantial corporate presence in Washington and thought Curley would bring it.

Prior to Curley's arrival, news service reporters would type out their stories, which would be edited and telecopied to Rochester. In Rochester, keyboard operators would punch the stories into perforated teletypesetting tape in a format that could be transmitted, via wire, to other Gannett papers. Gannett, however, had the wire only at night, which meant that papers with early deadlines got the reports late. Curley was charged with taking the news service from the linotype days into the computer age so papers could get the news on time.

In May 1977, Gannett acquired Speidel Newspapers, a Reno, Nevada–based company with thirteen dailies in nine states and a reputation for sky-high profit margins. The deal, consummated with a $170 million exchange of stock, added newspapers in California, Colorado, Iowa, Minnesota, Nebraska, Nevada, New York, Ohio, and South Dakota. "It was another giant stride by Gannett," wrote the *Washington Post,* "one which made it a truly national publishing company."

The acquisition was Gannett's largest to date and the second largest in U.S. history—exceeded by Newhouse Newspapers' $300 million purchase several months earlier of the company that owned *Parade* magazine. Yet Gannett—closing out the year owning seventy-seven newspapers and with revenues of $786 million and net income of $90 million—had even larger prey in sight.

Doug McCorkindale had become vice-president for finance and law and a member of Gannett's board of directors, with the principal responsibility for seeking out companies to buy. Around November 1977, he heard that the American Financial Corporation in Cincinnati—a significant stockholder in Combined Communications Corporation of Phoenix, Arizona—was thinking of selling its interests. A conversation in Miami that December with the president of American Financial confirmed the rumor. Neuharth met for preliminary talks with Karl Eller, president of Combined, that January. Serious negotiations began in February, with McCorkindale representing Gannett and Goldman Sachs and Company representing Combined. The meeting ended without agreement, but that April, Eller called McCorkindale and suggested the talks resume. The sides quickly reached an accord, which was approved at a joint meeting of the boards of directors.

The stock transaction's market value was roughly four hundred million dollars and would take nearly a year to maneuver through the Federal Communications Commission (FCC). At the time, under FCC regulations, a company could own a maximum of five VHF stations. The merger would have brought Gannett's total to six. (Combined owned two UHF television stations and five VHF stations—including highly rated properties in Denver, Atlanta, and Oklahoma City.) Gannett agreed to sell its television station in Rochester to Broadcast Enterprises Network, Inc., a black-controlled company in Philadelphia—helping to quell protests from a black media group that claimed Gannett had a poor history of hiring women and minorities.

The merger made Gannett a major force in outdoor billboard advertising and broadcasting. And it brought the *Cincinnati Enquirer* and the *Oakland* (California) *Tribune* into the company.

In McCorkindale's view, the purchase "sort of put us on the map for doing the bigger deals." Whereas Paul Miller's acquisitions had been through personal contacts, the Combined deal was so stunningly massive that henceforth anyone with a newspaper (or a television station or book company) to unload had to think of Gannett. Unfortunately, lamented McCorkindale, it led to the company being shown "almost all of the junk that [anyone] wanted to sell."

Though delighted by the company's moving into "a bigger league," Neuharth was not content: "We weren't in one of the ten top cities."

Following the merger agreement, Paul Miller, seventy-one years old, announced his retirement as chairman of Gannett, and Neuharth added chairman to his titles of president and chief executive officer.

Gannett—at least in media and financial circles—had made its name a household word. In Neuharth's first year as chairman, the corporation would generate revenues exceeding a billion dollars and pretax profits of $269 million. New people were pouring into the company. New ventures lay around the corner. And Neuharth, due to serve in 1979 as chairman of the American Newspaper Publishers Association, was on a roll that showed no sign of ending.

* * *

Robert Maynard, the former *Washington Post* editorial writer, had settled in the Oakland area, the site of the *Tribune,* Gannett's newest property. Maynard's move to California, however, had nothing to do with Gannett.

In Washington, the Maynards had invested in a home and quickly seen their twenty-five-thousand-dollar cash investment grow two hundred thousand dollars in value. One day the then-forty-year-old Maynard said to himself, "Here we are, sitting on a quarter of a million dollars, and we're . . . bored and unfulfilled. . . . This is dumb." His wife—a Washington correspondent for the *New York Times*—told him of a colleague at the *Times* bureau whom management was obviously attempting to force out. Someone asked the man why he simply didn't quit, whereupon the correspondent burst into tears and said, "I'm a *Times* man. I wouldn't know how to be anything else." Maynard's wife sighed, "Save me from that kind of thinking."

Whatever life held for them, the couple decided, they would never find it clinging to their jobs. They decided to take a couple of years to sort out their future and work with a journalism institute in California that trained minority journalists.

In the summer of 1978, Maynard received a call from John Quinn—a strong supporter of the journalism program and a personal friend as well. In the course of the conversation, Quinn told Maynard that Gannett had signed a letter of intent to acquire Combined Communications. Everything had worked out fine except for one small glitch.

A group of black executives at WVON, a Chicago radio station that came with Combined, were unhappy with Gannett's decision to sell its Rochester television station to Broadcast Enterprises. The WVON employees had formed their own acquisitions group and thought that they—who were, after all, inside the company—should have gotten first crack at the Gannett station. Why had they not received the opportunity? Neuharth, not knowing what else to say, replied that the other group had asked first.

"John, you've just taught me a very important lesson," said Maynard. "Among the assets you've just acquired is the *Oakland Tribune.*"

"Yeah," mumbled Quinn.

"Well, lest anybody else ask first, I'd like to be the editor of that paper."

Maynard talked at length of the great potential for the paper and the Oakland community. Despite Combined having gutted the property to trim expenses, Maynard was certain the paper could be turned around. The next week, Quinn told Maynard that Neuharth would be in Portland, Oregon, for a meeting. Could Bob and his wife, Nancy, join Neuharth and Quinn for lunch there?

During lunch, Neuharth turned to Maynard and asked, "You really want to be a newspaper editor? I thought you wanted to be a professor for the rest of your life."

Maynard replied that he was ready to get back into daily newspapering and that he particularly wanted to do so in Oakland, a market ripe with opportunity.

"In all the months we've been doing this deal," said Neuharth, "I've heard lots of references to the Oakland problem. You're the first person to ever mention the Oakland opportunity."

"I think it's a great opportunity," insisted Maynard.

"I do too," said Neuharth. "And as far as I'm concerned, here ends our search for an editor for Oakland." Maynard started his new job in late August 1979—becoming the only black editor of a major metropolitan daily in the United States. That same year Gannett named Dolores Wharton, president of the Fund for Corporate Initiatives, as its first black board member. Gannett also signed an agreement with the National Black Media Coalition pledging strong efforts to improve opportunities for minorities in the company.

Gannett's explosive growth inevitably led to a reexamination of the company's personnel policies. The casual approach that had worked for a small regional corporation was not adequate for a billion-dollar communications conglomerate.

Personnel had been one of the responsibilities of John Heselden, a former Gannett publisher who (in typical Gannett fashion) wore several hats—including that of head of the newspaper division. Neuharth decided personnel should have a full-time rather than a part-time boss and approved a senior vice-presidency for the position.

Madelyn Jennings, who was then a vice-president at Standard Brands, had met Neuharth through her work as a board member with Harte-Hanks Newspapers. She had long been interested in communications and leapt at the opportunity to build a human resources operation for Gannett.

Heselden had known virtually every executive and spouse in every operation. In a company expanding as quickly as Gannett, Jennings could never hope to duplicate that. Her task was to try to retain some of Gannett's closeness despite the fact that many managers inevitably would be unfamiliar names on pieces of paper. She also would have to put in place wage and salary packages, performance appraisal systems, benefits programs, and all the other human resource ornaments of a mature corporation—and to do so without corrupting Gannett's culture. The company prided itself on its "can do" spirit, lack of bureaucracy, emphasis on performance over credentials, and willingness to embrace untried managers and untraditional ideas. How, she would ask herself, could Gannett keep the good parts of that culture while simultaneously building a professional personnel operation?

Gerald Garcia, an executive with Capital Cities Communications, had watched the developments taking place at Gannett; and he had noted Maynard's appointment as editor in Oakland—taking it as a sign that Gannett might be willing to give minorities an even break. Over several months, and after numerous conversations with Gannett, Garcia finally decided to leave Capital Cities. Shortly thereafter, he became the nation's only Hispanic publisher of a general-interest daily. His appointment as publisher in Tucson, Arizona, was the realization of a dream similar to the one Neuharth had had as a child growing up in Alpena, South Dakota.

For much of Garcia's early life, his father was away—serving in the navy during World War II. A large part of the task of raising Gerald and his younger sister fell to his mother and his grandfather. Neither of his grandparents spoke English at home and the Anglo side of Beeville, Texas, was a different world. Yet he decided early that his future lay beyond the barrio.

"I just felt myself to be different than most people there. I mean, I spoke the language and I enjoyed the culture and I ate my beans and tortillas . . . but I thought that there was something better somewhere else."

Over one summer break from high school, Garcia had worked as a roustabout in the oil fields of West Texas. Previously he had helped his grandmother pick cotton. Although his grandmother would pick several hundred pounds a day, Gerald could barely manage a hundred. He had believed himself to be misplaced, just as he had when the Anglo crew chief would round up his Chicano crew and send them to the oil field while he sat in his air-conditioned truck. Garcia thought he should be the one in the truck.

Through his father's armed service contacts (and with the help of family friends who knew the local congressman), Garcia was assured an appointment to the U.S. Military Academy at West Point. A low score on the entrance exams dashed his chances. His knee—injured from football and a car accident—was in such bad shape that the academy would have been reluctant to take him anyway, he was told. Garcia was shattered and realized for the first time that the competition outside of Beeville was infinitely tougher than he had imagined.

He looked to sports as a possible avenue of escape and ended up attending Blinn College in Brenham, Texas—which he thought to be a great baseball school. In Brenham, he acquired a pretty blond girl friend, converted from Catholicism to Methodism, and met the owner of the *Banner Press,* who gave him a part-time job working for the paper and convinced him to make journalism his career. Garcia completed his education at Texas A & M University and discovered that the only paper that would offer him a job was in Corpus Christi, Texas—sixty miles from where he was born. "At least sixty miles is better than being in the same place," he told himself.

Garcia later went to the *Fort Worth Star Telegram* (where he remained when the property was acquired by Capital Cities) and handled several high-visibility assignments—including a redesign of the features section and serving as the paper's sports editor and assistant editor.

In 1977, several months after Capital Cities purchased the *Kansas City* (Missouri) *Star and Times,* Garcia was transferred to Kansas City as director of newsroom operations with responsibility to "reduce the employee census." He had three months to evaluate a full-time staff of some 350 people—plus hundreds of part-timers—and trim everyone not essential.

"You might survive all of this," his boss said at one point, "but the fact of the matter is that after you get finished doing what you're going to do, it will be like throwing a piece of raw meat to the lions every time you walk in the newsroom."

He was next appointed assistant to the publisher, and then given responsibility for recruitment and running Capital Cities' minority training program. Garcia enjoyed recruiting other minorities: "My conscience came back to me." Still, he craved a more challenging assignment. But the publishership Garcia had assumed would materialize seemed out of reach. He realized his "MBA from the barrio" wasn't impressing Capital Cities enough for the company to take a chance on him. Gannett, on the other hand, was offering great opportunity—though in a manner he found uncomfortable.

"I first got the impression that Gannett only wanted to hire me because my last name ended in a vowel," said Garcia. Part of Gannett's culture, he was beginning to believe, was an obsession with firsts—the first black editor, the first woman this, the first Latino that. Garcia wanted to be hired for his qualifications, not held up as a Chicano token.

Garcia was persuaded that Jennings, John Heselden, and others involved in his recruitment understood his position, that they wanted him—not just a Latino publisher. He was impressed that they were willing to be so specific in their commitments and felt, for the first time ever, that a prospective employer truly recognized his potential. Neuharth "didn't make me feel like I was wasting his time."

Gannett's team promised to teach him more than he had ever thought he could learn; Garcia believed them, and in 1981 joined the company. He would receive orientation and training at the Gannett paper in San Bernardino, California, and then take over the *Citizen* in Tucson.

CHAPTER 19

A BID FOR RECOGNITION

Gannett, although a $1.2 billion corporation in 1980, was still "a big company of mostly smaller operations," says Neuharth. The firm had flirted with *U.S. News and World Report* and a few other classy potential acquisitions, but a deal had never come together. That bothered Neuharth, who thought the lack of prominent properties limited the company's ability to attract and retain talent, and that creating or acquiring one could revitalize him and Gannett.

"The company was doing pretty well, but it was on automatic. It was easy. And anybody could have run that company and produced good earnings gains, won a few prizes, made a few more acquisitions. But we'd done all of that. . . . And for a hands-on guy, which I plead guilty to being, that was not a whole lot of fun. Just change the names of the cities, logos on newspapers, and you do the same thing over and over."

Moreover, Gannett had grown so large that buying more small newspapers contributed little to the bottom line: "No single acquisition could . . . unless it was another group."

Starting *Today* in Florida had been a high point for Neuharth. As he approached retirement age, he longed for another project that would generate excitement, that would allow him to exit as he had entered—bright lights and sirens going.

Also Neuharth, who considered himself a patriot, wanted to contribute something to his country. "I felt that some of the media were less than objective and certainly not very patriotic about [their] approach to covering the news. I felt that the media should be a unifier in the country, even when . . . critical of the establishment. . . . National newspapers in England and in Japan primarily, had, on many occasions through the years, developed a sense of unity in a country. . . . There was no publication in this country that could be a unifier because there was no national newspaper."

The picture presented by the dominant media, thought Neuharth, was "more troublesome, more discouraging" than reality. He aspired to start a publication to embody his "journalism of hope."

Neuharth's entire professional life had been pointing toward *USA Today*. *SoDak Sports* had showed Neuharth how to create a newspaper. *Today* had demonstrated how to make money at it. And numerous Sunday editions introduced by various Gannett newspapers had proved a successful start-up need not be a fluke. During New York's 1978 newspaper strike, Gannett had launched a *Today* in neighboring Westchester. The following year (using the *Tribune* as a base), Gannett had created *Eastbay Today* in Oakland. With each new paper, Neuharth had tinkered with his formula, experimenting with graphics, format, and price. Though the *Today*s in Westchester and Oakland died, they convinced Neuharth the basic idea was sound.

In early 1980, Neuharth selected four executives to secretly study the feasibility of a national newspaper: Tom Curley, then head of Gannett's newspaper readership research project; Frank Vega, *Oakland Tribune* circulation director; Paul Kessinger, a Gannett marketing specialist; and Larry Sackett, former production director for the *International Herald Tribune.*

The chosen four were given a $1.2 million first-year budget and a set of offices near Neuharth's residence in Cocoa, Florida. No decisions had yet been made, Neuharth told them. They were to be realists in assessing the merit (or lack of it) of his idea. Given Neuharth's obvious enthusiasm, however, the relevant question was not whether Gannett could create *USA Today,* but how.

By late 1980, the Cocoa team had developed a rough business plan. Neuharth and Quinn turned to Ron Martin, the former managing editor of Cocoa's *Today,* to oversee production of prototypes.

After two years in Cocoa, Martin had taken a year-long fellowship at Stanford University and then come to Rochester as managing editor of Gannett's *Democrat and Chronicle.* Martin's oldest son had developed severe allergies and asthma and required a more congenial climate. Unable to find a suitable location in the Gannett organization, Martin had gone to the *Miami Herald* as managing editor. Subsequently, he had helped run the *New York Post* and *US* magazine. He was editor of the *Baltimore News-American* when Quinn phoned in late 1980 to offer a position with the national newspaper.

Martin signed up in December and immediately began assembling a staff of Gannett editors to assist with prototypes. The entire operation—including the four original researchers—was moved to Washington.

Neuharth was getting increasingly specific about the newspaper he intended to create. *USA Today* was to be eye-catching, full of brilliant color, and bursting with information on news and sports; it was to have numerous indexes and summaries and few stories that jumped from page to page. Most important, it was to be fast-paced and compelling enough to interest the television generation.

Feedback on the first prototypes (circulated within and outside the company) was decidedly mixed. But if Neuharth was ruthless in tearing apart unduly rosy projections, he was also the guiding force behind the project's advocates. Little short of deposing him as chairman could have stopped the *USA Today* steamroller.

At year's end, Neuharth won approval from his board of directors and he and Quinn began assembling a team to work on the actual newspaper. Martin was informed that despite his back-breaking stint as planning editor, he would not be chief news executive of *USA Today.* A more administrative type was needed for that—one who could juggle a thousand different details and leave Martin free to work his editing magic. Martin, as executive editor, would report to John Curley, then publisher of Gannett's two Wilmington, Delaware, papers.

Nancy Woodhull would be managing editor for news. Other managing editors would head up features, sports, and business.

In many respects, Woodhull was a prototypal Gannett and *USA Today* editor—a driven worker from a small town with neither a family nor an academic pedigree likely to impress. She had entered New Jersey's Trenton State College intending to become a teacher, but dropped out of school to pursue a career at the small paper where both Curleys had worked—the *Perth Amboy Evening News.*

After five years, she quit the New Jersey paper and opened up an art gallery before being courted back and made features editor. At an American Press Institute seminar, she met an editor from Detroit who convinced her that she had outgrown her small New Jersey community. Woodhull concluded she had also outgrown her husband (her high school sweetheart) and left to become a sports features writer for the *Detroit Free Press.*

When she expressed an interest in management, her boss told her she wasn't editor material. Tom Curley, recruiting for his former position as night suburban editor in Rochester, said her possibilities would be unlimited at Gannett.

At Gannett, where Woodhull distinguished herself in several high-priority assignments—including a section-by-section redesign of the newspaper—she rose to managing editor of the *Rochester Times Union* and, subsequently, of the *Democrat and Chronicle.*

A few days past New Year in 1982, Woodhull was summoned to a brainstorming meeting in Quinn's Rochester office. The summons from on high did not strike Woodhull as unusual. She was surprised, however, to find John Curley waiting to see Quinn as well. She was even more surprised when Quinn came out and escorted them into the boardroom—which she previously had visited only on a tour. Ron Martin's presence struck her as stranger yet. And when Quinn asked if she wanted a glass of wine, Woodhull knew something peculiar was up.

The grand sliding door to Neuharth's office opened and the chairman appeared. His tone was conspiratorial. Everything they were to discuss, he said, was confidential. After quickly outlining his plans for *USA Today,* he turned to Woodhull and told her they wanted her as part of the team.

Overwhelmed, Woodhull murmured, "Well, gee, I'll have to think about this a little bit." At home she outlined the proposal to her second husband, who, without hesitation, replied, "We're going." She started work within a month, having found a house some fifteen minutes from the office, and convinced her in-laws to move in to help take care of her baby daughter, who was not yet a year old.

Even as Gannett's editors lined up behind *USA Today,* convinced they were making history, the sober numbers crunchers on the business side wondered whether Neuharth was merely creating headaches.

"During the early discussions," recalled Quinn, "the group quickly divided into two camps: one headed by [Quinn] the chief news executive, the other headed by [Doug McCorkindale] the chief financial officer. And other people rallied . . . on either side." The first year of research had convinced Tom Curley, Quinn's representative to the study committee, that the newspaper could be a winner. That was good enough for Quinn, who felt Gannett had no choice but to gamble on the national paper. "If we did . . . it, we might not succeed, but ultimately somebody would. And why shouldn't we be the first to try?"

McCorkindale perceived his role "as making sure that the company kept on the track to generate the earnings necessary to do what we wanted to do—whether that was acquisitions or . . . *USA Today.*" He, after all, was not a newsman; his specialty was not creating news products. His job was not to worry about a new newspaper, but about the entire company. "There was a rest of the company at that time," he pointedly observed.

In July 1981—with *USA Today*'s prototypes barely off the presses—Quinn and Neuharth left for Oakland to have dinner with *Tribune* editor Robert Maynard. After complimenting him on his work, Neuharth suggested Maynard needed another challenge and promoted him to publisher and president. Maynard was stunned, but not as much as a year later when the head of the news division called.

"I'm sorry to have to break the bad news," said Jack Heselden, "but as a result of our letter of intent today to acquire KRON [television in San Francisco], we're going to have to dispose of the *Tribune.*"

"Jack, I'd like to buy it," said Maynard on impulse.

"You would? . . . Well, that's going to be mighty difficult for you to do."

"Give me a chance to try."

Gannett soon agreed to Maynard's proposal and offered its lawyers to structure the deal. Maynard—concerned that a deal put together by Gannett lawyers might not be to his advantage—demurred and hired his own legal advisers. In a matter of months, he had purchased the paper for twenty-two million dollars, not using any of his own money. Gannett financed seventeen million dollars, with the remainder supplied by banks. As Maynard set off to pursue his dream with the *Tribune,* Neuharth did the same with *USA Today,* both facing a legion of unbelievers saying they were insane to try.

Reporters and editors—"loaners"—from other Gannett newspapers were arriving at *USA Today* in droves. Before the paper hit the streets in September 1982, more than two hundred journalists would be in place.

The staff was an unusual amalgam. Scrupulously balanced by Neuharth, Quinn, and company for race and sex, it boasted large numbers of women and minorities in visible positions. Several journalists were hired from outside Gannett, generally from large publications. They found many of the small-town journalists from Gannett unsophisticated; and many of the loaners, aware of the premium salaries the outsiders received, thought the newcomers were overrated and overpaid. The loaners were under particularly heavy pressure to perform. For those who did not do well were to be shipped back home, where their old jobs awaited them.

The various groups learned to work together. With Neuharth, Quinn, John Curley, and Martin sitting at the top, repeatedly kicking back copy, constantly demanding changes in approach—forever in search of the elusive "*USA Today* spin"—little time or energy was left for infighting.

John Curley tried to keep perspective by thinking of *USA Today* as just another Gannett launch: "I viewed it as a start-up . . . in which all the details had to fit so neatly that there couldn't be any screwups that would set us back."

One important detail that troubled *USA Today* editors was how to define news. *USA Today* reporters were constantly reminded that "the nation's newspaper" was to be different; it was to represent a fresh—perhaps even revolutionary—approach. Definitions were straightforward for three of the paper's four sections. "Money" was to provide basic business coverage, but with a strong consumer orientation—emphasizing, whenever possible, financial news that readers could use. "Sports" was to offer the most complete daily sports coverage available anywhere. "Life" was to report on current trends in health, education, and life-styles, as well as provide basic Hollywood, movie, and leisure-time coverage. But the news section—the so-called A section—had no clear mission.

The section, in John Curley's eyes, was to briefly recap the top news of the day and then cover whatever else people were interested in—or should be interested in. "That angle was difficult for us to define and communicate," said Curley. "I think it was also difficult for some—many—of the staff to grasp."

Woodhull, who had initial responsibility for the A section, defined its purpose a bit differently. The section was to "hit the hot buttons on what was the talk of the country," including the main events of the past twenty-four hours as well as likely events in the upcoming twenty-four hours.

Although *USA Today* was not to be "happy talk," said Quinn, its focus was to be on the future. And "when you look ahead, you're looking at solutions."

On September 15, the debut issue appeared in the first market (Washington-Baltimore), leading with a story titled "AMERICA'S PRINCESS GRACE DIES IN MONACO." A three-column color photograph of a plane wreck also ran on the front page, underneath the *USA Today* nameplate, with a headline proclaiming, "MIRACLE: 327 SURVIVE, 55 DIE."

The paper quickly sold out its first edition of 155,000 copies. And Washington journalists, among its first and most critical readers, concluded the paper's news judgment was more than a little weird. The same night that Princess Grace died, president-elect Bashir Gemayel of Lebanon was killed in an explosion. Why, the journalists wondered, had that story not led the paper? And why, they asked, would a paper trivialize a tragic airplane accident in Spain by calling it a "miracle"?

Editor John Curley was stunned at the intensity of the criticism. "The animosity from the working-level journalists was a heck of a lot more severe than I would have expected, because I could not envision in my wildest dreams that starting a newspaper would tick off as many people as it did . . . particularly in an industry where they've had enough failures."

Neuharth and other Gannett executives vigorously defended their decisions, arguing that Americans were more interested in the princess than in Gemayel, and that so many people surviving such a tragedy was, well, something of a miracle. More than five years later, Gannett executives were still explaining that first issue—and their approach to news.

The plane accident, pointed out Quinn, had occurred more than a day before *USA Today*'s editors made the decision on story play. "We had a great spot news color photo that was thirty-six hours old, and . . . we had to . . . figure out how to get it into the newspaper under a headline that wouldn't tell them something they already knew." The readership knew how many people had died; that news had been blaring from the television networks for the past twenty-four hours. The real news was how many had lived.

Ron Martin professed not to be bothered by the brickbats from other journalists; his only concern was whether the newspaper really communicated with its readers. He realized that for some of his *USA Today* colleagues the criticism was wrenching, "but I think the enthusiasm of the place and the common bond that we all had here . . . helped an awful lot of people through that period."

Within days of the Washington-Baltimore launch, the paper came out in Atlanta, the next week in Minneapolis, and the following in Pittsburgh. As *USA Today* opened in one market after another, everywhere the pattern was the same: heavy criticism from journalists even as their newspapers incorporated some of *USA Today*'s distinct features. Multicolored weather maps appeared in hometown papers in Atlanta, Chicago, and elsewhere—as did snazzy graphics and more extensive sports reports.

When editors realized the new paper did not represent a present danger to the existence of traditional local dailies, they continued to study it for ideas—particularly in packaging and presentation. If *USA Today* had not earned most journalists' praise, it was certainly receiving their attention—and forcing them to see Gannett in a new light.

"I think it showed not only people on the outside of the company, but a great many people on the inside of the company that they were capable of a great deal," said Martin, "that they . . . were able to function in the big leagues."

The visibility of *USA Today* also had a marked impact on Gannett's ability to hire. Recruits who previously would have scorned the company were more willing to sign up because the existence of *USA Today* revealed Gannett to be a bold, innovative company, said Quinn.

A striking and outspoken blonde, Cathleen Black, former publisher of *New York* magazine, joined *USA Today* as president in September 1983. The newspaper was then one year old and circulating just over one million copies a day. A week before Black's arrival, Neuharth had announced that *USA Today* would be available to 80 percent of the U.S. population in 1984. The New York launch had recently taken place. Cleveland and Boston had been added to the list, and *USA Today* was about to invade Dallas–Fort Worth. Advertising, however, was weak, and Black, who had made her reputation with *Ms.* magazine, was expected to help turn it around.

Born in Chicago and educated at Trinity College in Washington, D.C., Black had sold advertising for several magazines, including *Holiday, Travel and Leisure,* and *Ms.*—whose first advertising manager she had become in 1972.

Ms. executives had assumed that women working in big companies would open doors. Those assumptions had been naive. Female corporate executives didn't admit it, said Black, "but they were very threatened. . . . They didn't want to be identified with *Ms.* They didn't want to be the rabble-rouser in the company." Black realized that in order to be successful, she would have to become a missionary to the male advertising world—much of which thought *Ms.* to be run by freaks and weirdos. She had thrived in that tough environment. And *USA* should be no worse. If advertisers weren't panting to place ads in the "nation's newspaper," they at least weren't openly hostile to it.

During Black's courtship by Gannett, John Heselden, the long-time Gannett executive who was then publisher of *USA Today,* had talked at length about the company. At no point would Gannett stop growing, he had said. A new challenge would always be waiting, because Neuharth believed in pushing executives to their limits. After offering several positions (over numerous months) that Black had thought lacking in proper status, Neuharth had offered her the presidency of *USA Today.* "You could have saved yourself a lot of fancy dinners if you had talked about this last June," she told him.

In retrospect, Black would observe, "I should have talked to Al more about the parameters of the job as opposed to the title. That was my own ego getting carried away." Roughly a year after she was hired, Black was promoted to publisher of *USA Today* (but her responsibilities were generally limited to advertising). Though pleased with the promotion, she protested her lack of commensurate responsibilities. Neuharth made it very clear that he had no intention of giving her full responsibility for the paper, that with her one year of experience in the newspaper business she was presumptuous to think she could handle the job.

In another company, Black's title would have been advertising director, just as in another company the managing editors in the newsroom would have been section editors. But Neuharth had learned long ago that a job title's value lay in his ability to define it.

Black reconciled herself to Neuharth's ways and—aided by her spirited sales ability—the advertising picture brightened. Black was named to Gannett's board of directors and credited with helping *USA Today* turn the corner. In the process, she became one of the most visible and best-paid newspaper executives in the nation.

In April 1983, Neuharth promoted John Curley from the editorship of *USA Today* to the presidency of Gannett's newspaper division. One of Curley's first acts in his new job was to promote his brother Tom to the position of publisher of the *Courier-News* in Bridgewater, New Jersey—where John Curley had held his first publishing job.

Quinn (retaining his position as Gannett's chief news executive) took over as editor of *USA Today.* "I had been going to work in the newsroom every day," he said, "five to seven days a week, since I was seventeen years old. And then in 1971, I was led astray into becoming a corporate paper shuffler." Editing—particularly "in such a unique environment as *USA Today*"—offered more fulfillment than anything else he could imagine in the business.

John Curley was named president and chief operating officer of Gannett in March 1984. At the same time, Douglas McCorkindale was promoted to vice-chairman. For those who had assumed McCorkindale would be Neuharth's successor, the corporate moves came as a shock. Many believed McCorkindale's grudging support of *USA Today* to be the largest single reason for his fall from grace. Others noted that Neuharth himself had always wanted a journalist to follow him; that, at one point, he had even talked to people outside the company when the list of potential successors inside looked less than adequate.

Quinn surmised that, although McCorkindale's pessimism about *USA Today* and his lack of journalistic credentials had hurt him, McCorkindale could have overcome those deficits. Curley, after all, had not been an early or natural choice. McCorkindale had long been the most outstanding business person in the company—and no Gannett editor of his generation matched McCorkindale's stature. Only after proving he could juggle the daunting administrative tasks of *USA Today* had Curley emerged as Neuharth's successor. McCorkindale had an equal opportunity to step forward and prove he could run a news operation. If he had done so, said, Quinn, "I think McCorkindale could have overcome even my suspicion that he doesn't know much about running a newspaper, because he could have demonstrated that he could have. He elected not to do that. He elected to stay strictly a management person. And that's where I think he outlawed himself, not because he was negative on *USA Today,* but because he did not capitalize on the *USA Today* experience to demonstrate that he could run a news business rather than just a business."

As managerial intrigue swept the company, Gannett continued to grow ever larger and more confident of its ability to put together major deals.

It acquired the parent company of the highly esteemed *Des Moines Register* for two hundred million dollars. Gannett also flirted briefly with CBS, but CBS ultimately decided not to merge. In Gannett's largest acquisition to date, the company bought the Evening News Association—which counted among its holdings the *Detroit News,* four small dailies, and several television stations—for $717 million cash. (Almost immediately, Gannett sold four of the acquired stations for $200 million. Three of them—in Oklahoma City, Tucson, and Mobile—went to Knight-Ridder.)

Robert Giles, Gannett's editor in Rochester, was appointed editor of the *News* in Detroit. The day the news story ran that Gannett was considering bidding for the *News,* Giles had felt a tingle of excitement. For the first time in years, he saw the prospect of a job that truly thrilled him. *USA Today* had not struck Giles as his kind of paper. But he had played the good soldier and wished many of his star performers well as they marched down to Washington to contribute to the company's greater glory. But he knew, as they went, that much of Gannett's attention was going with them, that Rochester would no longer house the company's flagship publications. He knew also that Rochester could not interest him much longer; Detroit could.

The *News* was the dominant paper in an important city. And the competing *Free Press* was owned by Knight-Ridder, Giles's former employer, which he felt had unfairly allowed a rival to force him out as executive editor of the *Akron Beacon Journal* in Ohio. Giles relished the idea of taking on the chain in Detroit and had called Quinn and asked for the job.

Giles's appointment evoked no great fanfare at the company, but it signaled to Giles and to others that the day had arrived when moving up for an editor in Gannett need not be synonymous with moving out.

In Detroit and Des Moines, Gannett played the role of white knight, warding off hostile takeover attempts. And in both instances, it acquired newspapers that were more prominent than the vast majority bought by Gannett.

The pattern continued in 1986, as Gannett paid $319 million to acquire the Courier-Journal and Louisville Times Company of Kentucky. Again, Gannett had stepped into a messy ownership fight—this time among the feuding Bingham family owners—and, again, it emerged with a prestigious property.

The Louisville agreement had been announced just in time for the Gannett shareholder's meeting—held in May 1986 at Washington's Capital Hilton. The Detroit purchase had been concluded earlier in the year. In one twelve-month period, the company had invested more than $1.2 billion dollars in its acquisition program.

Neuharth took the podium for some final comments. The past year, he said, had been Gannett's best ever—thanks in large part to Gannett's emerging generation of leadership. Cathie Black had helped *USA Today* come of age. Doug McCorkindale had maintained Gannett's unbroken record of quarterly earnings gains and kept its acquisitions on track. And John Curley had helped run every phase of the operation.

But the older generation, said Neuharth, was showing its age. When he had been appointed CEO some thirteen years ago, Neuharth continued, the company had fifty-one daily newspapers, with a total circulation of 2.2 million. Now the company had ninety-three dailies, with a circulation of over 6 million.

In that same period, Gannett had gone from twenty-two Sunday papers to sixty-two; from one television station to eight; from one radio station to sixteen; from $288 million in annual revenues to roughly $3 billion; from no outdoor advertising operation to the largest such operation in North America; from a board of directors of white males, to the most diverse board of any media company in the nation. The facts, figures, and litany of accomplishments flew by, Neuharth adding one upon another, until he finally arrived—voice quaking—at the climax to his recital.

"When you add all that up, my instincts as an investigative reporter and editorial analyst tell me the time has come to take another step in the planned and orderly transition of Gannett's leadership to the next generation. Accordingly, when the Gannett board meets in its organization session right after this shareholder meeting adjourns, I will recommend that president John J. Curley be elected chief executive officer, succeeding me in that role; that I continue as your chairman, period."

Neuharth went on to discuss his plans to remain active in the company until the age of sixty-five, particularly in the areas of mergers, acquisitions, and new ventures; then he adjourned the meeting of stunned shareholders to view the new headquarters in Rosslyn, Virginia.

Madelyn Jennings, Gannett's chief personnel person, called the transition "one of the extraordinary cases where a chairman has his ego enough intact to do good succession planning. Al is making sure that when he retires, the person who goes into the job doesn't have everything to learn from day one."

A few months after Neuharth announced he was stepping down, *Tucson Citizen* publisher Gerald Garcia decided to leave the company. The events were not related.

Garcia had concluded that Gannett was not quite as perfect as it had once seemed. It was centralized to a greater extent than he had imagined, and was becoming more so.

No one had told him what to print in his paper, but Gannett

had been quite specific in telling him whom he could hire on his business staff, what he could pay them, and how he should price his paper—how, in general, he should run his operation. Since joining the company, Garcia had risen to the level of a regional vice-president in addition to publisher in Tucson, but acutely felt his lack of authority. He had argued interminably one day from a pay phone in the desert to get a manager a two-thousand-dollar raise. And he had felt impotent in his inability to remove a publisher under his supervision whom Garcia considered incompetent.

Garcia's complaints were no different from those of thousands of other executives at hundreds of other huge corporations. "Too many decisions," he said, "are having to be made at the top." He had not quite expected that at Gannett. And Garcia was not alone in wondering where Gannett was headed.

The company was drained from giving birth to and nurturing *USA Today.* So much energy and so many resources had gone into the paper—which finally went into the black in 1987—and into expansion, that very little had been left for nonpriority operations.

Robert Giles, the former Rochester editor, recalls that *USA Today* had been a considerable sacrifice for many in the company. "The local papers had less to work with. The increase in their operating budgets on the news side was less. There was less money for promotion. In some cases [the] news hole [or space allocated to the editorial department] was tighter. I think every honest editor in Gannett will say to you that there were moments when that was a deep frustration simply because we felt that our readers deserved better."

"Maybe we didn't make some investments over the last five years because we were focusing on other things," admits Gary Watson (who, as head of the metro newspaper division, oversees the company's larger newspapers), but he believes that some of those investments are finally being made. Gannett was getting around to starting some new Sunday editions and converting several papers from afternoon to morning editions and making other improvements that had been delayed as the push to prominence was taking place.

Neuharth's mother raised him to be a builder; and he built a company grander than anything its founder could have imagined. Then he moved its headquarters a stone's throw from the nation's capital and erected a bust of himself to sit inside the building housing its flagship paper. His successor is cut from very different cloth. The low-key John Curley, who is fond of neither limousines nor dramatic gestures, is bland in comparison to the theatrical Neuharth. Many within Gannett think that may not be so bad; after all the Neuharth-generated turbulence, a bit of calm might be nice.

"How much flamboyance can a company stand?" asked Quinn rhetorically. "How many marbled executive offices with fireplaces and gushing fountains do we need in Gannett?"

John Curley insists that, during his tenure, newspapers will remain the company's foundation. Gannett will continue to seek innovative ways to grow and will search for new ways to market and package information, but he doubts that it will begin to manufacture communications hardware: "I see evolution rather than large change."

The company "will continue to look at things that make sense to develop . . . not on the scale of *USA Today.* I think that's singular—at least I don't see anything that rivals that." He also expects acquisitions to proceed, but, as has been Gannett's custom, only when the target company wants to be bought.

John Curley talks of "the vision of tomorrow," an attribute he believes a lot of Gannett executives possess, an ability "to know where the world is going to be and make sure that you're somewhere in there." Curley has exhibited an uncanny knack for being at the right place at the right time. Whether he can position his company as skillfully as he has positioned himself is a question that will only be answered once Neuharth rides into the sunset.

In 1987, Neuharth set off on a fifty-state tour called BusCapade. He jetted back and forth to a forty-foot *USA Today* bus that was outfitted with work stations, a shower, and loudspeakers. And he rolled into state capitals like a visiting head of state and penned a column on his trips for Gannett newspapers. Afterward, he embarked on a similar JetCapade around the world. The trips were an opportunity for Neuharth to have fun while promoting *USA Today.* They also provided an excuse to give John Curley breathing room.

John Quinn appointed three Gannett executives to take over various portions of his job—and to sit on a Gannett news committee from which they could get a good overall view of the company. Curley would have a wealth of talent from which to choose a new chief corporate news executive if he wished—from among those three: Ron Martin, executive editor of *USA Today;* Charles Overby, vice-president of news and information (who is responsible for the Gannett News Service and serves as corporate liaison for editors at Gannett newspapers); and Nancy Woodhull, president of Gannett New Media Services (which oversees book publishing, radio and television news programming, electronic information, and other ventures).

With Gannett's success came a grudging admiration from its peers, particularly since Neuharth was moving Gannett along much the same path as other large media organizations—albeit in a spectacularly aggressive and flashy manner. Times Mirror, Knight-Ridder, the New York Times, and other newspaper corporations of stature were also growing, diversifying, and becoming more professionally managed.

Each company and its products were different, but in many respects they were not all that different—and they were becoming less so. *USA Today,* Gannett's boldest venture, was very similar in its attention to the market (and marketing) and to service journalism to the C sections of the *New York Times* and the "Style" section of the *Washington Post. USA Today* did not so much break the editorial mold as dramatically stretch it, prodding many newspapers into modernizing their appearance and modifying their journalistic approach.

As Gannett grew, it became a company where credentials and pedigrees didn't count, where results spoke, and where ambitious small-town strivers with degrees from little-known schools could, through sweat and dedication, hope to achieve success. In the later years of Neuharth's reign, as the emphasis shifted to prestigious properties—in television as well as in print—credentials began to matter a little more.

In the process, Gannett had become a company much too huge for any single executive to rule in the same hands-on manner as Neuharth had once done. By necessity—as well as by inclination—John Curley's management would be different.

Shaking up Gannett—as Neuharth had done—would be harder than in the past. A three-billion-dollar conglomerate moved more slowly than a three-hundred-million-dollar company. A new project—even of the magnitude of *USA Today*—would almost inevitably have less impact on the bottom line.

Neuharth had a passion for making his empire bigger, but, observed Tom Curley, "John [Curley] has a little less of that, more of a bent toward fixing what's here." The colossal corporation he inherited leaves him little choice. While Neuharth was a builder first and a manager second, John Curley will reverse the roles.

Knight-Ridder

Bernard Ridder, Jr.

P. Anthony Ridder

Alvah Chapman

Byron Harless

James Batten

CHAPTER 20

CONSOLIDATION

In August 1987, Al Neuharth sat in a hearing room in Detroit trying to convince an administrative law judge that two-newspaper towns were all but extinct. Several months earlier, Gannett and Knight-Ridder had announced plans for a joint operating agreement, under whose terms the advertising, circulation, and production staffs of the *Detroit News* and *Detroit Free Press* would be merged and combined Saturday and Sunday editions published. The Newspaper Preservation Act of 1970 required that the deal be approved by the U.S. attorney general—who had appointed the judge.

Several local organizations had objected to the agreement. Newspaper unions feared jobs would be lost. Suburban papers dreaded a stronger competitor. Some individuals suspected monopolistic abuses if the two largest (by circulation) newspaper chains in the country combined their largest local properties.

To Neuharth, the basic issue was strikingly clear. Unless the two newspapers were permitted to link their operations, one would surely die.

"It is a clearly demonstrated fact all across the U.S.A.—and I can name all of the markets if you wish," Neuharth told the judge, "that in a competitive situation . . . the dominant newspaper ultimately thrives, the weaker newspaper ultimately dies. . . . Since the end of World War II, it has happened in New York

City, in Boston, in Philadelphia, in Washington . . . in Cleveland, in Buffalo, in Hartford, Connecticut. . . .

"In every instance—every instance—the weaker newspaper has died or been saved by a JOA [joint operating agreement] or is presently in danger of dying. There are no exceptions in this country."

Knight-Ridder chairman Alvah Chapman, who followed Neuharth on the stand, made the same point. From 1977 to 1986, Knight-Ridder had put $176 million into Detroit: "We have not taken anything out." Such largesse could not continue. If the agreement was not approved, Chapman told his stunned audience, he would recommend to his board that the *Free Press* be shut down and its assets disposed of.

For Dave Lawrence, publisher of the *Free Press* since 1985 and editor since 1978, the situation was particularly difficult. Under a joint operating agreement, much of his job would be handed over to an administering agency responsible for the business affairs of the two papers. Since the *News* had been designated the healthier paper, Gannett would be in control.

"For years," said the intense young publisher, "I knew that something had to give." Knowing that had not made the news of a joint operating agreement any less jolting. "When you work as hard as people worked at the *Free Press* and as hard as I worked," there could be no preparation for the "stunning moment" when suddenly the rules changed.

Some two thousand *Free Press* employees needed his help to get through the uncertain period. He would do the best he could: "There are times in your life when you get paid not to be selfish."

For Knight-Ridder president James Batten, whose first editing job had been on the *Free Press,* the JOA process was painful as well: "I cared intensely about the *Free Press* and its people. . . . So to . . . set our foot on the [JOA] path was . . . anguishing." He and his colleagues had struggled over their decision, "but finally the imperatives of the Detroit marketplace . . . rolled over anybody's and everybody's emotional experiences and professional preferences. . . . Despite all the money . . . all the things we tried to do through the years . . . it's not working sufficiently for Knight-Ridder shareholders to bear the burden much longer."

The exigencies of the marketplace were driving Knight-Ridder and Gannett together, just as the marketplace had forced so many newspapers to come together—or die. Of the 1,526 U.S. cities that boasted daily newspapers in 1987, only twenty-five contained two or more papers that were separately owned and independently published—and the number was shrinking. At the same time, one newspaper after another was being snapped up by chains, and small chains were merging with ever larger chains—just as the Evening News Association had done with Gannett, and just as Ridder Publications had done with Knight Newspapers more than a decade earlier.

At the turn of the century, as newspapers sprouted across the United States, no newspaper executive could have envisioned an age in which single media companies would own one hundred newspapers or claim revenues of more than three billion dollars. Nor, in that period of robust competition between dailies, could publishers have foreseen an era where head-to-head daily competition was practically dead—or where newspapers started by individuals notable for their differences would end up largely owned by companies marked by their similarities.

Certainly, Charles L. Knight, who acquired one significant newspaper in his career, could never have dreamed that, in 1987, a company bearing his name would own thirty-one dailies, six nondaily newspapers, eight television stations, and take in annual revenues of more than two billion dollars.

As Frank Gannett was purchasing his first newspaper in Elmira, Charles Knight was investing in the sixty-seven-year-old *Beacon Journal* in Akron, Ohio. A former lawyer, cowhand, and free-lance writer born on a farm in Baldwin County, Georgia, Knight became the *Beacon Journal*'s advertising manager in 1900, publisher in 1907, and gained full control in 1915.

Like others of his generation, Knight treated his newspaper more as a base for political activity than as a business. A onetime southern Democrat turned Bull Moose Republican, Knight served in Congress and tried—unsuccessfully—to be nominated for governor of Ohio. But Knight had his greatest impact as a hurler of thunderbolts from the *Beacon Journal*'s editorial pages—from which he attacked the Ku Klux Klan and opposed entry into World War I.

Charles Knight's oldest son, John, born in 1894, wasn't convinced that newspapering suited him. He dropped out of Cornell University to go into the army during World War I and then headed for California (several thousand dollars richer, he would boast, from shooting craps in the service) to seek his fortune raising cattle.

His father lured John back to Akron and in 1925 bestowed upon him the title of managing editor. When Charles Knight died in 1933, John was left in charge of the *Beacon Journal* and the *Massillon* (Ohio) *Independent,* which the family had acquired in 1927.

Coming to power at the depth of the Great Depression and in the shadow of his father, John Knight began his stewardship cautiously. By 1936, he was confident enough to mount a front-page attack on a "Law and Order League" out to break a strike at the Goodyear Tire and Rubber Company factory—Akron's biggest employer. "We need no vigilantes here," roared the *Beacon Journal* editorial.

The next year, Knight bought the *Miami Herald* and dispatched brother James—fifteen years John's junior—to run it. Afterward, John Knight swapped the *Independent* for the *Miami Tribune* and promptly closed the *Tribune,* leaving only the *Miami News* as competition.

He also purchased Akron's rival newspaper, gaining a hometown monopoly. "I believe if the city wanted more papers, it would have them," he said.

The Knights acquired the *Detroit Free Press* in 1940, the *Chicago Daily News* in 1944, and the *Charlotte Observer* ten years later. For many years, James and his family had spent summers in a home they owned in Roaring Gap, North Carolina, where they became well acquainted with the *Observer,* of which James was named publisher and president while retaining responsibility for the *Miami Herald.*

Tall and imposing, John Knight became more famous than his father and was seen by many as the potential heir to the throne of the mythical William Randolph Hearst. While the Hearst empire was in decline, the Knight kingdom was fast ascending, but he claimed, "I'm not interested in acquiring papers simply to say that we have a lot of papers. I'm not chomping to go out and buy any more . . . I don't go wild." As if to prove it, he sold the *Chicago Daily News* in 1959.

Nevertheless, the chain continued to grow, adding the *Charlotte News,* the *Miami Beach Daily Sun,* the *Tallahassee Democrat,* and several weekly publications between 1959 and 1966.

Knight Newspapers had no corporate staff to speak of and no central management system of consolidated financial information. It was less a chain than a series of independent newspapers with common ownership. And it was becoming too large for the Knight brothers' casual management style.

John Knight turned seventy-two in 1966. James was nearly sixty. The future of the company depended on developing a strong organization and good successors. With no family members as likely candidates, they turned to outsiders.

Lee Hills, executive editor of the newspapers, was named executive vice-president of the company. Alvah Chapman, general manager of the *Miami Herald* and a former World War II B-17 bomber pilot, was also made a vice-president. Neither was related to the Knights. And for the first time, an outside member—E. J. Thomas of the Goodyear Tire and Rubber Company—was elected to the board. In a statement announcing the promotions in 1966, John Knight, chairman and chief executive officer, pointedly noted, "Behind the men promoted today are many others with capabilities to step into higher jobs as we continue to grow."

James Knight became chairman of the company the following year, and John moved into the newly created position of editorial chairman, staying on as head of the executive committee. Lee Hills was named president, continuing as publisher of the *Free Press* and executive editor of Knight papers. And Alvah Chapman was named executive vice-president, also remaining general manager of the *Miami Herald.*

With those promotions, the next generation of leadership was in place, but the work of restructuring the company was only beginning.

Chapman, in his forties and the youngest member of the executive committee, was frustrated by the lack of sophisticated financial procedures. Large amounts of cash simply sat in checking accounts. Chapman suggested to C. Blake McDowell, a lawyer and banker who handled Knight investments, that they put the money where the company could get interest. McDowell objected that to do so would "lose the friendship of the banks."

"It's our money," Chapman retorted. "It doesn't make any

sense to have ten million dollars in a checking account." In exasperation, he turned to E. J. Thomas, the newly appointed outside director, and persuaded him to talk to John Knight—whom they convinced to invest the money where they could get a return. With such small victories, Chapman tried to nudge Knight Newspapers into the modern age.

Long discussions were going on among Hills, Chapman, and the Knight brothers about the future of the organization, and they decided, for much the same reasons as other companies (including the desire to cash in equity and professionalize management), to issue public stock.

In April 1969, 950,000 shares were offered over the counter. In August, five million shares of common stock were listed on the New York Stock Exchange—selling at $36.25 per share. That same year, Knight purchased the *Philadelphia Inquirer* and *Daily News* (owned by Walter Annenberg) and the *Macon Telegraph* (owned by Peyton Anderson—Tom Johnson's former mentor—who was named to the Knight Newspapers board).

Knight Newspapers' senior management group gave its first presentation before the New York Society of Security Analysts early in 1970. The presentation went smoothly, but the tone was defensive. John Knight viewed the analysts in the wary manner of a virgin in a whorehouse. "We believe in profitability, but do not sacrifice either principle or quality on the altar of the counting house," he said.

James Knight, who followed his older brother, hammered on a similar point, talking at length about newspaper owners who had sold their properties to Knight for reasons that had nothing to do with money but because they believed in Knight and its tradition of community service and quality.

Lee Hills, Knight Newspapers president, defended Knight's preference for big-city papers even though many other chains were snapping up small-town publications.

In years to come, Knight executives would appear often before Wall Street groups, and the presentations would become matter-of-fact. But first time out, the Knights felt called upon to explain how—at least in their opinion—they were different from the pack, and to establish, as best they could, that they intended to stay that way.

As the Knights were sorting out the implications of their

pilgrimage to Wall Street, another prominent newspaper family was doing the same. Ridder Publications, Inc. (with newspapers in California, Colorado, Minnesota, and elsewhere) went public the same year as Knight—offering 625,000 shares of common stock at twenty-three dollars per share.

Herman Ridder had sired three sons; and his sons had produced eight sons and seven daughters among them. By 1969, the grandchildren (by then in their forties and fifties) had children and grandchildren of their own. Whereas the third-generation male heirs all drew good salaries from the business, the female heirs received only dividends from the stock. A stock offering was a way to generate cash for them.

Unlike the Knights (among whom the question had never come up), the Ridders discussed the possibility of having two classes of stock—which would allow the family to retain control of the public corporation. Some Ridder family members lobbied for the issuance of shares with limited rights. But the financial advisers were opposed, arguing that investors would find voting stock more desirable.

Bernard H. Ridder, Jr., a plain-spoken Princeton graduate and grandson of the patriarch, was then president of the company: "As far as I was concerned, as long as we were going public, I thought . . . , 'Let's come out with . . . voting stock and do it the way it should be done.' "

Though president, Bernard Ridder was really first among equals and was concerned about the ability of the business to continue to thrive without the discipline public stockholders would bring: "When you're in a family company and the only shareholders are family shareholders, each man . . . is his own boss. . . . Each publisher felt that he really wasn't responsible to anybody. Theoretically, he might be responsible to the board. But since the board was composed mostly of Ridder members and Ridder family members, he was an equal."

The family had come far since 1890, when Herman Ridder—a German immigrant and founder of the *Catholic News*—had become business manager of *Staats-Zeitung,* a New York–based German-language newspaper. Two years later, Ridder bought *Staats-Zeitung.* His three sons learned the business from the bottom up and inherited it when he died in 1915.

Bernard, who became president of *Staats-Zeitung* upon his

father's death, dabbled in poetry. Joseph was a mechanical whiz and sportsman—who played golf and raced yachts and horses. Victor, who as a result of infantile paralysis used crutches most of his adult life, spent his spare time on various Catholic and Boy Scout causes. The three men were as one, however, in their determination to break into the ranks of major U.S. English-language publishers.

They started with the *Long Island Press,* in which they purchased a controlling interest in 1926. The same year, they acquired control of the *New York Journal of Commerce,* and a year later of the *St. Paul Dispatch and Pioneer Press.* In rapid succession they added the *Aberdeen* (South Dakota) *American and News,* the *Grand Forks* (North Dakota) *Herald,* and a large minority interest in the *Seattle Times.* The rapid expansion outpaced the Ridders' ability to pay for it. And they had to sell their interest in the Long Island paper in 1932 to satisfy a bank loan.

The Ridders gained a reputation for caring a great deal more about money than about journalistic quality. They did little to dispel the notion. "We'll buy any newspaper we can buy at the right price and bet money we can make a profit," Victor told an interviewer several years after their first wave of acquisitions. "We are in this business as a business and if somebody offers us a good price for a newspaper we'll sell it."

By the middle 1950s, the eight grandsons of Herman Ridder were fully integrated into the family business, which included radio and television stations in Minnesota and in North and South Dakota and newspapers stretching from California to New England. (For roughly a year during the 1940s, the Ridders held a substantial interest in William Loeb's *Manchester Leader* in New Hampshire, notable mostly because the investment put them in the proximity of the *Sunday News*—just launched by recent Harvard graduate Blair Clark, former *Chicago Daily News* war correspondent B. J. McQuaid, and World War II veteran Benjamin C. Bradlee. "Those boys have no right—well, I guess they do have a *right*—but when we get going up there, they can't possibly stay in business," railed Joseph Ridder.)

Bernard's son, Joseph, was the most flamboyant. A handsome bon vivant with infinite self-confidence, Joseph promoted the *San Jose Mercury* (which he published) and himself by running stories of his month-long African safari and his forty-eight-hundred-mile journey through Russia. When one interviewer asked him for the secret of the family's San Jose success, he responded, "Let's just assume I'm a genius."

The pragmatic Bernard H., Jr., president of the company, concluded that too many of his relatives thought themselves geniuses and that going public might help keep them in line. The issuing of stock, however, did not work as well as he had expected. Family members continued to insist on "extra fringe benefits."

Ridder took the problem to a consulting firm, which recommended that he remain as chief executive officer but appoint an executive vice-president who could act as general manager for all Ridder properties. When Ridder tested the idea on the family, he found—as he had feared—that everyone thought bringing in a general manager would be great, as long as the new executive had no authority over them.

Security analysts told him that Ridder Publications' stock would never reach its potential as long as the company was run like a series of family fiefdoms. As he looked to the future and the possibility of even more family members coming on board, he concluded the only way the business would ever shape up would be to merge with a larger, more sophisticated organization.

Ridder was a close friend and golfing buddy of Paul Miller of Gannett, and the men had spoken several times about a merger. But Ridder—more impressed with Knight—had always put Miller off. Ridder admired the Knight organization's ability to produce high-quality newspapers—an area in which the Ridders were notoriously weak. Also, Knight had fewer geographic conflicts with Ridder than Gannett had—which meant most properties could be kept once a merger was completed.

Executives at Knight were also thinking a good deal about Ridder. Before the companies had gone public, some very brief discussions had been held about merging the two. The talks had come to nothing. But in early 1974, Alvah Chapman (who had become president in 1973) and Lee Hills (chairman of the board) decided to try again. Chapman called Bernard Ridder and arranged a meeting at the convention of the American Newspaper Publishers Association. After the meeting, Chapman was convinced the companies could strike a deal. Demand for

Ridder stock was weak; a merger with Knight should enhance its value—as well as resolve the dilemma of trying to find a successor to Bernard Ridder, who through saintlike patience had melded the family into a functionally cohesive group.

Some of the other Ridder family members thought Gannett might be a better choice, that the organization, which already had more than fifty dailies, was the chain of the future.

Bernard's major concern was his cousin Robert, who oversaw Ridder's broadcast concerns. Any merger, in order to get quick approval, would require the divestiture of the company's television and radio stations. To Bernard's surprise, Robert said he was willing to give up his chairmanship of the holding company that controlled the broadcast group. "If [Robert] had said, in effect, 'If you make a merger, you're selling me out of a job,' I would have had to back off," said Bernard. Instead, Robert said, "I think for the good of . . . my sisters and everyone else, we're better off making a merger."

The agreement for Knight and Ridder to exchange stock was announced in July 1974, with both companies pledging to dissolve all their broadcast interests. While awaiting formal approval by the boards, Lee Hills and Bernard Ridder talked at length about how to bring the companies together without bitterness and complications. Though some Ridder family members got cold feet, the merger was consummated in December, with Ridder becoming a wholly owned subsidiary of Knight. Alvah Chapman and Lee Hills continued as president and chairman of the board, respectively. Bernard Ridder became vice-chairman of the company and chairman of the operating committee.

The 1974 annual report boasted that the joining of the nineteen Ridder dailies and sixteen Knight dailies was "the largest merger in newspaper history" and that the combined company sold twenty-seven million newspapers a week, had annual revenues of $565 billion and had fourteen thousand employees. In 1973, Knight had nine thousand employees and revenues of $345 billion.

A letter to employees of Knight-Ridder from Lee Hills, Ridder, and Alvah Chapman, on December 2, 1974, the first official day of business for the newly merged companies, noted: "Today, each of us is a new employee of a new organization. Because of the changing nature of the newspaper business, we have new goals, we face new challenges and we have new problems which require new and better solutions."

No one could have predicted in 1974 that one of those new challenges eventually would be seeking a joint operating agreement in Detroit. At the time, the *Detroit Free Press* was gaining on the *News* in circulation and advertising. (The *Free Press* trailed by thirty-five thousand readers, substantially less than the eighty-four thousand difference that had existed only the year before.) Neither paper was losing money.

Some trends, however, were clear enough. Gannett, the New York Times, the Washington Post, Times Mirror, and a host of others had all made the trek to Wall Street. All had subjected themselves to a new set of rules that demanded growth (and therefore mergers) and efficiency (and therefore consolidation of competing daily newspapers). And all had done so for reasons very much like those of the Knights and Ridders.

The newspaper business, once run largely on ego and emotion, was being run more and more by hard-nosed calculations on investment of capital. And advertisers, happy enough to support two competing newspapers with much the same readership in an earlier age, were deciding that they too needed to be more scientific, more focused, less willing to spread their advertising around to papers that delivered much the same thing. (In August 1988, shortly before leaving office, Attorney General Edwin Meese overruled his advisers and approved the *Detroit News–Detroit Free Press* joint operating agreement. To reject the arrangement, said Meese, would ensure the financial collapse of the *Free Press.* The decision was subsequently appealed.)

CHAPTER 21

THE CHALLENGE

While the U.S. Justice Department pondered the fate of the *Detroit Free Press,* another Knight-Ridder paper was making national news. On Sunday, May 3, 1987, a photograph of presidential candidate Gary Hart appeared on the front page of the *Miami Herald* accompanied by the headline "MIAMI WOMAN IS LINKED TO HART: CANDIDATE DENIES ANY IMPROPRIETY."

The article below reported: "Gary Hart, the Democratic presidential candidate who has dismissed allegations of womanizing, spent Friday night and most of Saturday in his Capitol Hill townhouse with a young woman who flew from Miami and met him. Hart denied any impropriety."

The exposé laid out, in tantalizing detail, the movements of the woman, rumored to be an actress, who had flown from Miami to Washington and ended up, arm in arm, with Hart.

The article recorded Hart's denials that the woman had spent the night with him, along with claims by friend William Broadhurst that she had not come to see Hart. It reported that Hart appeared nervous when questioned and that sources claimed the pair had first met on a yacht in Miami and had held numerous telephone conversations since then. The piece closed with:

> [Hart] has insisted that the rumors have no basis in fact and, in an interview with the New York Times, challenged those who question his fidelity to follow him.
>
> He said the assignment would be boring.

The story sparked a heated debate on journalistic ethics and sent the candidate tumbling from his front-runner perch—but not before a reporter from the *Washington Post* confronted Hart publicly and asked whether he had committed adultery.

Heath Meriwether, the genial editor of the *Herald,* was not prepared for the uproar. The *Herald* had recently won a Pulitzer for its coverage of the Iran-contra scandal, and Meriwether—about to be transferred to Detroit—looked forward to leaving on a high note. He expected the Hart article to attract wide notice, but "I . . . never could have anticipated the intense scrutiny that the paper, the journalistic process, and I personally [were] going to face as a result of it."

The *Herald* had received a phone tip and pursued it "because of the largeness of the shadow it cast over the leading candidate for the Democratic presidential nomination at the time." The paper had assigned some of its best reporters and tried to be scrupulously fair, pleading with Hart, says Meriwether, to "let us talk to anybody who could shed more light." Certainly, mistakes had been made. Some critics thought the *Herald*'s surveillance had been sloppy, leaving open the possibility that the woman could have left the house unseen. Others criticized the *Herald* for tailing the candidate at all. By what right, they asked, were reporters licensed to pry into the most private details of a candidate's personal life?

The pat answer, of course, was that they were seeking insights into Hart's character—the same answer that applied when similar questions were raised about the *New York Times'* request to examine candidates' tax records and FBI files.

The more honest answer was that editors try to hold their readers' attention. Those readers—as editors increasingly understand it—crave personal information along with news and analysis, leading newspapers to devote as much attention to the life-styles and eccentricities of corporate magnates as to their business strategies. Vicious criminals rate profiles as well as reports on their crimes. Such stories are, in effect, the textual equivalent of a color photograph and reflect the growing intermingling of "soft" and "hard" news.

The personal lives of political figures—no less than the private lives of movie stars—have become fair game. To Gary Hart's misfortune, those developments coincided with his ascension as a political figure. John F. Kennedy happened to come along at a more journalistically congenial time.

Changes in journalistic practice, of course, have not been limited to Knight-Ridder, or to newspapers owned by chains. Yet, by striking coincidence, two of Knight-Ridder's largest newspapers—the *Free Press* (with its JOA application) and the *Herald* (with its Hart coverage)—were engaged in the 1980s in highly public inquiries into corporate governance and journalistic mission that would have been incomprehensible a generation ago. The fact is all the more arresting because Knight-Ridder is the megachain that has most emphasized continuity in values and traditions—and has made the smoothest transition into the modern age.

Instead of fighting the company's evolution, the Knight brothers embraced it and endeavored to diffuse their principles throughout their organization.

To a large extent, they succeeded. By continually emphasizing its values and hiring and promoting executives who share them, Knight-Ridder has won a reputation as one of the nation's best-managed and most quality-conscious companies. Whereas some chains boast of their rapidly rising revenues, Knight-Ridder points to the seven Pulitzer Prizes it won in 1986 and the five taken in 1987.

Responsibility for maintaining Knight-Ridder's traditions fell not only to Lee Hills and Alvah Chapman but to Byron Harless—a white-haired psychologist who has served as high priest of Knight-Ridder's corporate culture. As a student, Harless had set his sights on an academic career. But World War II exposed him to uses for psychology that he had never envisioned while at the University of Florida.

Drafted into the army just as the United States was gearing up for combat, Harless was assigned to the Pentagon. Working with several other psychologists and testing experts—many his former teachers—Harless devised tests to identify potential pilots, navigators, and bombardiers. The air force—after repeatedly watching trainees wash out—had turned to the psychologists out of frustration, and with a healthy dose of skepticism. When the tests worked better than anyone had imagined, Harless became hooked on the use of behavioral science in the workplace.

He set up a consulting firm and one day received a call from Nelson Poynter, owner of the *St. Petersburg Times.* Poynter dreamed of building a great newspaper and needed help selecting lieutenants. He had heard of Harless's work and thought the psychologist might assist him. Poynter persuaded Harless to come to St. Petersburg full time and rotated the psychologist through several positions at the paper, teaching him the newspaper business step by step; then Poynter and Harless proceeded to select and groom the future leaders of the *Times.*

In 1953, Alvah Chapman (then at the *Ledger-Enquirer* in Columbus, Georgia) was negotiating with Poynter to become general manager of the *Times.* Poynter, unwilling to hire Chapman without Harless's seal of approval, was embarrassed to tell Chapman about the psychological tests and arranged for an "accidental" encounter with Harless at the Tampa–St. Petersburg airport.

Feigning surprise upon spotting Harless, Poynter proceeded to make introductions. Harless and Chapman (who was headed to an industry meeting) flew to New Orleans on the same plane. No sooner had Chapman settled into his hotel room than the phone rang; Harless asked about his plans for the evening. Chapman mentioned a dinner party organized by James Knight. "You're not going," Harless said. "You're going to have dinner with me." Chapman obediently canceled his plans and stayed up until 3:00 A.M. taking Harless's tests. Poynter, after receiving Harless's report, offered Chapman the job the next day.

Harless and Chapman worked closely at the *Times.* And when Chapman left, in 1957, to become part-owner and publisher of a paper in Savannah, Georgia, he promptly recruited Harless as a consultant. After a short time, the appeal of Savannah faded. The majority partner, a banker, was getting complaints about the paper—which (under Chapman's direction) had supported higher taxes for the school system. Chapman had also advocated cleaning up the slums, though some of the banker's customers owned slum property. When the banker, in exasperation, sold his interest, Chapman cashed his in as well and moved to Knight Newspapers.

Harless began consulting for Knight and, shortly after the company went public, sold his firm to his partners and became vice-president for personnel of Knight Newspapers.

Douglas Harris, another psychologist, joined Harless and together they built an assessment and training system for all the properties. After the Ridder papers came into the company, Harris spent so much time hopping from one new paper to the next that peers referred to him as the "Ridder rabbit."

The primary objective was unchanging: identifying future leaders, motivating them, grooming them in the Knight-Ridder style. Harless and Harris sought employees with a strong sense of empathy and analytical minds—leaders who did their homework instead of flying by the seat of their pants. Over the years, Harless and his colleagues put together a management development system unlike anything ever seen in the newspaper world—complete with a training institute where managers took classes and an assessment center to give them feedback. Virtually every important Knight-Ridder executive was subjected to the process—a method of quality control that, as Harless saw it, could "provide a continuity of management with the same or similar value systems for years to come."

The practice was not without controversy. A 1978 article in the *Columbia Journalism Review* questioned whether psychological assessment properly belonged in the news business. "When such supposedly independent-minded people as . . . editors and reporters obediently bare their psyches on corporate orders, *that* is something to worry about," said the article.

Such criticism notwithstanding, the system of testing, training, assessment centers, and continual tracking allowed the organization to fill managerial positions efficiently and systematically—as it did in naming James Batten president in 1982, several years before chairman Alvah Chapman was scheduled to retire.

Batten's father, an agronomist, had settled in Tidewater, Virginia, where he built an agricultural research station. The station greatly improved the yield from the region's peanut, cotton, and soybean crops, and Batten's father became something of a folk hero. After the elder Batten died, the townspeople assumed Jim would carry on his father's work.

That had been Batten's plan during his studies at Davidson College in North Carolina, but after graduation in 1957, he discovered he would soon be going into the army. Rather than start a graduate program that would only be interrupted by military service, Batten got a job at the *Charlotte Observer.* "After a day or two," he said, "it was clear that I had looked through my last microscope. . . . I had found a much more interesting way to make a living."

His love of newspapering stayed with him through the army and studies for a master's degree in public affairs from Princeton University, after which he returned to the *Observer.* Later, Batten was transferred to Knight's Washington bureau—largely covering politics in the South and civil rights. His reporting permitted Batten to see his native South through new eyes and to bear witness to and rejoice in the ending of a way of life defined by race-baiting demagoguery.

After serving a stint as an editor in Detroit, Batten became executive editor of the *Charlotte Observer,* fulfilling his dream of leading a paper he had always admired for standing up for racial justice at a time when doing so was difficult.

All too quickly to suit Batten's taste, the assignment ended. The bosses in Miami had tagged Batten as the level-headed, team-playing type who should go up Knight-Ridder's corporate ladder. After agonizing over the decision for several days, he came to Miami in 1975 as vice-president for news.

Batten worked to integrate the Ridder papers into the operation and make them editorially respectable. Some of the Knight papers required work as well, and Batten appointed several new editors as he tried to master the economics of publishing.

Communities were loath to support more than one daily, but once a paper folded or was consolidated, the survivor's profitability generally zoomed. Bowing to the tide of the times, Knight-Ridder consolidated publications in several markets where it owned more than one—including Charlotte, Macon, and Lexington.

The moves were lucrative for Knight-Ridder and made the corporation less nervous about its long-term prospects and more interested in broad diversification.

Having shed its broadcast properties to facilitate the 1974

merger, Knight-Ridder had reentered the business in 1978 with the purchases of three VHF television stations. The next year the firm had invested in a newsprint mill and later expanded into cable television and Viewtron (a system to allow consumers to receive information via a computer terminal in their home).

Shortly after his promotion to president, Batten was designated point man for electronic diversification, making him responsible for moving the company even farther into the nontraditional marketplace—and farther away from dependence on newspapers.

The *Philadelphia Bulletin* went out of business that same year, giving Knight-Ridder, with its *Philadelphia Inquirer* and *Philadelphia Daily News,* a monopoly in the market. Within months, the *Inquirer*'s daily circulation had increased by some 150,000 and profits began to climb.

Three years later—in 1985—Knight-Ridder endured a wrenching forty-six-day strike in Philadelphia. The strike paved the way for automation in the mailroom. ("In the days of head-on competition [in Philadelphia] . . . nobody was really willing to go to the mat in the necessary way," said Batten, "because there was always the danger that one paper or the other could wind up being mortally wounded by a strike while the other guy continued to publish.")

Newspapers were looking better as Knight-Ridder's diversification efforts stumbled. The Viewtron project launched in 1983 had signed up only twenty thousand subscribers across the country by 1986, potential customers apparently seeing no reason to view news stories and advertising on a computer screen. Knight-Ridder shut down that operation and withdrew from the mobile telephone business. Knight-Ridder also sold its book publishing company, originally acquired, noted Batten, "on the theory that writers were writers, words were words, and print was print."

As the company backed away from its nontraditional investments (though it retained interests in business information services), it increased its stake in newspapers. In 1986, Knight-Ridder paid $311 million for a company that published six small dailies and two other papers in South Carolina and Mississippi. In 1988, the company bought Dialog Information Services (the world's largest computer-based data bank) for

$353 million. Later that year, Batten announced plans to sell the firm's eight television stations.

Knight-Ridder's newspapers were not without problems. In Miami, for instance, the *Herald*'s circulation was dropping—from 443,000 daily in 1985 to 419,000 in 1987; and the *Wall Street Journal* ran a story asserting the paper's editors had lost touch with the increasingly Latino city.

In the early days, said Batten, Knight-Ridder's editors had assumed that the melting pot would work in Miami, that the immigrants, largely from Cuba, would be assimilated. The assumption had proved to be naive, "partly because the people who came here came not so much as immigrants but as refugees, political exiles, many of . . . whose great hope was not to become assimilated . . . but [one day] . . . to go home."

In 1976, the *Herald* had launched a Spanish-language supplement, *El Herald,* in an attempt to reach its Spanish-speaking potential readers. By 1987, Knight-Ridder had decided that *El Herald* was not doing the job. The company brought in Robert Suarez, who ran Knight-Ridder's business operations in Charlotte, to help its Spanish-language publication and the larger paper find a place in Miami's Latino community—which generally saw the *Herald* as distant, hostile, and even pro-Communist.

Suarez, born in Havana in 1928, had originally supported Fidel Castro and spent time in prison for opposing Fulgencio Batista; but he had come to Miami in 1961 disenchanted with Castro's betrayal of the Cuban revolution.

In Cuba, Suarez had been a banker; in Miami he became a worker in the *Herald*'s mailroom. Five years later, he was named accounting manager for the paper's weekly publications and then controller. He left briefly to work in Honduras and in 1972 rejoined Knight-Ridder, in Charlotte, where he rose to the presidency of the subsidiary publishing the *Charlotte Observer.*

He thought *El Herald* "an embarrassment" and resolved to bring it to life with a redesign, a beefed-up staff, and a serious effort to cover the news. But the *Herald*'s problem, he believed, would not be solved merely through improving the Spanish-language supplement. The English version also needed work.

Heath Meriwether, the former *Herald* editor, agreed. Although he believed the creation of *El Herald* had been a wise and creative act, he later said, "If there had not been an *El Herald,* it would have forced the *Herald* . . . to better cover the entire community . . . including the Hispanic bastion."

Suarez's immediate concern was Miami; but given the growth of the immigrant population in the United States, he pointed out that other cities "sooner or later will have the same problem."

The problems in Miami were only the latest sign that newspaper executives could not take success for granted. That the *Detroit Free Press,* despite attracting nearly 650,000 readers a day, sought refuge in a joint operating agreement was another.

In the past, believes Batten, newspapers largely managed themselves. "In general, newspapers have been businesses that were hard to screw up. Good newspapers have succeeded [and] mediocre newspapers have succeeded." He finds today's market much less forgiving; in an attempt to adjust to that less benign environment, Knight-Ridder reorganized in 1976 and made one office responsible for the bottom line as well as for the editorial quality of Knight-Ridder's newspapers.

Paul Anthony Ridder, Herman Ridder's grandson, was named president of the newspaper division. Ridder had previously worked at the *San Jose Mercury News,* where he had been considered the star publisher in the company.

Ridder's father, Bernard (former chairman of the company), had never encouraged his son to go into the business. Once Tony had decided to pursue newspapering, he was told he could stay only if he proved himself to be good. He would start at the small (less than twenty thousand circulation) paper in Aberdeen, South Dakota; after that, no guarantees.

Ridder did well enough in Aberdeen to be sent to Pasadena and, subsequently, to San Jose, where he was when the company went public. He recalls feeling "in a way, slightly sad, that . . . [Ridder Publications] had been a family business all this time and we had reached the point where now we'd become a public company." But, like his father, Ridder concluded that the eventual merger was a good move, that it would help bring systematic management to the company.

In 1977, Ridder, who had started off as business manager, became publisher in San Jose. As Otis Chandler had done in Los Angeles, Ridder wanted to develop the paper into something he and his family could look on with pride. He lured Larry Jinks, then executive editor of the *Miami Herald,* to San Jose. Together they rebuilt the staff, modernized the production facility, pushed up profits, and turned a previously lackluster newspaper into one of the nation's finest. Ridder left San Jose with a feeling of deep accomplishment, and no longer haunted by the suspicion that he had moved ahead on the strength of his name alone.

He came to corporate headquarters committed to a philosophy of simplifying bureaucracy and holding down expenses. His newsroom in San Jose, he would point out, had grown from 165 to 350 in a very short time, but "we never . . . spilled a lot of money along the way."

The entire newspaper division, he felt, could do worse than to adopt that philosophy, which would allow Knight-Ridder to keep circulation and advertising costs down. The company, in his opinion, should also aggressively pursue growth and not concede the arena to Gannett.

As Alvah Chapman looked toward retirement, the competitive Ridder (who had distinguished himself in business operations) and the genteel Batten (who had risen from the editorial side) had emerged as Knight-Ridder's team for the future. Douglas Harris, the "Ridder rabbit" psychologist who had become vice-president and corporate secretary, observed: "They have different backgrounds, different interests, different personalities. . . . They are both intelligent, bright, quick, [and have] good instincts . . . strong abilities to empathize with others. They're careful. . . . Think before they act. . . . They're both vitally interested in communications . . . and [know that] running a communications company is different from running a shoe manufacturing company or a tire company."

The emerging leaders of America's most prominent papers differ in many respects. But they all talk the language of Wall Street. They all stress efficiency—in their newsrooms and their business operations. And they all value their relationship with the financial community.

John Morton, a former reporter who is now a financial analyst specializing in the newspaper industry, believes Al Neuharth was among the first to realize just how fruitful that association could be.

"You know . . . one of the jobs that Neuharth took upon

himself back in the seventies," says Morton, "was not just carrying the banner for Gannett, he was carrying the banner for the whole newspaper business in the public arena. . . . And he pretty much educated, almost single-handedly, the Wall Street community to what the newspaper business was really like in this country. Up until Gannett started doing their dog-and-pony shows, when a typical Wall Street analyst thought about the newspaper business, he thought of what was then the New York Times Company—all the problems they then had with strikes every three years. And every time the national economy went to hell, the *New York Times'* linage would go down. . . . And so they were turned off by newspapers because they couldn't see beyond the Hudson River."

Concern with finances has forced the industry to prove that great newspapers can be profitable—that great newspapering may even be an avenue to profitability. The features that make metropolitan newspapers outstanding—in-depth reporting, incisive writing, and an overall sophisticated approach to coverage—are the same features that attract affluent readers for whom advertisers are willing to pay premium rates.

Even many smaller papers have discovered that high journalism standards and profit do not have to conflict. Morton, for instance, cites the success of the New York Times Company, with its twenty-six small dailies and nine nondaily papers in places like Leesburg, Florida, and Santa Rosa, California.

More than a quarter of a century ago, A. J. Liebling foresaw the end of newspaper competition and wrote: "As the number of cities in the United States with only a single newspaper ownership increases, news becomes increasingly nonessential to the newspaper. In the minds of the average publisher, it is a costly and uneconomic frill."

Liebling was wide of the mark. As noted above, far from becoming a frill, for certain publications quality journalism has become an integral component of profitability; but quality journalism, as the phrase is generally understood, is not necessarily journalism that reflects the full complexity of a community. And as the disciples of marketing and journalism come together, the narrowing of journalistic sights becomes an increasing probability.

Newspapers have an unprecedented ability and inclination to direct different versions of the newspaper to different neighborhoods, and to direct features within the newspaper to specific categories of readers. As new presses come on-line, those abilities will increase. Richard Capen, publisher of the *Miami Herald,* noted, "We are a large metropolitan newspaper, but we also publish twenty-four local newspapers each week within the *Herald.*" Such zoning is only one aspect of the process of segmentation that the newspaper industry has embraced wholesale, largely because advertisers have insisted on it and profit plans appear to require it.

The danger in all the targeting, zoning, and segmenting is that newspapers can easily lose perspective—particularly of those communities not among the targeted.

Dave Laventhol, president of Times Mirror, recognizing the pitfalls, commented, "It is important that we don't define society totally by the people who read us. If we did that, we would be neglecting fairly important parts of our society."

Some editors have accepted the view that not all readers are created equal, that only the affluent are worth having. In trying to reach out to all of Washington, the *Washington Post* has registered a notable dissent. "That's ambitious as hell," observed Lance Primis, of the *New York Times,* "[and] . . . contrary to the way major companies now talk about trying to do more for fewer people."

For the *Post,* the strategy, so far, is working. At the very least, the experience there points up the merit of questioning whether the conventional wisdom is wisdom at all. Washington is a unique market; and the *Post* strategy may not work in many other places. But in an age of marketing, corporate efficiency, and specialization, newspaper executives could stand to give more thought than they have to where the trend lines will ultimately lead. For how a newspaper defines its audience will necessarily affect how it defines news. And the increased concentration on affluent consumers could very easily lead to the unthinking endorsement of middle-class cocoons—where unpleasant reality need not intrude.

In an age where good management has been put on a pedestal, it is easy to forget that much of "management science" is inherently unscientific. What passes for objective analysis is often rigorously applied nonsense.

Leaders make a point of looking beyond the neat projections and marketing charts.

As one institution after another moves faster and faster toward greater segmentation and specialization, newspapers remain one of the few vehicles that can act as a bridge between different parts of the population. For newspapers to refuse that role—and unquestioningly accept segmentation's inevitability—is ultimately to surrender the right to be treated as anything more than another disposable commodity for an increasingly insular, self-absorbed society.

At Knight-Ridder, the perhaps apocryphal story is told of John Knight's encounter with an editor who was lobbying for a more impressive title. "There is no higher title than editor," Knight is supposed to have said. Today, more than ever, editors seemed to believe there is no higher title than manager. Editors ideally have vision; managers have numbers; good newspapers demand both.

NOTES

PROLOGUE

Interviews

Benjamin C. Bradlee, February 25, 1987; Robert Erburu, August 5, 1987; Katharine Graham, May 13, 1987; William Hearst III, June 11, 1987; Larry Jinks, July 28, 1987; David Laventhol, May 27, 1987; Arthur O. Sulzberger, March 11, 1987; William Thomas, April 22, 1987.

Books

Alan Jay Lerner and Frederick Lowe, *Camelot* (New York: Random House, 1961); Richard H. Meeker, *Newspaperman* (New York: Ticknor & Fields, 1983); Harrison E. Salisbury, *Without Fear or Favor* (New York: Times Books, 1980).

Articles, Periodicals, and Documents

Alvah Chapman, transcript of testimony in joint operating agreement at U.S. Justice Department hearing, Detroit, August 12, 1987; *Facts about Newspapers '88,* American Newspaper Publishers Association; Michael Fancher, "The Metamorphosis of the Newspaper Editor," *Gannett Center Journal,* Spring 1987; "Knight Disagrees with Sulzberger on 'Chains,' " *Editor & Publisher,* June 14, 1947; Jim Ottaway, Jr., text of remarks delivered before the New England Newspaper Association, October 7, 1986; *Newsweek,* December 2, 1963; *Readers: How to Gain and Retain Them* (New York: Newspaper Advertising Bureau, 1986); Eleanor Randolph, "Grasping for the Keys to the Kingdom," *Washington Post,* January 9, 1986; James Reston, "Change Is the Biggest Story" (abridged address, Columbia University convocation), *Quill,* June 1963; *Time,* January 3, 1984.

CHAPTER 1. AN EDITOR AND HIS *POST*

Interviews

Benjamin C. Bradlee, February 25, 1987; Leonard Downie, February 23, 1987; Osborn Elliott, May 8, 1987; Katharine Graham, May 13 and June 4, 1987; Meg Greenfield, March 31, 1987; Robert G. Kaiser, April 2, 1987; David Laventhol, May 27, 1987; Robert C. Maynard, June 12, 1987; William Raspberry, May 19, 1987; Howard Simons, May 26, 1987; Roger Wilkins, April 29, 1987.

Books

Benjamin C. Bradlee, *Conversations with Kennedy* (New York: Norton, 1975); Osborn Elliott, *The World of Oz* (New York: Viking, 1980); Chalmers M. Roberts, *The Washington Post: The First 100 Years* (Boston: Houghton Mifflin, 1977).

Articles and Periodicals

Meg Greenfield, "The Prose of Richard M. Nixon," *Reporter,* September 29, 1960; Robert C. Maynard, "Black Nationalists Predict 'Race War,'" *Washington Post,* September 24, 1967; "The Right to Report," *Newsweek,* March 19, 1956; *Washington Post,* August 4, 1963; Roger Wilkins, "A Black at the Gridiron Dinner," *Washington Post,* March 26, 1970.

CHAPTER 2. MOVING INTO THE MAJOR LEAGUE

Interviews

Alice Bonner, April 17, 1987; Benjamin C. Bradlee, February 25, 1987; Milton Coleman, March 6, 1987; Leonard Downie, February 23, 1987; Katharine Graham, May 13 and June 4, 1987; Larry Kramer,

June 12, 1987; Robert C. Maynard, June 12, 1987; Howard Simons, May 26, 1987; Jacqueline Trescott, February 24, 1987; Roger Wilkins, April 29, 1987; Tom Wilkinson, February 24, 1987; Bob Woodward, May 14, 1987.

Books

Carl Bernstein and Bob Woodward, *All the President's Men* (New York: Simon and Schuster, 1974); Chalmers M. Roberts, *The Washington Post: The First 100 Years* (Boston: Houghton Mifflin, 1977).

Articles and Periodicals

Gary Arnold, " 'President's Men': Absorbing, Meticulous . . . and Incomplete," *Washington Post,* April 4, 1976; *Editor & Publisher,* July 17, 1954; "F.Y.I." (editorial), *Washington Post,* October 14, 1981; James L. Rowe, "Washington Post Stock Set at $26 Per Common Share," *Washington Post,* June 16, 1971; Sally Quinn, "The Politics of the Power Grab: Nine Rules of Notoriety," *Washington Post,* December 19, 1979; "The Ear," *Washington Post,* October 5, 1981.

CHAPTER 3. A NEW GRAHAM, A LAST STRIKE

Interviews

Loyce Best, June 5, 1987; Benjamin C. Bradlee, February 25, 1987; Herbert Denton (phone), June 23, 1987; Donald Graham, January 29 and March 5, 1987; Katharine Graham, May 13 and June 4, 1987; Meg Greenfield, March 31, 1987; Robert G. Kaiser, April 2, 1987; Frank Manzon, March 9, 1987; Robert C. Maynard, June 12, 1987; Donald Rice, April 29, 1987; Howard Simons, May 26, 1987.

Books

Chalmers M. Roberts, *The Washington Post: The First 100 Years* (Boston: Houghton Mifflin, 1977).

Articles and Periodicals

Robert G. Kaiser, "The Strike at the Washington Post," *Washington Post,* February 29, 1976; "The Post and the Presses" (editorial), *Washington Post,* October 3, 1975.

CHAPTER 4. CHOOSING A TEAM

Interviews

Nicholas Cannistraro, Jr., March 6, 1987; Thomas Ferguson, February 25, 1987; Donald Graham, March 5 and 31, 1987; Meg Greenfield, March 31, 1987; Boisfeuillet Jones, Jr., March 9, 1987; Larry Kramer, June 12, 1987; John B. Kuhns, March 9, 1987; Theodore Lutz, February 25, 1987; Frank Manzon, March 9, 1987; Thomas Might, April 2, 1987; Eleanor Randolph, June 3, 1987; Margaret Schiff, March 6, 1987; Richard Simmons, May 1, 1987; Alan Spoon, March 9, 1987.

Books

Howard Bray, *The Pillars of the Post* (New York: Norton, 1980).

CHAPTER 5. A NEWSROOM IN TRANSITION

Interviews

Alice Bonner, April 17, 1987; Benjamin C. Bradlee, February 25, 1987; Shelby Coffey, April 21, 1987; Milton Coleman, March 6, 1987; Leonard Downie, February 23, 1987; Robert G. Kaiser, April 2, 1987; Larry Kramer, June 12, 1987; John B. Kuhns, March 9, 1987; William Raspberry, May 19, 1987; Howard Simons, May 26, 1987; Jacqueline Trescott, February 24, 1987; Tom Wilkinson, February 24, 1987; Bob Woodward, May 14, 1987.

Articles

Milton Coleman, "18 Words, Seven Weeks Later," *Washington Post,* April 8, 1984; Janet Cooke, "Jimmy's World," *Washington Post,* September 28, 1980; Jonathan Friendly, "Writer Who Fabricated Story Tells of Pressure 'to Be First,' " *New York Times,* January 29, 1982; Bill Green, "Janet's World," *Washington Post,* April 19, 1981; Lewis M. Simons, "Addict, 8, Is in Hiding, Mayor Says," *Washington Post,* October 1, 1987.

CHAPTER 6. MATTERS OF RACE

Interviews

Alice Bonner, April 17, 1987; Milton Coleman, March 6, 1987; Leon Dash, April 30, 1987; Herbert Denton (phone), June 23, 1987; Dorothy Gilliam, June 4, 1987; Donald Graham, March 5 and 31, 1987; Cathy Hughes, October 5, 1987 (phone: conducted by Marchene White); Jay Lovinger, June 5, 1987; William Raspberry, May 19, 1987.

Books

Chalmers M. Roberts, *The Washington Post: The First 100 Years* (Boston: Houghton Mifflin, 1977).

Articles and Documents

Benjamin C. Bradlee, "F.Y.I.: The Washington Post Magazine," *Washington Post,* October 5, 1986; John Ed Bradley, "Murder, Drugs and the Rap Star," *Washington Post Magazine,* September 7, 1986; Richard Cohen, " 'Accused of Racism,' " *Washington Post,* September 16, 1986; Richard Cohen, "Closing the Door on Crime," *Washington Post Magazine,* September 7, 1986; Milton Coleman, Jeanne-Fox-Alston et al., *Blacks in the Newsroom of the Washington Post* (a report to the editors); *Conciliation Agreement* (Case No: YDC4-600), Equal Employment Opportunity Commission, Washington, D.C., 1980; Joseph Laitin, "A Cover Story, Two Lessons, Priests and Pagans," *Washington Post,* September 14, 1986; William Raspberry, " 'The Readers Are Right,' " *Washington Post,* October 6, 1986.

CHAPTER 7. FACING THE FUTURE

Interviews

Loyce Best, June 5, 1987; Benjamin C. Bradlee, February 25, 1987 (phone), September 25, 1987; Leon Dash, April 30, 1987; Thomas Ferguson, February 25, 1987; Donald Graham, March 5 and 31, 1987; Katharine Graham, June 4, 1987; Boisfeuillet Jones, Jr., March 9, 1987; Robert Kaiser, April 2, 1987; John B. Kuhns, March 9, 1987; Christopher M. Little, August 24, 1987; Thomas Might, April 2, 1987; Richard Simmons, May 1, 1987; Howard Simons, May 26, 1987; Alan Spoon,

March 9, 1987; Tom Wilkinson, February 24, 1987; Bob Woodward, May 14, 1987.

Articles

Kenneth Bredemeier, "Mobile Chief Testifies 6 Hours in Libel Suit," *Washington Post,* August 14, 1982; Kenneth Bredemeier, "Mobile Oil Corp. President's Libel Case Against the Post Begins," *Washington Post,* August 8, 1982; Leon Dash, "At Risk: Chronicles of Teen-Age Pregnancy," *Washington Post,* January 26–31, 1987 (six-part series); John B. Kuhns, "*Washington Post* Is a Staunch Believer in Collective Bargaining," *New York Times,* October 3, 1987; Sandra Polaski, "*Washington Post* Employees Want Negotiations in Good Faith," *New York Times,* October 17, 1987.

CHAPTER 8. IN PURSUIT OF PERFECTION

Interviews

Otis Chandler, June 10, 1987; George Cotliar, August 7, 1987; Robert Erburu, June 10 and August 5, 1987; Frank McCulloch, June 17, 1987; William Thomas, April 22, 1987.

Books

Marshall Berges, *The Life and Times of Los Angeles* (New York: Atheneum, 1984); Robert Gottlieb and Irene Holt, *Thinking Big* (New York: Putnam's, 1977); David Halberstam, *The Powers That Be* (New York: Knopf, 1979); Jack R. Hart, *The Information Empire* (Washington, D.C.: University Press of America, 1981).

Articles, Periodicals, and Documents

Ed Ainsworth, "Otis Chandler New Times Publisher," *Los Angeles Times,* April 12, 1960; Associated Press, "Publisher on West Coast Continues on Stand," *New York Times,* May 26, 1967: Gene Blake and Jack Tobin, "Teamsters Loan Extent Related," *Los Angeles Times,* October 24, 1962; Jack Nelson, "James Meredith Wounded by Gunman on Mississippi March," *Los Angeles Times,* June 7, 1966; Robert Richardson, " 'Burn, Baby, Burn' Slogan Used as Firebugs Put Area to Torch," *Los Angeles Times,* August 15, 1965; "The New World," *Time,* July 15, 1957; Nick Williams, letter to Advisory Board on the Pulitzer Prizes, January 28, 1966.

CHAPTER 9. KINDRED SPIRITS

Interviews

Dennis Britton, April 23, 1987; Otis Chandler, June 10, 1987; George Cotliar, August 7, 1987; Robert Erburu, June 10 and August 5, 1987; Tom Johnson, April 23, 1987; Dave Laventhol, May 27, 1987; Frank McCulloch, June 17, 1987; William Thomas, April 22, 1987.

Articles, Periodicals, and Documents

Peyton Anderson, Letter to President Lyndon B. Johnson, August 1, 1966; Peyton Anderson, letter to Tom Johnson, August 1, 1966; Max Frankel, "DMZ Is Exempted: Johnson Sets No Time Limit on Halting of Air and Sea Blows," *New York Times,* April 1, 1968; Lyndon B. Johnson, letter to Peyton Anderson, July 28, 1966; "Lyndon B. Johnson" (editorial), *Los Angeles Times,* January 23, 1973; Tom Wicker, "Surprise Decision: President Steps Aside in Unity Bid—Says 'House' Is Divided," *New York Times,* April 1, 1968.

CHAPTER 10. CONFLICT AND CONFUSION

Interviews

Dennis Britton, April 23, 1987; Otis Chandler, June 10, 1987; George Cotliar, August 7, 1987; Noel Greenwood, April 21, 1987; Tom Johnson, April 23, 1987; Dave Laventhol, May 27, 1987; John Lawrence, October 23, 1987.

Articles and Documents

Alfred C. Baldwin III, "Insider's Account of the Watergate Bugging," *Los Angeles Times,* October 5, 1972; Otis Chandler, letter to Tom Johnson, August 1, 1977; Herbert G. Lawson, "Price of Friendship: How Rich Acquaintances of California Publisher Evidently Lost Bundle," *Wall Street Journal,* August 11, 1972; Herbert C. Lawson, "SEC Says Otis Chandler and Audit Firm Deeply Involved in Alleged Geo-Tek Fraud," *Wall Street Journal,* March 25, 1975.

CHAPTER 11. PASSING THE BATON

Interviews

Dennis Britton, April 23, 1987; Otis Chandler, June 10, 1987; Shelby Coffey, April 21, 1987, May 9, 1988 (phone); George Cotliar, August 7, 1987; Frank Del Omo, June 10, 1987; Robert Erburu, June 10 and August 5, 1987; Noel Greenwood, April 21, 1987; Ron Harris, June 10, 1987; Tom Johnson, April 23 and June 11, 1987, March 16 and May 4, 1988 (phone); Dave Laventhol, May 27, 1987; James B. Shaffer, April 21, 1987; Frank Sotomayor, June 10, 1987; William Thomas, April 22, 1987; Donald Wright, April 22 and August 5, 1987.

Articles, Periodicals, and Documents

"Black Los Angeles: Looking at Diversity," a series of articles reprinted from the *Los Angeles Times,* 1982; Otis Chandler, letter to Tom Johnson, December 28, 1982; "Cruising Speed in L.A.," *Newsweek,* May 26, 1986; Eric Malnic, "Blacks Criticize Times Story on Inner-City Criminals," *Los Angeles Times,* July 20, 1981; Richard E. Meyer and Mike Goodman, "Marauders from Inner City Prey on L.A.'s Suburbs," *Los Angeles Times,* July 12, 1981; "Safe Choice," *Newsweek,* April 11, 1988; "Southern California's Latino Community," a series of articles reprinted from the *Los Angeles Times,* 1983; M. L. Stein, "Times Mirror Exec Raps Murdoch Formula," *Editor & Publisher,* April 7, 1984.

CHAPTER 12. LESSONS IN LEADERSHIP

Interviews

Walter Mattson, March 30, 1987; Arthur Ochs Sulzberger, March 11, 1987.

Books

Turner Catledge, *My Life and the Times* (New York: Harper and Row, 1971); Elmer Davis, *History of the New York Times, 1851–1921* (New York: Greenwood Press, 1969).

Articles and Periodicals

"Arthur Ochs Sulzberger Named Times Publisher," *New York Times,* June 21, 1963; "Orvil E. Dryfoos of Times Dies," *New York Times,*

May 26, 1963; Ruth Sulzberger Golden, "My Brother the Publisher, *Times Talk,* July–August 1963; A. H. Raskin, "The Strike: A Step-by-Step Account," April 1, 1963; James Reston, "Text of Eulogy of Orvil E. Dryfoos Delivered by James Reston," *New York Times,* May 28, 1963; Arthur O. Sulzberger, "View from the 14th Floor," *Times Talk,* September 1964.

Documents from the New York Archives

Francis A. Cox, memo to Arthur Ochs Sulzberger on need for higher profit margin, March 2, 1965; Edward S. Greenbaum, letter to A. H. Sulzberger on relief that Punch and not a businessman has been named publisher, June 26, 1963; Arthur Hays Sulzberger, letter to Christopher Chancellor on origin of Punch as a nickname, June 7, 1950; Arthur Hays Sulzberger, letter to Edward Greenbaum commenting on fears that Bradford might appear at Times board meeting, June 20, 1963; Arthur Hays Sulzberger, letter to J. D. Ferguson, outlining training program for Punch at the *Milwaukee Journal,* September 24, 1952; Arthur Hays Sulzberger, letter to Arthur Ochs and Barbara Sulzberger regarding "noblesse oblige," April 9, 1951; Arthur Hays Sulzberger, letter to Arthur Ochs Sulzberger, commenting on maturation during the strike, March 31, 1963; Arthur Hays Sulzberger, letter to Arthur Ochs Sulzberger, on Arthur Krock arranging employment at the *Milwaukee Journal,* November 20, 1951; Arthur Hays Sulzberger, memo to the file regarding plans to appoint his son publisher, June 6, 1963; Arthur Hays Sulzberger, memo to the file regarding Punch's desire to be king, July 21, 1934.

CHAPTER 13. A WHIRLWIND IN THE NEWSROOM

Interviews

James Greenfield, February 20, 1987; Sydney Gruson, March 16, 1987; Joseph Lelyveld, June 30, 1987; A. M. Rosenthal, September 15, 1987; Allan Siegal, February 12, 1987; Louis Silverstein, June 2, 1987; Arthur Ochs Sulzberger, March 11, 1987.

Books

Turner Catledge, *My Life and the Times* (New York: Harper and Row, 1971); Gay Talese, *The Kingdom and the Power* (New York: Dell, 1986).

Articles and Periodicals

Tony Brenna, "The Day the *World Journal Tribune* Was Born," *Editor & Publisher,* September 17, 1966; Damon Stetson, "The Herald Tribune Is Discontinued," *New York Times,* August 16, 1966; "*World Journal Tribune* Takes Merger Issues into Court," *Editor & Publisher,* April 30, 1966.

Documents from the New York Times Archives

A. M. Rosenthal and Lawrence G. Hauck, memorandum to E. Clifton Daniel on afternoon newspaper project, May 26, 1967; Arthur Ochs Sulzberger, memorandum to Joseph Alduino, Harding Bancroft et al. on problems facing the *Times,* June 2, 1965; Arthur Ochs Sulzberger, memorandum to Harding Bancroft, Turner Catledge et al. on opportunities presented by merger of three New York newspapers, April 4, 1966; Arthur Ochs Sulzberger, memorandum to department heads on structure of the *Times,* July 1, 1963.

CHAPTER 14. BUILDING A BUSINESS, TAKING A STAND

Interviews

Katharine Darrow, May 12, 1987; James Goodale, March 13, 1987; James Greenfield, February 20, 1987; A. M. Rosenthal, September 15, 1987; Allan Siegal, February 12, 1987; Arthur Ochs Sulzberger, March 11, 1987.

Books

Turner Catledge, *My Life and the Times* (New York: Harper and Row, 1971); Harrison Salisbury, *Without Fear or Favor* (New York: Times Books, 1980).

Articles and Periodicals

Neil Sheehan, "Vietnam Archive: Pentagon Study Traces 3 Decades of Growing U.S. Involvement," *New York Times,* June 13, 1971; Hedrick Smith, "Vast Review of War Took a Year," *New York Times,* June 13, 1971; "The Times Shifts News Executives," *New York Times,* August 1, 1969; "Times Raises Dividend by 10 cents, a 4–1

Stock Split Is Approved," *New York Times,* September 12, 1968; "Times Trust Sells Big Block of Stock," *New York Times,* December 4, 1968.

Documents from the New York Times Archives

Arthur Ochs Sulzberger, memorandum to Joseph Alduino, Harding Bancroft et al. on problems facing the *Times,* June 2, 1965.

CHAPTER 15. REMAKING THE *TIMES*

Interviews

Katharine Darrow, May 12 and 27, 1987; Max Frankel, October 13, 1987; Guy Garrett, Jr., January 28 and February 9, 1987; James Goodale, March 13, 1987; James Greenfield, February 20, 1987; Sydney Gruson, March 16, 1987; John Lee, February 4, 1987; Joseph Lelyveld, June 30, 1987; Walter Mattson, March 30, 1987; Donald Nizen, September 2, 1987; Peter Passell, February 26, 1987; Lance Primis, May 8, 1987; A. M. Rosenthal, September 15, 1987; Jack Rosenthal, March 11 and 12, 1987; Roger Starr, March 18, 1987; Arthur Ochs Sulzberger, March 11, 1987; Seymour Topping, May 19, 1987; Roger Wilkins, April 29, 1987.

Books

Harry Levinson and Stuart Rosenthal, *CEO* (New York: Basic Books, 1984); Richard H. Meeker, *Newspaperman* (New York: Ticknor & Fields, 1983); Leonard Silk, *The American Establishment* (New York: Basic Books, 1980); Gay Talese, *The Kingdom and the Power* (New York: Dell, 1986).

Articles and Periodicals

"Times Unifies Its News and Sunday Departments," *New York Times,* April 6, 1976; "Times Widens Top News Team as Part of Its Expansion Program," *New York Times,* December 18, 1976.

Documents

James Goodale, statement on termination agreement relating to the women's class-action suit against the *New York Times,* October 6, 1978; Leonard Harris, press release on out-of-court settlement of nonwhite employees' class-action suit against the *New York Times,* September 17, 1980.

CHAPTER 16. SULZBERGER'S LEGACY

Interviews

William Connolly, January 15, 1987; Paul Delaney, February 6, 1987; Max Frankel, October 13, 1987; Gerald Fraser, August 8, 1987; James Goodale, March 13, 1987; Sydney Gruson, March 16, 1987; Warren Hoge, May 20, 1987; Dave Jones, January 22, 1987; Joseph Lelyveld, June 30, 1987; Russell Lewis, May 7, 1987; Erich Linker, May 12, 1987; Walter Mattson, March 30, 1987; Tom Morgan, April 16, 1987; Lance Primis, May 8, 1987; A. M. Rosenthal, September 15, 1987; Jack Rosenthal, March 12, 1987; Allan M. Siegal, February 12 and March 3, 1987; Arthur Ochs Sulzberger, March 11, 1987; Arthur Ochs Sulzberger, Jr., October 1, 1987; Seymour Topping, May 19, 1987; Craig Whitney, March 5, 1987, November 20, 1987 (phone); Tom Winship, April 7, 1988 (phone).

Articles and Periodicals

Fox Butterfield, "A Correction: Times Was in Error on North's Secret-Fund Testimony," *New York Times,* July 13, 1987; George Garneau, "Goodbye Gray Lady," *Editor & Publisher,* July 25, 1987; Tamar Lewin. "Changes at Times Approved," *New York Times,* September 19, 1986; Eleanor Randolph, "Questions Too Pointed, N.Y. Times Editor Says: Paper Backs off from Request to Candidates," *Washington Post,* June 20, 1987; "A. M. Rosenthal Leaving Executive Editor's Post at the Times, and Max Frankel Is His Successor," *New York Times,* October 12, 1986; "Several Top Executives Promoted by The Times," *New York Times,* April 20, 1988.

CHAPTER 17. EXPANDING HORIZONS

Interviews

Phil Currie, May 14, 1987; Brian Donnelly, September 18, 1987; Ron Martin, April 21, 1987; Allen Neuharth, October 8, 1987; John Quinn, March 31, 1987.

Books and Monographs

Ben Bagdikian, *The Media Monopoly* (Boston: Beacon Press, 1983); Paul Miller, *The Gannett Group: 50 Plus 50* (Rochester, N.Y.: Gannett,

1974); Richard Polenberg, *Frank E. Gannett: A Progressive Publisher in Politics* (Rochester, N.Y.: Gannett Foundation, 1988); Peter Prichard, *The Making of McPaper* (New York: Andrews, McMeel & Parker, 1987).

Articles and Periodicals

"A Voice for Brevard," *Today,* March 21, 1966. "Frank Gannett Dies at 81: His Empire in Foundation," *Editor & Publisher,* December 7, 1957; "Frank E. Gannett: He Accumulated Newspapers to Make Them Strong," *Editor & Publisher,* December 7, 1957; "Gannett Buys Westchester group of 9 Daily Papers," *Editor & Publisher,* April 4, 1964; "Gannett Co. Income Tops $100 Million," *Editor & Publisher,* April 29, 1967.

CHAPTER 18. BUYING INTO THE BIG TIME

Interviews

John Curley, April 15, 1987; Thomas Curley, April 30, 1987; Brian Donnelly, September 18, 1987; Gerald Garcia, May 3, 1987; Douglas McCorkindale, May 5, 1987; Robert Maynard, June 12, 1987; Allen Neuharth, October 8, 1987; Charles Overby, May 15, 1987; John Quinn, March 31, 1987; Nancy Woodhull, April 29, 1987.

Monographs

Paul Miller, *The Gannett Group: 50 Plus 50* (Rochester, N.Y.: Gannett, 1974).

Articles and Periodicals

William H. Jones and Laird Anderson, "Gannett: 73 Papers and Still Counting," *Washington Post,* July 30, 1977; "Paul Miller to Retire as Gannett Chairman; Neuharth to Get Post," *Wall Street Journal,* September 11, 1978; Francis W. Wylie, "Gannett: Where Local News Is Global Money," *Finance,* April 1973.

CHAPTER 19. A BID FOR RECOGNITION

Interviews

John Curley, April 15, 1987; Thomas Curley, April 30, 1987; Brian Donnelly, September 18, 1987; Gerald Garcia, May 3, 1987; Robert

Giles, July 21, 1987; Jimmy Jones, May 14, 1987; Douglas McCorkindale, May 5, 1987; Robert Maynard, June 12, 1987; Allen Neuharth, October 8, 1987, December 4, 1987 (phone); Charles Overby, May 15, 1987; John Quinn, March 31 and November 16, 1987; Gary Watson, May 15, 1987; Nancy Woodhull, April 29 and 30, 1987.

Books

Peter Prichard, *The Making of McPaper* (New York: Andrews, McMeel & Parker, 1987).

CHAPTER 20. CONSOLIDATION

Interviews

James Batten, August 27 and September 3, 1987; Alvah Chapman, September 2, 1987; David Lawrence, July 21, 1987; Bernard H. Ridder, September 1, 1987.

Articles, Periodicals, and Documents

Alvah Chapman, transcript of testimony in joint operating agreement at U.S. Justice Department hearing, Detroit, August 12, 1987; "Bernard Ridder, Publisher, Dead," *New York Times,* May 6, 1975; "Charlotte Observer Is Purchased by Knight Newspapers for $7 Million," *Charlotte Observer,* December 30, 1954; "Foray in Yankeeland," *Time,* November 25, 1946; John S. Knight, James L. Knight et al., "A Presentation by Knight Newspapers, Inc." before New York Society of Security Analysts, February 24, 1970; "Knight Newspapers Buy Fifth Daily—the Charlotte Observer," *Tide,* January 15, 1955; Ward Morehouse, "Jack Knight a Big Factor in Revitalization of Akron," *Editor & Publisher,* June 17, 1939; Allen Neuharth, transcript of testimony in joint operating agreement U.S. Justice Department hearing, Detroit, August 10 and 11, 1987; "Our Respects to Robert Blair Ridder: Third Generation 'Publisher' Is Electronic Journalist," *Broadcasting,* June 24, 1963; "Publisher Joe Ridder: How to Expand a Newspaper Dynasty," *Printer's Ink,* June 27, 1958; "Ridder Publications Is Set to Go Public," *Broadcasting,* October 6, 1969; Richard E. Rothman, "Knight, Ridder Set Newspaper Merger," *Washington Post,* July 11, 1974; Helen M. Staunton, "It's all in the Family: Newspapering That Is," *Editor & Publisher,* October 18, 1947; Kennedy Stewart, "The Man Who Bought theChicagoDailyNews,"*PM Sunday Magazine,* December 3, 1944;

"Victor F. Ridder, 77, is Dead; Publisher and Scouting Leader," *New York Times,* June 15, 1963.

CHAPTER 21. THE CHALLENGE

Interviews

James Batten, August 27 and September 3, 1987; Richard Capen, September 29, 1987; Alvah Chapman, September 2, 1987; Byron Harless, September 1, 1987; Douglas Harris, September 1, 1987; Larry Jinks, July 28, 1987; Dave Laventhol, May 27, 1987; Heath Meriwether, July 21, 1987; John Morton, April 1, 1987; Lance Primis, May 8, 1987; Bernard H. Ridder, September 1, 1987; P. Anthony Ridder, September 29, 1987; Roberto Suarez, September 29, 1987.

Articles and Periodicals

Roger Lowenstien, "The Herald Is Wooing Cuban Readers, but It Risks Loss of Anglos," *Wall Street Journal,* March 5, 1987; Jim McGee and Tom Fiedler, "Miami Woman Is Linked to Hart: Candidate Denies Any Impropriety," *Miami Herald,* May 3, 1987; Francis Pollack, "Knight-Ridder Wants to Know the *Real* You," *Columbia Journalism Review,* January–February 1978.

Books

A. J. Liebling, *The Press* (New York: Ballantine Books, 1961).

INDEX